Class Not Dismissed

Praise for Anthony Aveni

THE END OF TIME: THE MAYA MYSTERY OF 2012

"Anthony Aveni is a passionate scholar and a vivid and engaging writer. He is a polymath, too, with an astounding range of interests and knowledge. Like Jared Diamond, Aveni is a brilliant synthesizer, and a delightful one."

Oliver Sacks, author-neurologist

PEOPLE AND THE SKY: OUR ANCESTORS AND THE COSMOS

"A triumphant exploration of the reasons why a wide variety of human societies have sought patterns in the sky, of the human exploration of the 'cosmic sweep of life.' This engrossing book is destined to become a classic."

Brian Fagan, author-archaeologist

BEHIND THE CRYSTAL BALL: MAGIC, SCIENCE, AND THE OCCULT FROM ANTIQUITY THROUGH THE NEW AGE

"A vastly entertaining inquiry into the roots of magic and science . . . with unflagging wit and a sharp critical eye."

Evan Hadingham, author-editor, PBS Nova

CONVERSING WITH THE PLANETS: HOW SCIENCE AND MYTH INVENTED THE COSMOS

"In this intriguing work, Anthony Aveni writes with a mastery and polish that is wonderfully accessible, akin to an engaging classroom lecture."

New York Times *Book Review*

EMPIRES OF TIME: CLOCKS, CALENDARS, AND CULTURES

"One of the best books on a scientific theme for the serious general reader that I have read for some time."

John Barrow, author-physicist

Class Not Dismissed

REFLECTIONS ON UNDERGRADUATE EDUCATION
AND TEACHING THE LIBERAL ARTS

ANTHONY AVENI

University Press of Colorado
Boulder

© 2014 by Anthony Aveni

Published by University Press of Colorado
5589 Arapahoe Avenue, Suite 206C
Boulder, Colorado 80303

The University Press of Colorado is a proud member of
the Association of American University Presses.

The University Press of Colorado is a cooperative publishing enterprise supported, in part,
by Adams State University, Colorado State University, Fort Lewis College, Metropolitan State
University of Denver, Regis University, University of Colorado, University of Northern Colorado,
Utah State University, and Western State Colorado University.

∞ This paper meets the requirements of the ANSI / NISO Z39.48-1992 (Permanence of Paper).

Library of Congress Cataloging-in-Publication Data

Aveni, Anthony F.
  Class not dismissed : reflections on undergraduate education and teaching the liberal arts /
Anthony Aveni.
    pages cm
  ISBN 978-1-60732-302-0 (paperback) — ISBN 978-1-60732-303-7 (ebook)
  1. Education, Humanistic. 2. College teaching. 3. Lecture method in teaching.
4. Undergraduates. I. Title.
  LC1011.A896 2014
  370.11'2—dc23

                              2014010469

Cover illustration © razihusin / Shutterstock.com

23 22 21 20 19 18 17 16 15 14   10 9 8 7 6 5 4 3 2 1

To the teachers we all remember best.

Contents

Acknowledgments

I am grateful to Darrin Pratt and his staff, especially Laura Furney, Dan Pratt, Cheryl Carnahan, and Kelly Lenkevich, at the University Press of Colorado for working with me on my books for more than ten years, to Diane Janney for serving as my assistant at home base for fifteen years, to Faith Hamlin for representing me these past twenty-five years in the literary world, and to my wife, Lorraine Aveni, for supporting me for an even greater length of time than I've spent at Colgate. Finally, to all those connected with every aspect of Colgate University, I have decided to cop out of making a list. First, it would be too lengthy, and second, I would fear leaving someone out. So, especially to my fellow teachers and students: you know who you are, and thanks so much for contributing to my life in learning.

Class Not Dismissed

1

Introduction

At first I had in mind a set of memoirs filled with lasting moments in and around my classroom, interactions with students and colleagues, the worst and best experiences on campus, moments of reflection about those I hold dear who mentored me in my career as teacher and scholar: what you might expect from a prof who has held one and only one job his entire professional life, a job—how I hate to call it that—he's loved from day one and continues to cherish. Having completed my fiftieth year of service at Colgate University, a small liberal arts college in upstate New York, I have told so many teaching-related stories that friends have suggested I ought to catalog them by number.

Then I began to think more about the serious, complex issues involved in the process of teaching and learning. I had thought about them before, discussed them with fellow educators, even played a role in implementing new ways of educating young people at the college: How do you measure effective teaching? Is there really a conflict between creating knowledge (scholarship) and disseminating it (teaching)? How do you hold to a college's mission

DOI: 10.5876/9781607323037.c001

1

to offer the very best education in a changing world, a world in which the teacher and what he teaches has lately been cast in shadowy light? I needed to deal with these pressing issues too. I wondered: Does all that I have to share about what I have lived and learned from more than half a century in the classroom, a time that covers more than one-fourth of the entire existence of the venerable institution I still serve, require two separate books?

Almost never having come across a book about education that wasn't as dry as dust, I decided to use salient memories to support and enhance themes related to modes of acquiring and disseminating knowledge to young people. *Class Not Dismissed* is my attempt to parlay what friends call my natural sense of humor with my take on the profession by threading stories, some laughable, others deeply serious, into a narrative that gets at things I believe are important to both teachers and students (I've italicized them in the text). My goal is to share real stories about everyday college life that might help promote a dialogue on serious educational issues, many of which, even after all these years, I still haven't fully worked out.

As is obvious from the table of contents, I have chosen the standard journalistic "why? what? how?" format to set up the narrative. "Why I Teach" (chapter 2) begins with the qualities I remember best in those who inspired me to make life choices. I also take account of what fellow teachers have to say about their memorable mentors and why they share my profession. As you might guess, it's all about passion. So much of what delights us as teachers emanates from paying witness to what I like to call the "breathing process." Learning is like being born. It begins with a gasp, an unsteady, assisted intake of knowledge and ideas in a strange, threatening environment. Then it gradually grows, settles in, becomes more deeply rooted and more controlled. Effective learning has so much to do with your ability to take over and breathe on your own. To breathe life into my account, I've incorporated stories of my own unsteady breaths as a novice teacher.

Chapter 3, "What I Teach," opens with the horror story of the first time I was asked to conduct a class in a subject area I knew little about. My initial resistance to the liberal arts processual mandate of helping students become aware of the values that lie at the core of their identities loomed as a frightening task. There I was, stranded in an intellectual wilderness, worlds away from home discipline. I also share my thoughts and feelings about another uncomfortable struggle in which I tried to balance dedication to my own specialty and an increasing desire to contribute to a new interdisciplinary inquiry.

My narrative necessitates dealing with a little history about where the idea of the liberal arts originated and how it developed and changed in the American academy, especially at my home institution. Little did I realize, when I entered Colgate as a yet-uncertified professional astronomer at age twenty-five, that I would be called upon to spearhead the first major revision of the college's general education program in the post–World War II era. Some of the bizarre suggestions I received from fellow profs about how to revise gen ed (a task I've likened to moving a graveyard), though sincerely intended, are too precious not to share, especially those I encountered in dialogues with my imaginative colleagues next to the fancy espresso machine I purchased with a large chunk of my first year's budget—all in the spirit of promoting academic discourse.

What does it mean to be educated? Is it only about acquiring a body of knowledge, or does it have as much to do with experiencing the process of how you come to know what you never knew before? Product vs. process: that's the essential tension between the two goals that challenge all teachers. I deal with this in chapter 4, "How I Teach." Because I believe in learning by sharing both negative and positive experiences, I begin with stories that taught me how *not* to teach. Much of my "how" section focuses on method and the big debate about whether to lecture or lead discussions. Both are viable teaching techniques, and each requires a lot of time and thought for a teacher to become really effective. Rather than simply resort to boring lists of how to do this or how not to do that, again I thought it best to convey my ideas on methods of teaching through storytelling. I want to share some engaging tales of life experience in the classroom as a way to raise questions about how we all might make teaching more effective.

Chapter 5, "Questioning Teaching," is a bit more opinionated. Here I single out what I believe are the most pressing problems and issues confronting teachers and students: Should professors be given tenure, essentially a guaranteed job for life? Where do the roles of parents and teachers crisscross one another? How should we assess quality teaching? How much attention should be paid to student as opposed to peer evaluation? Can vocational training and the liberal arts coexist constructively? Where does technology belong in the classroom? What's behind the current lecture-on-a-laptop trend? Will the

Free Internet College transform the future of American education? Finally, I end on one of today's most hotly debated questions. Being a student today is a far cry from what it was when I enrolled in college: the debt crisis didn't exist, and there were jobs aplenty. So, why go to college anyway?

Having been involved in interdisciplinary studies long before it became fashionable, my perspective on education tends to be a bit broader than that of most college teachers. Though I was trained in the sciences, I hold a joint appointment in the social sciences, a result of venturing long ago outside my discipline of astronomy into what stargazing means in other cultures. (They call that anthropology in the academy.) I've also held visiting appointments in the humanities at other universities. And I have written books, including two for children, that cut across the trinity of curricula: the sciences, social sciences, and humanities.

In sum, I wrote *Class Not Dismissed* because I felt the need to say something about what academic life is like in practice. I want to share the joy and the despair, the high and the low points in a profession I would trade for no other. Passion. That's the single quality I wish those who read this book would feel about what they do with their lives, no matter what profession they may choose. So whether you're a fellow teacher, a student in or about to enter college, or one who has been there and has had occasion to reflect on your experience of college life, I hope my stories about life and learning connect with you.

2 | Why I Teach

In studying the convoluted orbits of the stars my feet
do not touch the earth, and, seated at the table of Zeus
himself, I am nurtured with celestial ambrosia.
—*Claudius Ptolemy*[1]

To get an education you have to hang
around until you catch on.
—*Robert Frost*[2]

I Love You, Miss Cohen

I dedicate *Class Not Dismissed* to Miss Sarah Cohen, my second-grade teacher at the Truman Street School in New Haven, Connecticut. Because it is so often the case that someone's gift to us early in life goes unappreciated until much later, I've lost track of her. I'm not even sure whether her version of Sarah comes with an "h."

DOI: 10.5876/9781607323037.c002

Miss Cohen was tall, dark, late-thirty-ish, with a slightly raspy voice (she was a heavy smoker). Gentle in her demeanor, extremely patient, and—as anyone would know who spent five minutes in her classroom or only peered through one of its glass windows and watched her move and smile and gesticulate—totally in love with her kids. She was also way ahead of her time as a classroom innovator, and this is where she touched me most deeply. Sure, she taught the three Rs, but she also gave her kids plenty of rope to explore. And she indulged our passions unabashedly. She would often respond to a question with "let's do it and find out!" You know the type.

What Sarah Cohen kindled in me was chutzpah in a *positive* sense—a kind of audacity that manifested itself in my building up enough self-confidence to dare to do something I initially thought I couldn't possibly pull off. When I told her I wanted to be an author, she didn't simply encourage me to try writing a book; she made an entire class project out of it. Miss Cohen asked each student to volunteer a task: research, illustrations, arrangement and labeling of figures, cover design, sectioning and title making, indexing—even book binding. I would be the lyricist.

The book's title was *The Queen's Dilemma*, the story of a ruler who leaves the castle because she's overworked and underappreciated. She undergoes a series of travails: wandering in the forest, meeting strange people, encountering wild animals, and nearly starving to death. Finally she meets her prince charming, who awakens her with a kiss while she's fast asleep under a tree. I pirated the story line out of a combination of Cinderella and Snow White, minus the Seven Dwarfs. Now that I think about it, my mother, a beleaguered homemaker who also worked full-time, was likely the archetype of my lead character.

All the kids in Room 2 got excited when it came time for the class to work on joint projects. Less constrained than today's teachers by curricular mandates, Miss Cohen would set aside the hour following lunch break for student collaboration. Every step of the way, she'd make sure we were all aware of how every facet of the process of creating a work of literature needed to be carefully coordinated. The sentences in our book needed to be grammatically correct, the printing squared off and tidy. All the illustrations had to be placed at the correct positions in the text for the story to make sense. There were endless production questions: Would the queen really wear an outfit like that when she was running through the forest? How much glue do you need to add to the binding to make the book strong enough to resist repeated openings and closings? Are you sure you worked out the price of the book to cover the cost of all the materials and still make a reasonable profit? Sarah Cohen had a knack for knowing when to loosen the tether and when to give it a gentle tug to help guide her young charges along the path of learning by doing.

The Queen's Dilemma took about three weeks to complete, from ruling the lines on the page that would frame the inch-high pencil print to the binding process, done in decorative wallpaper glued to heavy cardboard. I got to keep the finished product, and I cherish its tattered pages to this day. My mother loved to trot it out when she bragged, all too frequently, about her son's first book, written at the age of seven.

Sarah Cohen was a daring experimentalist who ventured far beyond rote teaching and curricular norms. Every time I come across *The Queen's Dilemma* in our family memorabilia box, it reminds me of the care I must give and the confidence I must try to instill in my own students, incentives reinforced in Miss Cohen's neighborhood school classroom. I regret that I missed the opportunity to thank her in person for all she gave me.

Dreams of Skywatching

My moment of revelation about the wonders of the universe began when I was eight years old. It happened as I lay half awake, sprawled face-up in the back seat of my father's '38 Dodge. We were returning, as we did late on most summer Sunday nights, from visiting my mother's family in the nearby town of Ansonia. Looking almost straight up out of the sharply angled rear window, I noticed the way the stars reflected the car's turning motion by rotating in the opposite direction. A band of faint light that stretched all the way across the sky caught my eye. Like the stars around it, the luminous streak kept shifting direction with each turn, first parallel, then perpendicular to the back window.

When we pulled into the driveway, I distinctly remember opening the car's heavy rear door and stepping out into the cool night air, the silence broken only by chirping crickets. I looked up and my mouth opened wide as I beheld the black night sky blanketed by dazzling starlight. There was that milky white band in the sky that ran from the top of the garage straight up overhead and disappeared behind the roof of the house. I could make it move all by myself just by rotating my body. What was that fuzzy luminescence? And where did all those stars that blanketed the rest of the sky come from? There must have been millions, billions, zillions of them, I thought. What were they? How far away? In his chapter on mysticism in *The Varieties of Religious Experience*, William James wrote: "When I walk the fields, I am oppressed now and then with an innate feeling that everything I see has a meaning, if I could but understand it. And this feeling of being surrounded with truths which I cannot grasp amounts to indescribable awe . . . Have you not felt that your real soul was imperceptible to your mental vision, except in a few hallowed moments?"[3]

That late summer night was the first time in my life I recall feeling the emotional state of excitement we call *passion*. It was an almost breathless feeling, and it nearly brought me to tears. I became consumed with an overwhelming desire to find out as much as I could about the stunning spectacle I'd just witnessed. When I told Miss Cohen about it, she explained that the band of light that enthralled my soul was known as the Milky Way—the edge of the galaxy we live in, part of an even bigger universe made up of billions of galaxies. How big was it? "You need to go and find out," she said, pointing me toward Dewey Decimal Section number 523 of the Truman Street School Library. There were only three or four astronomy books among the minuscule holdings in the humble neighborhood cache of knowledge, scarcely enough to satisfy the immediate needs of my curiosity. But the vast collection at the City of New Haven Public Library, just a nickel ride downtown on the Washington Avenue streetcar, held the potential to temporarily quench and then further accelerate my desire to answer a flood of questions that popped into my head: Where did the stars come from? What makes them shine? Why do they have different colors? How come some are bright and others are scarcely visible? I spent hours in the reading room after school pouring over Camille Flammarion's detailed illustrations of the Milky Way in his thick *Dreams of an Astronomer*. I fantasized over the imaginative drawings of what life in a space station might be like in Willy Ley's *Conquest of Space*. I rummaged through the entries in the *Catalog of Celestial Objects for Common Telescopes* by the pioneer celestial photographer Edward Emerson Barnard. I copied notes, drew charts, even made my own star catalog. Over the next four years I managed to save up seventy-five dollars of allowance money to buy my own telescope. What a feeling of excitement, this opening of the mind, this newly acquired capacity to pursue on my own the truths about a world I'd never encountered before.

I acquired great joy in collecting information about the vast extent of the creation of the universe in space and time. I learned that the span of existence of our entire human family, from cave dweller to ancient pyramid builder to me and all of my lived activities, was as small in comparison to the age of the universe as was the thickness of the coat of gold paint on the dome of the New Haven Public Library compared to the height of the building itself. I found joy too in understanding *how* astronomers had come to know that it would take more than a human lifetime to travel to the nearest star in the space vehicles Ley promised would one day take us to the moon.

My zeal for acquiring information was soon accompanied, for reasons I can't explain, by a deep desire to share my knowledge with my friends. My teaching career began at age eleven in an abandoned coal bin in the shared basement of a second-story coldwater flat my mother, father, younger brother, and I rented in a two-family house in East Haven, Connecticut. The coal bin, an 8-ft. × 10-ft. wood-slatted chamber, open at the front, lay empty, as most of them did in the early 1950s. By then, postwar American homes were heated largely by oil.

That extinct coal bin would become my classroom, the place where my brain child, the East Haven Astronomy Club, would meet every Tuesday after school. The number of enlightened pals in my neighborhood middle-school class interested in the pursuit of the life of the mind was surprisingly large—maybe 15 percent, which amounted to five or six boys. Today we'd call them "geeks"—still my most cherished classroom treasures. We all pitched in sweeping, cleaning, and decorating the walls with picture cutouts of planets and galaxies from *Life* and *National Geographic* magazines. Sitting on makeshift benches, each made of pieces of discarded 8 × 10 boards nailed together, at desks fashioned out of vegetable crates found in the trash bin behind Green's Neighborhood Market, we crowded into the cozy coal bin–turned-classroom to share our ideas.

Most of the lessons—gee-whiz stuff that excites the young adolescent mind—were given by me. I recall teaching *my* students how to find constellations with the aid of a homemade sky map, replete with labels for magnitudes, distances, and colors of member stars and fashioned out of a discarded window shade. Each of us chose a favorite star. Mine was the bright blue super-giant Rigel in Orion, the Hunter, 800 light years distant and 50,000 times brighter than the sun—imagine! We'd also convene at night during the summer to look through my 2-inch refracting telescope. Because we lived near a wetland, mosquitoes plagued us. To ward them off, we would station ourselves inside a circle ringed with dry cattails stuck in the ground. Once we'd ignited them, the smoke, an awful-smelling blend of swampy incenses, kept us protected—though it didn't help the seeing conditions.

When our landlord heard that his basement was periodically crammed with kids who could only be up to mischief, he evicted us. Undeterred, we built a second classroom out of twigs and thatch in the woods behind the widely spaced houses in our neighborhood, but it gradually got taken over by kids from the next block whose alternative goal of building a "smoking fort" (a place where they convened to smoke cigarettes) conflicted with the more lofty pursuits of the scientific mission of the coal bin academy.

But other opportunities to share in the joy of learning awaited me. My paternal Uncle Carl, a whiz of a grade-school teacher (seventh and eighth grades), periodically invited me to conduct a class. On one occasion I brought my telescope, took it apart, and ran a little seminar on how it worked. He taught me how he "hooked" his kids with a provocative question like, how come two lenses 3 feet apart make faraway things look big? Why are the images upside down? Here, you try it. Then he'd hand a pair of lenses to one of his kids to experiment with.

I don't know why I stuck with the stars. Scarcely a day of my life in middle and high school passed when astronomy wasn't on my mind. Well, there were a few times . . . My high-school chemistry teacher, Esther Barnett, was a soft-spoken diminutive woman who, as far as I could judge, knew more about her subject than all my other teachers combined seemed to know about theirs. Her lessons were anything but rote. She seemed so absorbed when she engaged us, constantly throwing out questions. She would ask us to guess what might happen when she poured the contents of one test tube into another. She had a way of building excitement with each response. Then she'd smile and pour. Now, what could the weird-smelling gas be that's bubbling up out of that test tube? Or, here's mercury. It's a silvery liquid as dense as lead. So how come when we bind it with oxygen it turns into a red powder? Amazing! Esther delivered the goods, the mystery of the chemical elements. She didn't just engage me; she also encouraged me to pursue my own studies beyond the classroom.

I got so turned on to chemistry that in my senior year of high school I spent most of my earnings, acquired from working part-time in the family-owned diner, on chemicals and test tubes in an effort to set up my own home chemistry lab in our basement. I lessened the burden of my mother's concern about the noxious fumes that emanated from my chem lab by offering a project on science in the public interest. I would test her urine, as well as that of all five of my maternal aunts. (Sugar diabetes, as they then called it, ran on her side of the family.) But an unanticipated incident dealt a death blow to my nascent chemical research. Among the depleted items in my stock was hydrochloric acid. Caustic and volatile, it's really necessary if you want to isolate some of the more exotic chemical species. Since my dad contemplated a stop at the drugstore on the way home from work one day, I asked him to pick up a bottle for me. That evening as the family car (a '49 Mercury coupe had replaced the '38 Dodge) approached the driveway, I heard the brakes screech. Looking out the window I saw the vehicle stopped in mid-turn. My father had flung open the door and flown out of the car. I saw him dash randomly around the yard, as if chased by some wild animal, a trail of smoke emanating from his coat pocket. Now, doesn't everybody know you don't stuff a bottle of HCl into your overcoat pocket, at least not when your car heater is turned on full blast and you're driving over a bumpy road? The bottle had exploded and burned his upper thigh (not seriously). By the time my father burst through the back door, he had discarded his coat and his smoking pants were down to his knees. The accusative pointing finger at the end of his extended arm told me, even before he could deliver the dictum in a loud angry voice, that all chemical operations in the house would be shut down immediately.

College wasn't easy for me at the outset. My second-generation American parents had needed to quit high school to earn a living. Though they were incapable of mentoring me in my studies, they did give me a good work ethic to help overcome my poor preparation for college. In the inner-city high school I attended, my trig teacher doubled as a basketball coach and my physics teacher spent more time in the neighborhood bar than in the lab. Esther Barnett was a welcome aberration. I barely made it into Boston University and struggled in my first semester to cling to a 2.7 GPA. Away from home for the first time and never having socialized much, in the early part of that semester I fell in with the wrong set of compañeros who happened to room in the vicinity of 501 Myles Standish Hall, the quarters I shared with four other freshmen. Drinking beer and playing cards (cribbage was big in the 1950s) filled my need for inclusion in the social norm. I remember in my one low-enrollment class that fall, Freshman Composition, feeling intimidated by responses from students who seemed vastly wiser than I. "The last two books I read by Sartre were mostly about communism," responded Lois to the question "what is communism?" Who's Sartre? I was surprised to learn through the grapevine that Lois ended up with a B-minus in the course, same as me. It was a struggle, but once I got up enough courage to seek help from the graduate student TA in my physics class, I began to learn strategies for problem solving. I also realized that the time I needed to study to *really* understand the material was vastly greater than I had anticipated, compared to my experience in high school, where fewer than a fifth of the class went on to college.

The Ones I Remember

I had favorites in college too. Caleb Wroe Wolfe, my geology professor at Boston University, inspired throngs of students with his dynamic presentations on volcanoes and earthquakes. I could sense in him that feeling of wanting to communicate the sheer joy of learning I spoke about earlier. He chose every word so carefully, expressed every idea so clearly; the rocks he held in his hand almost seemed to come to life. He turned me on. His electrically charged classes drove me to the library. Field trips to the Berkshires and the North Shore added an active, hands-on component to the classroom learning experience. Under Wolfe's spell, I seriously considered majoring in geology, though eventually I'd return once again to the stars. But the desire to teach never left me.

Gordon Stipe was my favorite physics teacher. US Navy man schooled under the GI Bill, southern gentleman, soft-spoken. I had him for three courses. He'd sit and talk with me or ask me how school was going, then how my physics homework was progressing. He was approachable, and our conversations helped me lose my fear of looking stupid if I asked my instructor a question.

Then there was Ray Weymann, the scourge of all astronomy grad students at the University of Arizona, where I earned my PhD. Weymann was not a master lecturer. He influenced me in a different way. Ray was a strict disciplinarian and an unrelentingly critical perfectionist who rode herd on his students, never seeming quite satisfied until he could be assured they had left no stone unturned in whatever territory they explored. As a theorist, he cared mostly about *ideas*. Though his area of research was pretty far removed from my own, he ended up offering me more constructive criticism on my largely empirically based dissertation than any of the other readers.

Weymann was neither charismatic, in the Wolfian sense, nor outgoing like Professor Stipe. Nothing took center stage away from the world of *ideas*, not even his personal appearance. Hair uncombed, his white shirttails never tucked in, he'd cast a squinty-eyed look, especially when he badgered his charges with questions like "why didn't you do *this*" or "how could you overlook *that*?" He was unrelenting and frankly a bit intimidating. Call me a masochist, but I found myself going back to his office. I reasoned that Weymann really cared about me. Why else would he spend so much time critiquing me and helping me perfect my work? So what if he worked overtime not to show it? Was he worried about violating some imagined decorum in the teacher-student relationship? Several years later, when I spent my first sabbatical leave at the University of Arizona, engaged in research on the birth of young stars, Lorraine and I ran into Ray and his wife, Barbara, at a departmental colloquium. Lorraine reminded the couple of the time they had invited Ray's seminar class over to the house for popcorn and conversation. "That meant a lot to us," she said. Ray Weymann's squinty eyes suddenly welled up in tears, and he compelled himself to turn away. Strange man, but I loved him.

The facets that make up the mosaic of qualities of my favorite teachers are colored and shaped differently. If Sarah Cohen was my role model for self-confidence, Ray Weymann, who continually pressed me to go further than I wished, became my archetype of perseverance. Gordon Stipe showed me that some teachers aren't too busy to help you integrate your personal life into your life as a student. From second grade through graduate school, they all played a role in making me who I would become in the classroom.

I've collected a host of answers to the question, why were they your favorite teachers? She was accessible: her door was always open. He meticulously prepared his lectures. She had an almost magical capacity to stimulate me to perform at the highest possible level I could achieve. I wanted to please her, especially. He was a great storyteller who had a knack of relating just about anything in the assignment to some true-life experience. He was an amazing synthesizer. I could ask her what now appear to be the stupidest questions without worrying that she'd put me down. She cared about me personally. He was entertaining, scholarly, precise, loud, animated, and friendly to boot. He showed that he was fallible by the wonderful gift of being able to laugh at himself—a real human being. Every time I'd ask her a question she'd ask me to explain, to work out the answer for myself. At first I found this habit annoying, but later I realized that she gave me a real gift of how to learn—by teaching myself. He had a challenging mind that made me realize I would benefit greatly just from being around him. If there's a common denominator in these disparate answers to who was your favorite teacher, I wager you'll discover it in the root response by those of us in the profession to another question: Why do you teach?

Archetype of the Professor

Back in the 1980s I used to attend biweekly seminars on Andean anthropology at Cornell University, a 90-minute commute from my home in Hamilton, New York. In addition to the faculty and graduate students at Cornell, scholars and students interested in Andean studies would drive over from the universities in Binghamton, Albany, and Buffalo to participate in the sessions. These seminars usually consisted of a presentation by one of the members of the group, followed by a lengthy discussion. Among the attendees was Bernd Lambert, a brilliant social anthropologist, linguist, and longtime member of the Cornell faculty. Attired in tweed tattered at the elbows, he usually sat slumped over in his chair during the presentations, his eyes half shut, still awake but with his head bowed. Lambert said little, but he always had a look of deep concentration; his face, what you could see of it, was screwed into odd contortions. Frequently, he would move his index finger in a wiggly, yet controlled, motion from left to right across the blank space of the table immediately in front of him. Then he'd return the finger to its starting position and repeat the complex linear movement all over again. Hypnotized by his actions, I realized that he was writing—sans paper and pen. Later I learned that Lambert was a campus character noted for "doing his linguistics" in the midst of meetings and seminars.

Though deeply absorbed inscribing his thoughts invisibly on horizontal surfaces of campus furniture, on occasion he would pose an insightful question or make a cogent observation.

Of moving fingers and professorial super-concentration, I recall Colgate psychology professor Nicholas Longo, an expert on dolphin and porpoise behavior, holding forth in one of our old campus lecture halls. The venue featured a long stone table equipped with gas, air, and water jets and various other ports and outlets to accommodate demo equipment. I noticed that the more absorbed Nick got, the greater the attraction his right index finger seemed to acquire to a half-inch-diameter circular hole cut through the thick slate slab that comprised the top of the table. "And . . . uh-h-h . . ." Nick thought extra hard as he attempted to phrase the precise terminology to explain delphinic eye-brain coordination mechanisms, all the while worming his finger deeper into the aperture. "Let me write it down for you," he said; and he turned to move toward the blackboard behind the table. But Nick's finger refused to follow. It got stuck fast in the circular hole, and all attempts at turning and twisting the digit to release it failed. A gentle tug, a strong pull, then he cast a hopeless gaze into the assembled throng and sighed, "Jesus—I'm stuck!" It took five minutes and the help of a bar of soap and gentle massaging by three of us seated in the front row to put Nick back together again. Then, fully focused, he clicked back into his insightful presentation.

I have witnessed many other examples of deep thought–concentration overtaking all other concerns in the classroom. Robert Nesbet, my physics instructor at Boston University, often neglected to return the zipper on his trousers to the full upright position once he'd left the men's room prior to class. On one occasion he appeared in class with a foot-long thin strip of tissue hanging like a stalactite from the hinge that attached the rim to the lens frame of his eyeglasses. Later in the term, having broken his spectacles and evidently not holding their repair in high priority, he taught our quantum mechanics class for three weeks with the vision-enhancing device held precariously in place by a single rim. As he lectured, his head would gradually tilt to one side to compensate for the gravitational shift of his unbalanced optical headgear. Periodic readjustment righted his spectacles with his cranium and another ten-minute cycle ensued. One day, as he worked up a concentrated head of steam and began to immerse himself deeper and deeper into the theory of the shell model of the hydrogen atom, Professor Nesbet raced around the front of the room excitedly waving and gesturing an account of what was happening in his brain as a torrent of words spilled out of his mouth: "The likelihood of a transition in this electronic state of the atom depends on . . ." Suddenly, his trajectory was violently halted frontally at pelvic level by the sharp corner of the desk. Momentarily doubled over in pain, he quickly caught his breath and finished his sentence: "the probability coefficient of the energy levels involved."

Some professors consciously play into the popularly conceived role of the academic lost in a world of his own. For example, a young instructor in our physics department used to love to act out his imagined version of the late-nineteenth-century Gilded Age professor (a time when physics first began to undergo revolutionary developments). At one of his colloquia I attended (in the aforementioned classroom) he appeared in a dark pinstripe suit, replete with vest, pocket watch, and bowtie. He sported a goatee to enhance the image and even faked a slight British accent. Some students hated it—said on their evaluation forms that they found him distant and pretentious—but others really got into it. As he sashayed around the room expounding on relativistic principles (he claimed to have been a student of a student of Einstein), the professor sidled over to the front of that same big slate table—the formidable barrier between the authority behind the desk and the unwashed mass in front of it. Perhaps with thoughts of altering the atmosphere in the direction of informality, he attempted to hoist himself up into a seated position at one end of the table. Unfortunately, as he lifted himself, his bottom made perfect contact with a two-foot-square plywood board that covered up a small sink built into the slate desktop. The board flipped out from under him and his rear end plunged into the sink, leaving his arms and legs thrust upward. The professor flailed in a vain attempt to extricate himself. His wild wriggling caused his pant cuffs to descend downward toward his knees, revealing a pair of elastic garters attached to his stockings. Once again the faithful front-row faculty caregivers leaped to the rescue, but not before the classroom descended into howling chaos. Embarrassing! But maybe there's a moral: be who you really are in the classroom.

My stories fit the typical academic portrayed in the popular media as an absent-minded professor who comes to class wearing rumpled clothes—the old tweed jacket and unpressed trousers with cuffs cut well above the ankles if a man; hair in a bun, thick glasses, and an overly lengthy, out-of-date print dress if a woman. At formal occasions he appears in a tux three sizes too large, his untied cravat dangling down his wrinkled shirt and his hair flared out in Einsteinian fashion. She travels about town on a worn-out single-gear bike or manages to get around in a clunker. *The Nutty Professor*, both the earlier 1960s Jerry Lewis version and the later 1990s remake with Eddie Murphy, come to mind. Portrayed by comic "Professor" Irwin Corey, "the world's foremost authority" (older readers will remember him), the professor exhibits a panoply of nervous tics and speaks in an incomprehensible mushy jargon: "To make the gezakstehagen you connect the rubber gungus to the orange kelted klyme." Though Corey made me laugh, his egghead impression troubled me a little because it represented people in my profession as oddballs, totally tuned out of anything mainstream. Yet I am forced to admit that Corey did effectively portray the behavior of a few odd characters in the academy I've known—and dared tell you about in amusing little vignettes. But they are rare and they impact mass cultural perception disproportionately.

So why this image? I believe it stems not so much from academics immersed in a separate world completely detached from reality but more from not necessarily seeing the world the way most other people do. Teacher Mark Edmundson thinks the best teachers are the ones who encourage their students to think about the world in alternative ways.[4] Good teaching, he says, is about thinking in ways most of us see as "counterintuitive." For example, the historian sees an election not through the latest news bites but in the historical framework of American politics. The biologist views the natural world as "not calmly picturesque but a jostling, striving, evolving contest of creatures in quest of reproduction and survival." The literature professor, unimpressed by the usual clichés, "demands bursting metaphors and ironies of an insinuatingly serpentine sort." And the philosopher seeks out an argument "as escapeproof as an iron box: what currently passes for logic makes him want to grasp himself by the hair and yank himself out of his seat."[5]

Why are the best teachers often described as "dispassionate" or "disinterested?" Now if one of my students should tweet Mom or Dad and tell them "Professor Aveni says he's disinterested in astronomy . . .and he's not passionate either," I might get a complaint that I'm not really into my job. Notice that I didn't say *not* passionate or *un*interested. Being *dis*passionate means not falling prey to trendiness. And *dis*interest means I don't have an ax to grind, a personal opinion driving my explanation of an idea or issue. A good teacher can be passionate about what he teaches but dispassionate when it comes to the issues he raises.

Learning, Loving, Breathing

Love is the answer. Love of knowing. Love of wanting to help someone else to know. Love of watching students grow and change. In *The Symposium*, Plato speaks of the "erotic-educational" relationship between teacher and student. Plato differentiates between Common Love, which is purely physical, and Heavenly Love, which develops only in those who become capable of seeking virtue by developing the capacity to reason. Plato's dialogue on love and learning still rouses controversy today (you can see why if you read it carefully):

> The correct way, she said, for someone to approach this business is to begin when he's young by being drawn towards beautiful bodies. At first, if his guide leads him correctly, he should love just one body and in that relationship produce beautiful discourses. Next he should realize that the beauty of any one body is closely related to that of another, and that, if he is to pursue beauty of form, it's very foolish not to regard the beauty of all bodies as one and the same. Once he's seen this, he'll become a lover of all beautiful bodies, and will relax his intense passion for just one body, despising this passion and regarding it as petty. After this, he should regard the beauty of minds as more valuable than that of the body, so that, if someone has goodness of mind even if he has little of the bloom of beauty, he will be content with him, and will love and care for him, and give birth to the kinds of discourse that help young men to become better. As a result, he will be forced to observe the beauty in practices and laws and to see that every type of beauty is closely related to every other, so that he will regard beauty of body as something petty. After practices, the guide must lead him towards forms of knowledge, so that he sees their beauty too. Looking now at beauty in general and not just at individual instances, he will no longer be slavishly attached to the beauty of a boy, or of any particular person at all, or of a specific practice. Instead of this low and small-minded slavery, he will be turned towards the great sea of beauty and gazing on it he'll give birth, through a boundless love of knowledge, to many beautiful and magnificent discourses and ideas.[6]

Though Plato couches his discussion of love in unmistakable sexual language, relating it to social relationships between aristocratic men and boys, he makes clear that Virtue can be attained only when "someone is willing to put himself at someone else's service in the belief that the other person will help him improve in wisdom, or some other aspect of virtue."[7]

In an essay titled "Loving Teaching," English professor Peter Beidler likens his love of the profession to romantic love.[8] The two share several common elements, such as trust, encouragement, praise, self-revelation, discovery, risk taking, and selflessness. For example, loving teachers try to build trust. Good teachers are not afraid to put aside the mask of the teacher and show some of the uncertainty within; and the truly selfless teacher and the student in whom she confides are involved in the fragile process of discovering new feelings and new truths together. Like the selfless lover, the good teacher wants not what is best for him but for his students.

Teaching is like the process of breathing. Beidler tells us that "being a teacher is being present at creation, the day a student begins to breathe . . . Nothing is more exciting than being there when the breathing starts . . . I occasionally find myself, quite magically, catching my breath with them."[9]

My Colgate colleague, biologist Nancy Pruitt, describes the successive stages she has witnessed in the breathing process. Her greatest moments in teaching happen mostly in the sophomore classroom. At the outset of the term, the students still want to know what they need to memorize and which pages of the text they will be tested on. By the middle of the term, one or two students begin to ask questions that connect an idea with the problem at hand. Another dares to become critical of one of the methods used in a study. Still another brings ideas from a different class to bear on a problem the class is working on. Now the breath of life in the learning process has begun to take hold. By the end of the semester, Pruitt tells me, her linear thinkers are gradually transformed into independent creative individuals.

What educator isn't familiar with the stages of learning development in her students' breathing process? Most initiates think all questions have definite answers. To get the answers you consult the experts (your professors) for the correct information. I recall one of my freshmen dropping by the office after we had spent part of a class discussing the question "why is there so much intellectual apathy on this campus." He flopped into my guest easy chair that seems to possess the magical quality of rendering students more conversant and said, "Okay, professor. You convinced me. I want to be more intellectual. Now tell me what to do." For the beginning learner, all truth is absolute. That's Stage One.

Pruitt's sophomores had begun to realize that Stage Two in the breathing process happens when you come to realize that many problems don't have a single fixed answer. The opinions of the experts determine how they will respond to questions—opinions informed by their experience and beliefs. But there's no real basis for judging these opinions; all truth is relative.

Finally, Stage Three in the breathing process comes only with continued exposure to ideas. Only then will the student discover that in many cases judgment *can* be evaluated on the basis of better reasoning and more solid evidence and that perhaps the problem itself can be restructured in a better way. In the transformation from "ignorant certainty" (Stage One) to "intelligent confusion" (Stage Three)—and here I employ former Harvard president Derek Bok's labels[10]—the student becomes a critical thinker. There's irony in realizing that to be educated, you must pass from a perceived state of knowing to being content without knowing.

The psychologist and educational researcher William Perry, who conducted a lengthy study of cognitive development in a group of male Harvard students in the 1960s, came to pretty much the same conclusion. He was able to discern four basic developmental stages of self-perception, beginning with Dualism, wherein knowledge is an absolute entity and any point of view that challenges it is unacceptable.[11] In Multiplicity, the second stage, students view their teacher as the expert. Relativism is the third stage and I think the most difficult to transition to because it involves confronting complexity. The student who perseveres begins to realize, slowly and painfully, that knowledge isn't simply acquired by direct transmission. You need to participate in the process. Now students begin to acquire an appreciation for forming their own viewpoint, which may incorporate their experiences and beliefs. Commitment, the fourth stage, happens when students start to acquire the responsibility to reflect upon and integrate what they learn from others, so they can create ideas on their own.

The Russian developmental child psychologist Lev Vygotsky calls commitment the "zone of proximal development," that uncomfortable domain that lies between knowing and not knowing something.[12] Applied to more mature young people, Vygotsky's assertion would be that a more capable person can help a student learn skills that pass beyond his level. In other words, development *follows* one's intellectual maturational potential to learn. It doesn't just depend on a student's independent abilities. It's a teacher's duty to push her students into that tenuous zone, as discomforting as it might seem in the teacher-student relationship.

Now for the bad news. Many educators feel most people who go to college never get much past Stage One. The lively mind doesn't come into being through mere exposure, even if you take Robert Frost's advice quoted in my second epigraph to this chapter and "hang out."

I think being there when the lights go on, when the pupils dilate (sorry for the pun), is for me one of teaching's greatest moments—Perry's third stage especially. But, like lighting a fire in the woods without matches on a damp day, getting the breathing process going can be tedious and time-consuming. It requires thought and attention—dry leaves over dry sticks, rubbed together vigorously, continuously. But when the few fragments on top burst into flame, warmth becomes satisfaction. So it is in the classroom. If you rub the wrong way, callously, hastily, there is no fire, no breath, no life.

The challenge of actually trying to transfer my analytical and synthetic thought processes to the brain of another, that's what attracted me to teaching, writes professor of Spanish literature Fernando Plata. "This *is* as hard as it sounds," he admits. "Knowing the cosine of an angle or a Greek accusative may be enough to get you by on an exam, but to really explain these phenomena requires a deep level—you need to reach a deep level of understanding."[13]

Getting there isn't easy because all brains are not the same. As William Perry's research has shown, gender, ethnicity, religious beliefs, and social status are among the multitude of factors that have a bearing on how we understand things. If I fail to convey an idea that seems clear enough in my mind, I have no business assuming that my student is incapable of grasping it. Physicist Carl Weiman calls this the "curse of knowledge,"[14] the idea that when you know something it is difficult to think about it from the perspective of one who does not. Try tapping out melodies of familiar tunes with your finger and see how many a friend can identify. A classic experiment of this kind showed a rate of success 1/20th of what was anticipated by those doing the tapping.

Like starting that campfire, sometimes you need to go to great lengths to get things to ignite. I recall spending my entire two office hours one day with a single student trying to explain Wien's Law, the reciprocal relationship between temperature (T) and peak wavelength (λ) in the continuous spectrum of stars, which we had been dealing with in my elementary astronomy class. "The higher the temperature the lower the wavelength, in direct pro-portion," I said. My student cast a bewildered look at me. "T equals 1 over λ," I continued. "So if I drop the temperature from 6,000 to 3,000 degrees, what happens to the wavelength?" Again a blank stare, no response; then, "I don't get it." Finally, after many unsuccessful attempts at trying to explain Wien's Law had begun to frustrate me, I blurted out, "Look, it's like y equals 1 over x." "Oh," his face lit up. "Sure, now I get it! That's just like what we learned in math class." I realized that I'd simply been speaking to him in an unfamiliar language, the language of physics. It was not until I used the alphabet with which he was acquainted, the simple x and y of algebra-speak, that he got it. It took time, but I had found a domain breakthrough in his sphere of knowl-edge. We finally stood on ground where we could communicate.

Sometimes the failure to communicate resides at the most basic level you can imagine. John Okello, a Kenyan immigrant enrolled in my astronomy class, had flunked my first hour-long exam on atomic structure. I make a habit of inviting all students who fail an exam to come to my office to see if we can find out why. When John came in, we started reviewing the test material on atomic energy levels electrons can jump to or from as they move closer to or farther from the atomic nucleus, emitting or absorbing energy as they transition. I quickly realized that I was speaking to a person who, before he had entered my classroom four weeks earlier, had never heard of the particle theory of matter; that is, he knew nothing of the idea that matter is composed of minuscule entities called atoms. How could I expect him to understand what I was trying to teach him? Though atoms may never have been part of his educational background, John was an extraordinarily bright and motivated young man. With persistent tutoring during office hours, he soon caught up to, and passed, most of his classmates. John went on to major in math-econ at Colgate, graduating with honors. I've always been proud of him and the many others I've taught who don't give up.

Educate. It comes from the Latin verb *educare*, "to go forth" or "to go out." Education is a process of liberation. The truly educated person becomes free to continue on her own. But to be an effective teacher, you need to learn to sense when students arrive at the point in their studies where they are able to *go on*. University of Wisconsin political philosophy professor Charles Anderson thinks this "going on" stage of learning is quite different from a student simply *catching on*, which is usually signaled by the response "oh, I get it" (like my student in the Wien's Law example).[15] We can pass on our knowledge to students and, by testing them wisely, get a pretty good feeling of whether they *catch on*. One good indicator is the degree to which new knowledge knocks students off the normal track of how they tend to see things. (I always marvel at the shock my students exhibit when they realize that if two cars are each traveling 30 mph on a head-on collision course, then either driver who measures the relative speed of approach of the other will *not* arrive at the anticipated common sense answer of 30 + 30 = 60 mph. The correct answer, proven by lab experiments—not with cars but with atoms— is 59.9999 . . . mph, thanks to the theory of relativity.) Understanding that the real world is *not* the world of everyday experience is one of the great "I got it" experiences in science.

When we deal with "going on," Anderson argues that we enter the world not of the receptive mind but rather of the *active* mind. He offers this simple example, taken from one of the philosopher Ludwig Wittgenstein's classes: teacher writes down the numbers 1,5,11,19,29. Student responds, "yes, I can go on: 41,55,71 . . ." Now, did the student just spot the increasing series of differences between that chain of numbers 4,6,8 and extrapolate? Or perhaps, possessing a mathematically oriented mind, might he have developed a mathematical formula $x = y^2 + y + 1$ to continue the series? Either way, or through a host of other ways of understanding, does the student's capacity to "go on" mean the student has already *understood*? I believe a student has arrived at Anderson's "going on" stage of learning when she can take what I give her and apply it coherently and constructively *to her own worldview*.

I love seeing the breathing-learning process at work, watching it take hold, witnessing linear thinking lose its grip and give way gradually, often painfully, to a more sophisticated kind of inquiry, one capable of truly beginning to deal with complexity. I can only describe what I feel as a shared sense of joy between me and my students, what Plato calls love. So why do I teach? Why do I want to be a proselytizer in the world of ideas? Why do I want to share in the excitement of being disproportionately curious and reflective? Quite simply, because seeing my students progress from a simple state of knowing to a more complex one makes me feel good. I love it. Call me indulgent. Call me selfish. It's why I teach.

But the teacher himself should not be held to any creed;
nor should the question be whether his own opinions are the true ones, but whether he is instructed in
those of other people, and, in enforcing his own, states
the argument for all conflicting opinions fairly.

—*John Stuart Mill*[1]

From Mountaintop to Classroom

How far you go in the stream of life depends on the speed and course of the current that carries you. That's the "life is like a river trip" analogy. Fortunately for me, the current was pretty swift when I stepped in.

Vestigial remnants of memory bites about how I got my first (and only) job emanate from my early days in graduate school. It was the summer of 1963 and I had just passed my astronomy prelims at the University of Arizona. I'd begun collecting data with the new Kitt Peak telescopes for my dissertation on the birth of stars. It was an exciting time for all of us doing space-related studies in southern

DOI: 10.5876/9781607323037.c003

Arizona. The mountain had recently been selected as the site for the new National Observatory, a consortium of universities that would make Tucson the highest per capita city in the country for astronomers. As a result, UA's astronomy department doubled its faculty in the three years I happened to have been studying there—pure serendipity.

Lorraine and I had been married nearly four years. She had given birth to our daughter, and our son was well on the way. I recall sitting on the platform high up at the Newtonian focus of the 36-inch scope, outfitting the machine with the equipment I'd use that night to photograph the spectra of a dozen odd T Tauri stars (young stars still surrounded by the residual interstellar matter out of which they had recently formed), when I spotted Lorraine coming across the metal walkway from the dorm, presumably to announce a lunch break. There was an announcement all right, but not the one I'd anticipated. I heard the wind-driven doorway below slam as Lorraine made her way up the stairs to the dome. "Guess what? We're out of money," her voice reached me well before she appeared. "What do you mean out of money," I replied. Lorraine was a doctor of budgetry. She figured things out to the dime: rent ($55 a month in our tiny two-room blockhouse of an apartment; the place was so small it had a fractional street number: 429½ E. 3rd St.), groceries ($23 a week), car payment ($50 a month) . . . How could we be broke? I've got a $2,200/year teaching assistantship, and she's raking in $50/week on a split shift at Ma Bell. As we munched on our Spam sandwiches, Lorraine showed me the figures. They reeked of vermilion. What to do?

Later that day Aden Meinel, my dissertation adviser (an outstanding instrument designer responsible for the world's first multi-mirror telescopes), showed up on the mountain to do some data gathering of his own and to check up on me. Lorraine cooked dinner in the kitchen complex attached to the dorm, and as we chatted I felt compelled to answer his obligatory "how's it going" by quoting Lorraine's "we're out of money." Aden wasn't the sort of guy who might second-guess you with comments like "who told you to have kids" (he'd fathered five). He responded almost reflexively "So, get a job." He continued, "You've finished your coursework. No need to stay here in Tucson. Get a higher-paying teaching position at some out-of-the-way college and come back here periodically to collect your data. You can write your dissertation in absentia—people do it all the time. Come back to Tucson next summer and defend it."

Sounded like a plan to me. So I asked, "How do I get a job?" "When you kids [the generic term guys had not yet been invented] get back to Tucson, just go to the *bulletin board outside my office. There are lots of job notices there. See what appeals to you and then we'll talk." The summer of '63 was just two years after President Kennedy's vow that we'd put a man on the moon by the end of the decade. Because the space program was well under way, anybody even close to a degree in a space-related discipline faced a host of open doors to high-paying jobs: NASA, McDonnell-Douglas, Grumman Aircraft . . . And there were college teaching jobs aplenty at the lower end of the salary scale ($6,000 a year plus). Lorraine and I spotted at least a dozen notices in that category pinned to the corkboard: Montana State, Florida, Oregon, US Naval Observatory at Flagstaff (Aden advised against that one because he thought it would involve too much administrative work, though I was tempted by the attractive $7,500 a year salary), Colgate, Ohio State, Kalamazoo College . . . We were particularly attracted to Colgate because it was situated in the Northeast and we were native New Englanders. Aden thought it wasn't a bad choice. "It's small, looks like a pure teaching institution. That sort of job will give you plenty of time to work on your research. Stay there a year or two, get some teaching under your belt, and you'll be ready to move up."*

It also happened that Harold (aka "Tycho," a tidbit for astronomy insiders) Lane, the only astronomer at Colgate, had been spending his sabbatical in Tucson working on flare stars, not too distant relatives of my T Tauris. He had just accepted a new post at the National Science Foundation, which created the vacancy. I talked to him about Colgate and what it was like: a small liberal arts college in a pleasant upstate rural environment. He didn't mention the winters (more on that later).

After mulling for a few days, we called the phone number on the ad: "2" in the local phone system (Hamilton, New York, was among the last places in the country to switch over to dial telephones). The town operator put me through and Professor Clement Henshaw, chair of the physics department, picked up at the other end. Less than five minutes into the conversation he said, "Well, you're hired. Be here by September 10. You'll teach elementary astronomy, physics labs, and a section of Core science." Then he US-mailed me a map. Within a week (it was now mid-August) we were on our way cross-country, the three-and-a-half of us in our non-air-conditioned 2-cylinder Renault Dauphine. Little could Lorraine and I have imagined that that journey would take us (she about to turn twenty-one and me barely twenty-five) to our single port of disembarkation along our shared river of life. And we'd ride the rapids all the way.

Postscript to student readers: How dare I tell this story? I am acutely aware of your plight. I have had many conversations with my seniors about their impending entry into the real world of joblessness that lies ahead of them. One recently wrote on her job application "I implore you . . ." and "I really need this job." (I advised her that that level of fervency was likely to hinder her chances.) Most of my students know that in the contemporary degree-inflated buyer's market, their Colgate BA may not be enough. Clerk or cargo manager, receptionist or rental manager, today you need a diploma to do just about anything. An Atlanta-based study conducted by the Brookings Institution in 2012 revealed that 39 percent of postings for administrative assistance required a BA.[2] Ironically, most employers are wary of hiring over-qualified college graduates because they would be tempted to leave as soon as they find a *real* job. I try to point out that it's a long way from *here* to *there*, and many pathways branch along the road in between. Follow your passion, broaden your options, remain open to all possibilities. You never know where it may take you. I know—easy for me to say, isn't it?

Assignment One

A member of the Colgate faculty for twenty-five years, Don Berkey was a wonderfully supportive colleague in the department. The day I arrived at Colgate this gray-haired, pudgy prof began my personal tour of the campus. I say began because the tour lasted a day and a half. I saw everything, from Don's research lab to the college cemetery, where the remains of Colgate dons of yesteryear had been entombed. Even though times were tough and his salary was lean (I doubt he was making five fig-ures), Don still managed to invite junior faculty to his modest home at 16 University Avenue for a welcome-to-Colgate dinner. Just a few days after we were installed in our first of two sabbatical rentals that year, Lorraine and I were greeted by Jean and Don at the front door of the Berkey residence, along with two other young couples, one from physics, the other from geology. As the eight of us snacked on Spanish peanuts offered with a glass of modest vintage white wine, we conversed about a variety of topics. One of them pertained to our new environment, a rural town in the bucolic countryside of upstate New York, where we had all staked our claim to bring new insights to higher learning. After half an hour Jean called us to the dining room table.

The chatting continued as we were seated and the food was brought in. She placed a chrome-domed oval platter at the center of the table and flanked it with small bowls containing mashed potatoes and string beans, along with a basket of dinner rolls. Novice geologist Jim McLelland, known for his voracious appetite, glanced at me with furrowed brow at the apparent sparsity of veggies in the two bowls. His eyes seemed to speak: "This mere nibble of food for eight people? You gotta be kidding!" When Don lifted the shiny cover of the main platter, it was clear that a subsistence crisis loomed. There, in the middle of the vast porcelain terrine, was a piece of corned beef measuring no more than 5 inches on a side. Our host carved—at best—3/16-inch slices off one end and deposited them on the dinner plates. Jean added—again at most—two tablespoons of mashed potatoes, count- 'em-on-one-hand string beans, and a bun about the size of a modest plum to each plate. (Even for 1963, these were scant portions.)

Immediately, the race for who would get seconds was on. Jim had the advan- tage—a bigger mouth—but before he could lick his plate, our host had taken gold and was forking the single thin slice of meat remaining on the platter onto his own plate, grabbing the only remaining bun in the basket on the way back. As he began to reach for the last few string beans, Jean broke off her conversation with Jim's wife. Her facial expression scolded Don silently, and she must have kicked him under the table. That's the only explanation I can think of for the way Don winced and lurched back- ward for an instant. Then, directing the party's collective attention to a wall at the opposite end of the table, Jean pointed to a picture and said in a voice clearly audible across the room: "My sister painted that. You'll notice the Baptist Church in the foreground, and if you look closely you'll see the water tower on the low hill behind." We all turned our heads and, as if instructed telepathically, Don sneaked the meat and veggies back into their respective receptacles and announced as his wife's voice trailed off, "Now, who's ready for seconds?" Rarely does a faculty dinner at our home take place today without my recalling memories of the "Derkey Shuffle."

Though Lorraine and I were born and raised in coastal Connecticut, which gets its share of snow, a few years in graduate school in Tucson had dulled our habit of driving at a constant velocity during icy conditions. Those of us who reside in snow country know from experience that you avoid braking as much as possible. We'd been in Hamilton scarcely two months when the first major snowfall occurred: about 2 feet, just before Thanksgiving break. Living downwind of the Great Lakes, especially Lake Ontario, which is too deep to freeze, means we get a lot of white stuff—an average of 120 inches a year. Half our distance from the lake, you can easily double that. Now, two feet of snow can produce four- to six-foot drifts. Piles of freshly plowed snow by the roadside are known to top eight feet. (Snow removal in Hamilton operates pretty much 24/7 from November to April.) I had managed to get up the hill the morning after the storm. Luckily, I was following a vehicle that dispersed salt on the road. By late afternoon, when I got into my little Renault to make my way home, the roads had iced over, the result of plummeting temperatures that usually follow a storm as high pressure works its way into the area.

I wheeled out of the parking lot onto Academic Drive, then headed down the steep slope and curve past the Ad Building, continually downshifting to decelerate. (Here's my theory about why small liberal arts colleges are located on hills: it's to be closer to God, the source of all true knowledge. At least that's what the profs told those who enrolled at Colgate when it was largely a missionary training school.) As I approached the flat, I picked up speed. A mountainous chevron of freshly plowed snow lay piled at the center point where the road forks at a 30° angle into two segments just ahead of me. I chose the right branch, but my Renault seemed to prefer the left. We compromised and together hit the snow pile, penetrating the barrier like a torpedo.

We're all aware of that instantaneous reaction to a sudden bodily twist or turn or a fall. We collect ourselves momentarily. Anything broken? Any pain? Am I alive, I thought? I needed to think further on that last self-inquiry because it was dark, except for a faint glimmer of light that penetrated the snow covering the rear windshield. I imagined the horror experienced by someone caught in an avalanche—smothered, about to be suffocated, unable to move. But I could move, even if I was unable to push open a door. I felt like a tortoise imprisoned in its shell. The tight-fitting Renault had completely shielded me from the outside world—except that I felt very uncomfortable in that confined condition. The next few minutes unfolded like an eternity. Then I felt my mini-car, the motor still running, being rocked back and forth by unknown forces. Had salvation arrived at last? Large mitten-clad hands cleared the windshield and side windows. Their possessors jerked my wheeled coffin out of the pack and lifted it three feet above the surface of the earth—four large athletes they were. I rolled down the window and poked my head out at my saviors. I smiled nervously and made vocal expressions amounting to embarrassed thank-yous. "Which way do you want it pointed, sir?" inquired the largest of the four, his face barely visible through a heavy hooded parka. I signaled with my right hand, whence my pall-bearers turned to the right and laid me down in the middle of the roadway. I waved another feeble thank you and sped off, hoping none of them were enrolled in my class.

"You're hired." Those words, conveyed by telephone by the venerable chair of Colgate's Physics and Astronomy Department, rang happily in my ears as I experienced my first semester of teaching at Colgate over fifty years ago. While I was exhilarated at the prospect of being able to realize my dream of becoming both a professional scholar *and* a teacher, I was puzzled, maybe even a little put off, when I began immersing myself in the tail end of the teaching assignment announced over the phone. Teaching physics labs sounded reasonable enough. After all, I had an undergraduate degree in physics; and what *is* astronomy but a specialized branch of physics? It was the "Core science" that bothered me, especially when I read the course description in the catalog:

Core II. The Physical Sciences
   The nature of science is studied in several scientific inquires of the past.

The inquiries included selections from Aristotle, Galileo, Lavoisier, Dalton, Avogadro, and Mendeleyev. Each was treated as a case study in exploring the roots of science: Galileo's experiments with falling bodies as a foundation for the discovery of gravitation, Mendeleyev's invention of the Periodic Table leading to an understanding of the foundation of chemistry, and so on. All of this was capped by readings from science philosophers on scientific thinking in general and the place of science in society.

I wasn't coming to Colgate to teach *about* science, I thought. I *am* a scientist. I *do* science. Shouldn't what I do in my profession be the sole focus of attention in my classroom? Besides, Lavoisier and most of the rest of those archaic characters were chemists—dead ones at that. I'm not an expert in chemistry. What business do I have teaching that stuff? How would my students feel about being taught by a non-expert? Would you go to a foot doctor for neck pain? Why waste time dwelling on the science of the past given all the amazing discoveries being made in my field today—the expanding universe, big bang cosmology, the birth of stars?

Those were my initial thoughts. In hindsight, I realize that they reflect an attitude common to novice teachers fresh out of grad school, especially if they have been narrowly educated, as was I. While I was grateful for the opportunity to teach at a quality institution of higher learning, I felt uncomfortable about being forced out of my specialty. At twenty-five I was, understandably, not ready to stretch, not open to embrace learning across the disciplines.

My skepticism about Core science followed me into the weekly staff meetings with fellow teachers from the other scientific disciplines who taught sections of the common syllabus course. Every Monday afternoon we'd meet in the lounge for an hour or two to discuss the forthcoming readings for that week and set up tests and quizzes for the half-dozen sections of twenty–twenty-five students in this required course. My arms folded, I remained a passive skeptic for the first few weeks. Then I began to catch on. The so-called inquiries, many of them told in the first person and in original eighteenth- and nineteenth-century language, portrayed great scientists speaking to their contemporaries. The readings related their attempts to persuade fellow scientists of the validity of their theories and interpretations. This was a lot different from my approach in the astronomy survey class I also taught that first semester. There, a thick textbook served as my guide and authority. As is typical in most science survey courses, I viewed my mission as one of transmitting a basic body of contemporary astronomical knowledge. I dwelled more on questions of *how* rather than *why* science gets done and paid little attention to why science as a way of knowing matters in the world. On the contrary, the hallmark of Core had to do with studying the diversity of methods applied to a wide range of case studies of scientific problems. Casting science in a historical vein served the purpose of setting the stage for *why* changes take place in the ways we interpret the natural world. Core dealt not only with understanding scientific ideas but also with the reasons why some theories fail while others can be modified, or even replaced, in the face of new experimental evidence. Gradually, I began to emerge from my own zone of proximal development. I got it: Core was all about focusing more on the process, the argument, and less on the information, the discipline.

To give an example, when I taught Galileo in my astro survey course, I focused on the discoveries he made with the first telescope in the seventeenth century—the moons of Jupiter, spots on the sun, mountains and craters on the moon—and how these new findings challenged the accepted theory of his time. Before the telescope, people believed the earth was the center of the solar system, but this new evidence overturned all that. Galileo's interpretation supported a radical new idea: the heliocentric, or sun-centered, solar system devised by his predecessor Copernicus. My encounter with Galileo in Core was a bit different. While the class discussed all the revelations delivered by Galileo's telescope, we also dealt with similar discoveries made in the budding disciplines of chemistry and geology. Now on less familiar ground and learning along with my class, I began to understand why parallel developments in the old disciplines occurred when they did and how they were connected. The excitement I acquired at walking this new turf spilled over to a class that now seemed easier to connect with. Maybe it was because I became open to revealing gaps in my knowledge. In Core I was no longer cast purely in the role of expert. Discussions about the value and uses of scientific knowledge and its pursuit, even if initially somewhat uncomfortable and strained for me, soon developed into one of the most engaging segments of my curriculum.

It took a semester or two, but eventually I became a convert to the case study, cross-disciplinary method. This isn't to say I gave up my role as a purveyor of new knowledge. In my view there will always remain a healthy tension, an endless dialogue, between the pedagogical poles of learning through transmission and learning via process. Notwithstanding, like a born again ex-smoker or ex-drinker, I became an ex-Core skeptic—a Core apostle. I even began to devise my own approaches to how to conduct my Core science class. Some things worked. Some didn't.

Good teachers should always be alert to new methods, new techniques—novel spins to get a basic point across. Teaching science offers the advantage of using gadgets and gimmicks. To explain the workings of the natural world, the exemplary teacher can take advantage of the demonstration to engage students. Take physics. A thousand words describing how bodies fall to earth can't measure up to a single moment of the direct interaction with nature one experiences by carefully watching things plummet for oneself. True, it takes time to organize a classroom demo, but it can be a grabber, get a student intrigued in the workings of nature. The "ooohs" and "aaahs" of witnessing a surprise, something that might not have been anticipated, are ample reward for all the effort that goes into setting up an effective live demo.

Clem Henshaw, the tall, soft-spoken, relatively expressionless Colgate prof who hired me, would not have thought of entering a classroom without coat and tie; he always reserved the lecture room in Lathrop Hall for the entire period prior to his scheduled 10:20 a.m. elementary physics class. During that prep period, he'd fill the top of the four-foot × twelve-foot slate table in front of the board with c-clamps, ring stands, rubber hoses, test tubes, inclined planes, bells, and whistles—whatever equipment he'd need to win over his assembled acolytes to the efficacy of the laws of physics. Most of his students were pre-meds who hated physics, which they were required to take; notwithstanding, Clem was there to turn them on to nature—not so much by word, for (as I have hinted) he was not a very dynamic character, but rather by deed. You learn by doing, by experimenting; that was Clem's motto.

One of Professor Henshaw's in-class gems was designed to show that any object (regardless of what it's made of), when released from on high, accelerates as it falls under the influence of gravity. Only the medium through which it falls—be it air, water, or motor oil—can alter gravity's perceived effect by slowing the speed of descent by varying amounts. Example: You're coming out of a supermarket carrying a bag full of goodies. All of a sudden the bag rips open and out topple a container of marshmallows and a can of beans. Instinctively, you reach for the beans because you know they will hit the ground first. That's because heavier objects fall faster in air. Ah, but remember the astronaut who simultaneously dropped a golf ball and a feather on the surface of the moon? Both hit the ground at the same time, didn't they? Nature's true behavior is revealed only under ideal conditions. The moon has no atmosphere to resist the falling motion.

Clem's earthbound drop-ball experiment used a number of inch-wide spheres of different weights—lead, steel, aluminum—and a very expensive graduated glass cylinder about eight inches wide and three feet tall that you could fill with liquids of varying viscosity. A camera mounted on a stand, its shutter permanently opened in the darkened room, would record each ball's ponderous descent as the instructor carefully dropped them in the cylinder one at a time. Next to it, a stroboscopic light flashed rapidly on and off to reveal the location of the falling object every tenth of a second. Each student would get a photographic print of the recorded descent of the balls. They'd use it to measure how far the balls fell during each interval so they could calculate their velocity and acceleration.

As a novice teacher, I'd watched Clem perform this demo a few times, and I was so convinced of its effectiveness that I decided to introduce it into the curriculum of one of my Core science classes. When Professor Henshaw performed this demo, he would begin by dropping the heaviest ball—the one made of lead—in air alongside the cylinder. He would time that drop. Then he'd drop the steel ball, the aluminum ball, and so on. Next he'd turn his attention to what would happen in a watery medium. He'd fill the cylinder nearly to the brim with tap water and drop each ball in turn into the liquid, again making photographic records of all the drops. I recall the students' eyes drinking in the stark blinking imagery, the room dead quiet in anticipation but for the clicking noise of the strobe light. Once a ball reached the bottom of the cylinder, it would land on a wire mesh net neatly fitted to its circular bottom. The professor would pull on a handle hooked over the rim of the cylinder attached to the net, thus drawing its contents all the way to the top of the cylinder, where he would retrieve each sphere. Once he had allowed the retrieving net to fall back to the bottom, the professor was ready to drop—and retrieve—the next ball.

Having concluded and duly recorded the ball drops in air and in water, Henshaw would announce "now let's try a more viscous medium." He'd carefully walk the brimming water-filled glass cylinder over to the sink and empty it. Then he'd bring up from below the desk a case of 1-quart cans of 10W-40 motor oil. Popping each top with a "church key," he'd carefully pour the contents into the cylinder. As he worked, the professor would toss in a few informative asides about how Galileo used to conduct experiments just like these over 400 years ago and how his experiments, as well as those in which he rolled balls down inclined planes, helped lay the foundation for the discovery of Newton's universal law of gravitation. All the while, the syrupy, greenish, transparent liquid could be seen rising higher and higher up the cylinder, past the 1- 2- 3- 4- . . . liter marks, until it reached within an inch of the top.

Professor Henshaw concluded the experiment by dropping and timing the balls—brass, aluminum, steel, lead—through the oily medium, pulling each back up with the retriever. The slower descent of the lighter balls, especially the aluminum ball, which took several seconds to reach the retriever net at the bottom, was obvious to the eye and appeared clearly indicated by many more flash points crowded together on the photos. All of this took a lot of time, care, and patience.

The better you innovate, the greater the opportunity to educate. My contribution to advancing scientific experimentation would be efficiency. When I did the experiment, I decided to drop balls both in and out of the cylinder at the same time. Such a technique, I thought, would offer the added advantage that students could witness the differences in the speed of the dropped balls immediately and directly. How would I accomplish such a feat? Easy: I'd hold one lead ball between thumb and forefinger and another lead ball between ring finger and pinkie. With my middle finger draped along the cylinder rim, I'd carefully position one ball over the oil inside the cylinder and the other over the air just outside the cylinder, then release both balls at the same time. This was my plan.

There I stood one Friday morning behind the stone demo table, confronting a classroom full of anticipatory faces, about to simultaneously launch the two spheres. Like any savvy performer, I built up the tension prior to the event by asking *my students to think about what might happen if we tried this experiment on the moon or on Mars. Shutter open, strobe light on, "3-2-1-launch." I released both pallid dense spheres and they obediently began to plummet earthward, stroboscopic clicks documenting every step of the descent. The air ball raced downward in the bat of an eyelash, while the oil-bound one fluttered along behind. Then a strange noise—a crackling, no, a cracking—more like glass shattering. Then a tipping. The cylinder lurched, then slowly leaned class-ward like some vitreous Pisa tower. My first instinct was to jump backward. Instead, I thrust my hand forward toward the cylinder in nightmarish slow motion as I attempted to prevent the column of glass from toppling. The air-dropped lead ball had hit the base of the cylinder, shattering it. My efforts to catch a falling cylinder placed second to Newtonian dictates; and the entire apparatus (now in real-time motion) slammed down onto the stone table, smashed into a million pieces, and jettisoned oil-covered shards and spurts of 10W-40 as far out as the fourth row of the classroom. There followed a reaction you might expect from the youthful set—laughter, raucous belly-rolling laughter at the sight of their teacher screwing up. Oil-drenched shirts, pants, shoes, and socks. The front-row guys who sopped up the bulk of it seemed to laugh the loudest. To their credit, they were the ones who stayed the longest with mops and towels to help their embarrassed instructor clean it all up. Moral? Look before you leap. Practice before you innovate. Or maybe just don't innovate?*

Epilogue (A "Non-Scratching" Retriever): Reporting these failed efforts to my austere mentor, a man who prided himself on being careful, rigorous, neat, and precise, required a weekend of screwing up my courage. When I finally faced the music the following Monday morning, Clem was calm and understanding. He didn't even raise his voice. What concerned him most was the tragic loss of the precious graduated glass cylinder, which had been in continuous use at Colgate for more than fifty years. I would be required to provide a new one and pay for it out of my own pocket, he told me. That seemed fair. But when I scoured every scientific supply catalog for such an item, I found that no one manufactured a glass cylinder that large. I couldn't even get a used one. Finally, I settled on a company that sold sections of plastic cylinders. I made sure I got one wide enough to accommodate the metallic ball retriever; then I cemented it to a square plastic base. The replacement cylinder was far less scientific-looking than the original, which had graduated marks labeled with fancy-looking numbers in an old-style font. But at least it would work.

The next semester when drop-ball season returned, Professor Henshaw gave the new apparatus a go. He filled the cylinder with water, did the drop, pulled up on the

*handle of the retriever, and scr-r-r-a-a-tch. The metallic netting at the edge of the
ball retriever scraped against the sides of the plastic cylinder, leaving long stria-
tions. With every ascent, it scraped some more. At the end of the demo the professor
came to the back of the room where I had been sitting and uttered a statement that,
unless context is provided, might seem better suited to a dog show than a physics lab,
"Well, Tony, it looks as if you'll be in the market for a non-scratching retriever."*

*This is still not the end of the story, for even though the old metallic retrieving
net was replaced with a new one made of plastic, things still weren't right. Plastic
floats, so you need to weigh it down, which presents additional problems (I could go
on). Alas, to this day the original drop-ball experiment, simple in scope, elegant in
design, exquisite in procedure, has not been replicated in ideal form. But even with
flawed equipment, showing sure beats just talking about gravity.*

Several live witnesses to my failure in that class have returned to visit me,
usually on alumni weekend. They have laughed with me about my innovation deprivation and the limits of efficiency in classroom experimentation.
The vulnerable side I exhibited in my Core liberal arts science class that day
did a lot to bind teacher and student.

Acquiring the Tool of My Trade

*The astronomer's chief techno-item is the telescope, and the story of how I acquired
one for my little corner of the knowledge factory is a bit unusual. It was my first
year of teaching and I was going to do it all. New courses, new programs, even a
community outreach program—all of it directed toward revealing the wonderful
insights of my chosen profession to a wider world. For outreach I'd give a lecture
the first Monday night of every month to Hamilton-area townsfolk on a popular
topic: "Life in the Universe," "When Will We Put a Man on the Moon," "How Do
Stars and Planets Form?" Then I'd follow with a session at the observatory. Kids
liked that part best—looking at the moon, Venus, nebulae, and galaxies through
Colgate's telescope.*

*Now, the telescope I had inherited from my predecessor, Harold "Tycho" Lane, was
not the sharpest knife in the drawer. It was a 12-inch reflector (that's the diameter of
the mirror at the base of the tube) about 12 feet long. The telescope tube was made of
heavy compound cardboard and was mounted on a gargantuan cement pier accessed*

by a platform that could be made to ascend or descend over a four-foot range of elevation. So, anyone's eye could be placed at the level of the eyepiece, which happened to be positioned at the top end of the tube. To get up to the viewing position, you'd adjust the half-ton rolling elevator (to judge by its size and the way it dwarfed the instrument, you'd think the elevator was more important than the scope) by raising and lowering a pair of parallel vertical control rods. This created a noisy grinding sound, second in decibel level only to the chirpy, rattling motor that powered the rotating hemispherical dome, which was fashioned out of an old silo top. The dome was equipped with a set of sliding doors mounted on rollers that could be turned so that light entering the dome slot would pass down the telescope tube to the mirror.

Despite the inferior equipment, public response to my outreach efforts in the culture-starved region of northern Appalachia known as Madison County, New York, was enthusiastic. Proactive science teachers—bless them!—brought their classes by the busload. They came from Boonville and South Otselic, Norwich and Skaneateles—more than an hour away—to hear my sky talks and peep at the stars and planets through the old scope. Neither ultra-cool autumn nights nor frigid winter darkness would deter the aspiring adolescent astronaut or astronomer from this splendid extracurricular at the nearby college. I know the feeling. As a twelve-year old I savored the monthly New Haven–area Amateur Astronomical Society meetings at the Yale Observatory in my own hometown. I'll never forget the night I mustered enough courage to ask Dr. Dirk Brouwer, head of Yale's astronomy department, for advice about how to pursue a career in astronomy. "Study mathematics and physics, my boy," he responded, to my surprise.

One chilly, clear November night, following my third lecture in the series, I found myself accompanying a cadre of fifth and sixth graders, high schoolers, townies, and a handful of interested Colgate students, faculty, and spouses on the 10-minute walk up the hill from Lathrop Hall—the science building where I held classes—to the observatory. A couple of student assistants had set up the 12-inch telescope and pointed it at the crescent moon, which lay low in the west. The dome accommodated about a dozen people. (Space for another dozen would easily have been possible were it not for that cumbersome elevator.) Since there were more than 100 in attendance that night, a long line of stargazers had already formed. By the time I got to the observatory door, the queue ran back down the stairs through the narrow lower-level entryway and well out onto the grass. I managed to wedge my way through the crowd and up the stairs to the telescope. I positioned myself near the elevator to help old folks and tiny tots ascend as I answered the oft-anticipated

questions fired at me out of the darkness: "How far can you see with this telescope?"
A better question might be: "How faint an object can you detect?" "How much does
it cost?" Not much. It was designed and put together by a local chiropodist who
donated it to the university back in 1948. The optics were decidedly inferior, at least
in the eyes of a specialist fresh out of the great discovery center of experimental
astronomy known as the Kitt Peak National Observatory.

I still love standing by the telescope watching young people's expressions as they
gaze at the stars for the first time. I'm especially drawn to the dilating pupil, the eye
opening wide to drink in the concentrated light that pours down the tube into the
eyepiece from some vast object light years away. I enjoy witnessing the delight in the
eye of the beholder and on the face that invariably breaks out in a wide smile. That
night was one among many when I knew I had met my calling: sharing the wonders
of the night sky with people of all ages.

The dark figures jostled about—kids and grownups climbing up and down the
elevator to peep through the scope, each experiencing personal, one-on-one live
contact with a piece of the vast universe, conveyed to their wide eyes through a very
modest telescope. One among the moving shadows, a diminutive man in an overcoat
and fedora hat (still very popular in the early 1960s), sidled over to me during the
observing session and inquired sotto voce, "This telescope any good?" I didn't recog-
nize him; his face was half hidden by a scarf. Had the feeble moonlight rendered me
a view, it isn't likely I would have recognized him anyway. Lorraine and I hadn't
been in town long enough to get to know many people. My gut response was an hon-
est one: "To tell you the truth, it's a piece of junk. Wish we had a better one." Then
I moved on to the next questioner.

Out late that night, I didn't arise until after 9:00 the next morning. Not a prob-
lem because, as a night owl astronomer, I'd been freed of the necessity to teach ear-
ly-morning classes. Early that afternoon the office of the dean of faculty phoned me.
"The dean would like to see you. How's this afternoon at 4:00?" queried his secretary.
"Sure," I replied, wondering what the matter was. The broken glass cylinder? Nah.
I'd already settled that affair with Professor Henshaw.

I taught my two Tuesday afternoon classes, held office hours, and, when the
appointed hour arrived, made my way to the office of the dean of faculty. I waited
only a few minutes before being called to the inner sanctum housing the man who
essentially ran the university. (University presidents are largely fund raisers.) Jim
Storing, a red-cheeked, middle-aged man of slight stature, had been a political sci-
entist prior to entering the deanery. I'd heard his demeanor could be austere, but his

faculty regarded him as a square dealer and an excellent mediator between teachers and administrators, well deserving of the title (genitive case) his office bore. Profs called him the "ombudsman," reflecting in part his Scandinavian descent. The instant his grinning Nordic countenance greeted me, I knew why I had been called to Dean Storing's office. "So, you think our telescope is a hunk of junk, do you?" he queried, pursing his lips and raising a suspicious eyebrow. "Well, er, I guess what I meant was . . ." I stumbled, tongue-tied, wondering how long a period of grace he would allow me to seek employment elsewhere before issuing my letter of termination. As I stammered, every molecule of saliva evaporated from my mouth. My blood supply plummeted to my feet and the metallic taste of nervous welled up around the periphery of my tongue.

Then the ombudsman shocked me: "Well, why don't you do something about it?" "Really? What? How?" as I struggled to regain my social equilibrium. "I have someone down in the Ad Building I can get to help you write a grant proposal. They have an educational support division down at the National Science Foundation in Washington. A new telescope would go a long way toward helping you start up that new program for an astronomy concentration I overhead you talking about last night." He knew about that? And how could a political scientist be hip to the NSF? Storing was one impressive ombudsman!

Within a month I had that meeting with the grant writer. Colgate even sent me to Washington to plead my case. It happened that one of President Johnson's "Great Society" achievements was the establishment of enhanced programs for funding the improvement of undergraduate science education. He really had lived up to the tag claimed by every campaigner for the White House since: "the education president." Within two years we'd replaced the chiropodist's 12-inch telescope (and cumbersome elevator) with a brand new, all-electronic, 16-inch Bausch and Lomb precision instrument. One of Jim Storing's final acts (he succumbed to a heart attack in his early sixties, just two years after our encounter at the observatory) was to approve the establishment of my proposed program for a concentration in astronomy and physics at Colgate University. How well you succeed in your job has much to do with how caring and supportive your mentors are.

Why had Jim Storing made it a point to pop in on me in my sacred domain that night? Did the dean know our instrument was in need of an overhaul? Had the ombudsman deliberately set out to catalyze a new employee he'd heard was ambitious and eager to make positive changes in this little college in the Chenango Valley? Or was he just out for a bit of fresh air? I'll never know.

Incidentally, *Colgate's astronomy outreach program continues today. It's a little less ambitious because the duties of the office have multiplied. Today a planetarium (we call it a "visualization laboratory") accompanies the observatory, a huge asset in a cold, often cloud-bound environment. But the memory of my encounter with the ombudsman sticks with me as I now play the role of enabler—one who takes seriously the task of raising the hopes and attempting to facilitate the thoughtful wishes of inspired younger colleagues. If that's not part of the job description of a college teacher, please rewrite it.*

Encountering the Liberal Arts

Ask any informed academic what the term *liberal arts* means and he will tell you that it has to do with the study of knowledge not directly related to professionalism or to technical or vocationally directed learning. Students encounter the liberal arts when they take, either by their own choice or because they are required to do so, courses offered by departments that make up the university that lie outside their intended fields of concentration or, in the case of a Core program, when they enter a special set of required courses beyond the domain of the departments that specialize in bringing together generalized areas of inquiry.

In retrospect, I can understand my initial skepticism about engaging the unity of knowledge concept that serves as the centerpiece of many core general education programs. I'd been educated at large universities where I enrolled in large classes in gen ed programs with few requirements outside my major field. Colgate was my first encounter with an institution that sought well-roundedness in students by requiring them to deal with considerable subject matter outside their intended areas of concentration. I had heard the mission rhetoric about acquiring knowledge, developing critical skills, and learning to reason and think for yourself; but I'd never thought much about what you're supposed to achieve by going to college beyond acquiring special skills in a specific discipline. My intense focus on astronomy didn't come with an agenda that included where it all might fit into some sort of larger social or cultural framework.

Who is to say what the overarching purpose behind higher education ought to be and how one ought to go about achieving it? Scholars who have written volumes on such questions offer a variety of responses. Most agree that, at a purely intellectual level, one of the basic duties of a college teacher should be to help students integrate specialized fields at a deep enough level to be able to deal with *bigger questions*. Some proffer the added behavioral goal of developing personal values, like sound moral character and active citizenship. Others go further still, advocating that colleges and universities should be collectively responsible for cultivating our national culture.

Everyone seems to agree on the need to teach students to communicate, both orally and in writing, and to be able to think critically. Trouble is, most of those who are thrust into the classroom fresh out of graduate school are more interested in teaching in their own field than in developing basic skills oriented to the needs of the student. "I wasn't hired to teach writing," complained a novice teacher I met recently. I could sympathize with her. Rarely do we learn how to teach in graduate school anyway. The sole skill my graduate school members concentrated on was how to conduct and present specialized research.

Even among the few mentored in acquiring teaching skills in graduate school, there is wide disagreement on how to go about achieving the goal of helping students think critically. Some argue that mastering a huge body of knowledge supersedes any serious attempt to deal with it critically. As I began to teach in Colgate's liberal arts Core program, I came to realize that the case study strategy of teaching how to make the argument in science Core classes offered a valid response to this goal because it covered multiple sides of an issue. In addition, it showed how similar methods of reasoning and experimentation could be applied to diverse problems. These encounters offered students broader questions to think about.

The goal of developing personal values in the Core liberal arts approach to learning, I think, is by far the most controversial. Whose values? Which values take precedence? Which, if any, should be held highest? Even if educators agree on what aspects of ethical behavior to stress and even if we show our students the way to confront complex multifaceted moral problems, how do we go about applying these concepts *in practice,* as active citizens? It is here that we encounter what Derek Bok[3] calls "easy relativism," that simple way of thinking students acquire early in their education. Basically, they think that different people have different views and there is no way to really make any valid judgment of one's opinion of another.

There's more to the college experience than broad requirements like Core. Mastery of a body of knowledge and the requisite skills that go with dealing critically with new knowledge are at the base of the concentration requirement. You need depth, an understanding of the basic resources and arguments that make up a particular area of study; and the only way to acquire it is by focusing the heart of your education on a discipline. You need a major, a cluster of eight or more interrelated courses of increasing sophistication that comprise a discipline.

Today, most students select a minor (four or five courses) that usually complements the major, or they double major (37% of my students do so, which is typical). Examples include geography and environmental studies, anthropology and Native American studies, physics and astronomy, mathematics and economics, or art and Renaissance studies. But I've seen combinations as spread apart academically as psychology and theatre, neuroscience and art, and English and anthropology. I think the current widespread fad of double majoring is connected to students' uninformed perceptions of *why* they ought to attend college. When asked the question, most students, at least for as long as I've taught, respond that a college degree is mainly about acquiring gainful employment, so why not get as many skills under your belt as you can to enhance your options? It looks good on the résumé.

"What can she do with it," parents of my advisees often ask me, especially when their offspring is about to declare a major in art, cultural anthropology, or philosophy as opposed to chemistry, economics, or international relations. Are there realistic possibilities for earning a living if my offspring doesn't become another Pablo Picasso, Margaret Mead, or Jean Paul Sartre? Concerns about narrowness place a close second to worries over relevance. At first glance, the facts of life-after-college support the case. Students in highly specialized technical or professional majors, such as computer science, social work, or nursing, are more likely to secure employment.[4] The same is true when it comes to levels of earning.[5] For the Class of 2010 nationwide, accounting majors ended up the most employable (46%); business majors registered 44 percent, and engineers in all categories—chemical, mechanical, computer, industrial, and environmental—were not far behind. When it came to annual starting salaries, aeronautical engineers led the financial rolls with $60,000, while economics majors averaged $50,000.[6]

There's another chapter to the story of what you end up doing with your education. Highly concentrated training only gets you so far. I've had dozens of conversations with former students who tell me that after a few years of employment or graduate study, the broader thinking and exposure to the interrelationships among the diverse fields of learning acquired in the liberal arts curriculum, especially the complex of required Core courses and free electives they took to explore their broader interests, made them wiser in the long run. All of this makes me wonder how I had managed to survive intellectually without ever really understanding the meaning of a liberal arts education until I became a teacher. How odd it is that the encounter with my liberal arts peers and the Core science teaching assignment I had so stridently balked at undertaking turned out to mark the true beginning of my own education.

Little did I know when I engaged my first teaching assignment that I was standing on the tip of a huge intellectual iceberg, the depth and breadth of which ought to be seriously explored by anyone seeking to engage students in a liberal arts college, or in any setting for that matter. To pay homage to our thoughtful predecessors and to know where we came from, I think it's worth thumbing, if only briefly, through the pages of the story about the origin of the liberal arts.

A Little History

How did all those "ologies"—geology, biology, psychology, anthropology—get into our college catalogs? Who divided the turf of human inquiry this way? Why did they do it? Originally codified by fifth- to seventh-century encyclopedists, the liberal arts once numbered seven—the magic number of creation in Genesis and the number of days in a week, not to mention the number of moving celestial bodies (the sun, moon, and five visible planets). That made sense because all knowledge was believed to have been ordained in heaven. The seven pillars of knowledge were divided into two parts: the verbal arts (the *trivium*)—grammar, rhetoric, and logic or dialectic—and the mathematical arts (the *quadrivium*)—arithmetic, music, geometry, and astronomy. This classical canon was passed on to the Middle Ages, when the so-called scholastic movement redirected the curriculum from acquiring and transmitting knowledge for its own sake toward the highest of all possible goals: interpreting holy writ. The disciplines, as they came to be called, were used to solve problems, such as proving the existence of God and the associated conflicts between faith and reason, free will and intellect.

The Medieval period was also responsible for the structure of the *university* as we know it today. We hear that word, along with *faculty, master,* and *student,* used for the first time about AD 1200. The young men who entered such an institution would be directed along different career paths, from law and medicine to the arts and the clergy. The tremendous outpouring of new ideas and information in the fifteenth- and sixteenth-century Renaissance required an expanded institutional structure for the transmission of new knowledge. So the university, as we have come to know it, was born.

When we read about Copernicus's mental invention of the sun-centered solar system, I often tell my astronomy class what college life was like when the great Polish astronomer enrolled at the University of Kracόw (Poland) in the very year Columbus arrived in America. Imagine Copernicus conversing in Latin with his fellow students, I tell them, and debating with his professors as well. Questioning your profs was a requirement in those days. That would happen in the evening after a long, hard day that began at 7:00 a.m. listening to the masters' lectures on Euclid, astronomy, geometry, and philosophy. I tell them that even students here at Colgate had it pretty rough as recently as the twentieth century. For example, if you wanted your dorm room heated, you would need to set up and stoke the fireplace yourself. You'd go out to the snowy quad on winter mornings and fill your pail at the big coal pile deposited there. I remind them, too, that Copernicus's education, like that of students at most small liberal arts colleges, was directed toward religious pursuits. At least up to the 1920s the same was true at Colgate, which was in the business of turning out Baptist missionaries.

During the great scientific revolution that began in the late seventeenth century, the study of the natural world began to enter the university as a series of organized disciplines, each with its own distinct subject matter and methodology. Out of medicine grew specialized interests in plants, animals, and minerals; thus the seeds of the disciplines of botany, zoology, and geology were sown. Alchemy, once endorsed in the university, would give birth to chemistry. That happened largely as a result of attempts to organize and synthesize salts once it was realized that they could be broken down into more basic chemical elements. Behold the reductive power of science taking root!

The oldest of the sciences was astronomy; it dealt largely with the study of the motion of celestial bodies (dynamics) as it took its place alongside physics. This happened after experiments in terrestrial laboratories and the invention of the theory of gravitation made it evident that the two shared both a theoretical and a mathematical approach to explain how the material world functions. Two other "ologies," psychology and archaeology, were twentieth-century latecomers to the academy; they still reside on the periphery of the exact sciences and are housed in the social sciences in some universities. Since then, specialization has further subdivided the scientific "ologies" into immunology and epidemiology, behavioral psychology and neuropsychology, organic and inorganic chemistry, sedimentary geology and petrology, planetary and stellar astronomy, nuclear and solid state physics, and so on. Still more recently, disciplinary tools and methods shared by more than one discipline have created *inter*disciplines, such as geophysics, biophysics, planetary geology, neuropsychology, and my own cultural astronomy.

As the disciplines grew, they became silos unto themselves, more complex, more focused, more exacting, and more voluminous in the sheer storage and output of their own sort of knowledge. Fields like sociology and archaeology that scarcely existed a century ago began to burgeon. New approaches to philosophy and literary criticism posed alternative ways of redefining our values. Each discipline, especially those in the sciences, also developed its own specialized jargon. Increased specialization led to enormous breakthroughs, such as understanding how the brain works, how the subatomic realm operates, and how the earth was formed. But these advances at the frontiers of knowledge, which required more time and effort for practitioners to keep up with, came at the expense of the diminution of the broad-based corpus of knowledge familiar to most scientists—remember the "Renaissance Man?" This left them with a reduced understanding of, and appreciation for, the other disciplines. Today this development poses major problems, especially when it comes to teaching undergraduate science.

Here's a cardinal rule that seems to govern disciplinary perception: scholars immersed in one discipline tend to see uniformity in all the others and fine distinctions only within their own. For example, a cultural anthropologist has no more comprehension of what evidence derived from the application of universal laws means to a physicist than does a physicist of what evidence derived from a poststructuralist analysis of myth means to a cultural anthropologist. Secure in the valid methodologies germane to our own specialties, we can easily become suspicious of the other. I call it academic xenophobia. The liberal arts strive to reconnect the silo disciplines.

Peter Beidler writes that in the liberal arts "one discipline touches another, meshes with it, and becomes, paradoxically, a great net to hold an infinite number of questions, and at the same time to release possibilities, intuitions, sometimes even answers to the problems of the 'real world.' "[7] Conventionally, the liberal arts are housed in undergraduate institutions that are independent of professional and graduate schools. Though the heart of the Bachelor of Arts degree remains the disciplinary concentration, to promote well-roundedness most colleges also include some form of general education as a requirement. The courses that comprise most or all of gen ed consist of a host of free electives. That usually includes a distribution requirement in which students select a minimum number of electives (most often two) in each of the basic divisions of knowledge: the humanities, the sciences, and the social sciences. Read the catalog description of any liberal arts institution and you'll see that it advertises a curriculum that imparts general knowledge and develops rational thought and intellectual skills. The idea is to complement the more specialized, professionally directed, technical or vocational curricula.

Many institutions add another requirement that seems to run counter to the idea of professionalism; that's where Core comes into the picture. Core is a program of study in which all students are required to enroll, and it's often made up of specially designed courses separate from the usual departmental offerings of major/minor requirements and free electives, though the departments are expected to supply faculty. Many of whom are reluctant to teach these courses to students who are equally reluctant to enroll in them because they don't like to be told what courses to take.

To understand how general education, of which Core is a part, came about and where the ensuing tension between requiring courses and allowing students to elect them originated, we need to back up a couple of centuries. With the advent of the French Enlightenment in the late eighteenth century, followed by the establishment of the secular nation-state in Europe at the beginning of the nineteenth century, came the idea of constructing great factories of knowledge. Especially in the German universities, unbound by political and religious dictates, professors would be free to teach whatever suited them. Their students, however, would not share in that freedom. They would be required to take Latin and Greek, for truths about the past could only be understood fully when confronted in the primary sources, or those written in the language in which they were originally expressed. Coursework in logic, grammar, and rhetoric would be required too. Only then would a student be deemed ready for advanced studies in mathematics, natural philosophy, geology, biology, and astronomy. The capstone at the end of the college experience was usually a course in moral philosophy, often taught by the president of the university.

The post–Civil War reform era did not bypass American education. Harvard, Cornell, and a handful of other great bastions of learning challenged the rigidity of the Teutonic classic curriculum. Attacking the metaphor "eat your spinach; it's good for you," reform-minded Cornell president Andrew White argued that "to give mental discipline by studies which the mind does not desire is as unwise as to give physical nourishment by food which the body does not desire."[8] (Why hasn't the fast food industry latched on to this authoritative endorsement?) By the end of the nineteenth century, Harvard had abolished all requirements except for a semester of English composition and the study of a foreign language. This was a bit extreme. For example, I checked a 1900 Colgate catalog and found that about half of the courses were elective. The average was about 70 percent in US colleges. That figure dropped to 40 percent in 1940. Presently it is less than 25 percent.

Today, about a quarter of my college's offerings are free electives, courses you're entitled to choose among after you've accounted for requirements for your concentration and the general education/core courses you must take. When I came to Colgate in 1963, the figure was more than a third. I recall posing the question to my freshman advisees: In which semester would you like to take your elective?

I feel it's my responsibility to push my students outside the rigid confines of today's curriculum. I can sit for hours with my advisees making suggestions about options and choices through which they can broaden their education, often to no avail. I find it more successful to bring knowledge peripheral but still relevant to my discipline into the classroom setting. For example, in my astronomy course, when I present the mystery of Stonehenge and the theory that the Bronze Age megalithic architecture may have functioned as a prehistoric astronomical observatory and computer, I give my students readings and we have discussions on the archaeology of Stonehenge: how radio-carbon dating works, and how the archaeological record supplies us with a kind of unwritten knowledge about why Stonehenge was built. Recently, one of my students dropped by the office and asked, "Do you know anything about the archaeology courses I could take here?"

Some institutions, like Brown and Cornell, offer a higher percentage of electives because of reduced or nonexistent Core programs. At the other end of the spectrum, St. John's and Concordia, which advocate a highly structured common Core education, allow few or no electives. The University of Chicago, long known for its hefty twenty-one-course Core curriculum, reduced the program to fifteen (six quarters each in the humanities and natural sciences, three in social sciences) in 1999, largely on the grounds that too many requirements proved unappetizing to prospective undergrads. Increased specialization, along with the appeal of free choice to the mind of the average eighteen-year-old, has sped up the downward trend in requirement rigidity. Trouble is, little effort has been made to look into what free choices are actually being made.

I think the "you pay, you choose" philosophy is unwise. Consider the dislike most students exhibit toward science. Few non-majors take science courses at Colgate beyond the two-course distribution requirement in the Division of Natural Sciences and Mathematics. When they do, psychology is by far the most popular choice. Likewise, I don't know of many of our science majors who elect art, music, or literature because they have an innate desire to look, listen, or read. People just aren't sample-oriented; they don't come equipped with a curiosity to pursue new interests. Still, I do wonder whether the proliferation of minor concentrations may be a positive sign that at least some students manifest a desire to broaden themselves. Finally, there's the matter of taking "gut courses" (an old term for an undemanding course that guarantees an A; the term probably comes from gutting or excerpting) that maximize out of class activities. Yale's 2007 most gut class-listing included "Modes of Thought," "Computers and the Law," and "New York Mambo."[9]

While American free elective reform had the advantage of loosening the reins of authority and promoting entrepreneurship, with it came the obvious disadvantage of allowing students to seek paths of least resistance through the curriculum. By the turn of the nineteenth century, three-quarters of

Harvard undergrads pursued no major course of study, and more than half elected a majority of introductory courses. At the same time social clubs and fraternities, along with intercollegiate athletics, began to proliferate on college campuses. By the 1920s, going to college in America had become less a serious intellectual experience and more a means of making social contacts and enjoying the good life. As a reporter for the *Illini News* wrote in 1920, "The man who has taken no part in the social side of life usually comes a very long way from having all the characteristics that the world implies in the use of the term 'a college man.' "[10] Today's student body would not seem so out of place: 73.6 percent of freshmen rank "being well off financially" as an essential goal of going to college. Compare that to 39.6 percent who place "acquiring a meaningful philosophy of life" ahead of that goal.[11] The only time those numbers were reversed in my lifetime happened in the midst of the campus revolutions in the late 1960s and early 1970s, but more about that later.

The research university was another product of the late-nineteenth-century Euro-academy. It was only natural that if universities allowed professors to pursue their own interests and if they hired the best historians, authors and literary critics, chemists and biologists, then institutions of higher education would necessarily become places where knowledge is not simply transmitted but also *created*. If universities are knowledge factories, the disciplines are its workshops. Any legitimate workshop must acquire its own specialized tools (methods) and materials (the organized body of knowledge) to be productive. The chief skilled laborers are the professors. Their output at the end of the assembly line consists of the journals, societies, and associations to which they contribute knowledge and, above all, the cadre of disciples they produce in the discipline. Mimicking graduate institutions, my own college takes great pride—especially in the sciences—in promoting joint student-faculty research. This is implemented through summer programs and advanced study or honors courses, usually taken in the senior year.

As specialization and depth took hold in American education, many of the most inspired researchers exhibited little interest, and even less patience, in doling out the fruits of their labor to an ever-less-interested, post-adolescent student body. True, a love of learning could be inspired by the rare scholar with a natural aptitude for good teaching, but such a magical combination of top-notch scholar-teacher was rare in the academy.

The Core of the Liberal Arts: What Is It and What's It Good For?

Publish or perish. I began teaching in the early 1960s, a time when the tension between teaching and research in American liberal arts colleges was just beginning to develop. Dean Storing had his own suspicions about the conflict between depth and breadth in the college curriculum. He wrote, in fairly uncompromising terms: "And, though one hesitates to say this, some of the teachers who have gone all-out for general education have been decidedly second-rate; some have gone into general education with a vengeance because they feared or knew they were second-rate. They may have had the feeling that if they could not compete with their more learned colleagues in their own fields they might be able to compensate for this by becoming the evangelists and protagonists for the 'new' approach to the liberal arts, namely, through a program in general education."[12]

Had Storing not harbored such an attitude about beefing up scholarship at the college, I doubt that I, along with the dozen other young men (women were not admitted to Colgate until the early 1970s, prior to which there were fewer than a handful of women on the faculty) with a demonstrated commitment to research, might not have been hired. Prior to my coming to Colgate, the only criterion for academic tenure was a demonstrated record of sound teaching, judged solely by the department chair and the dean. Many Colgate faculty did not possess PhDs, nor had most contributed to the scholarly literature. Most small liberal arts schools used to be finishing schools for young men from wealthy families—what one old Ivy dean termed "touring car education," an air-conditioned first-class coach trip through the cultural landscape designed to tailor you to offer up clever remarks in social company.

Gen ed distribution and Core are about breadth, but that doesn't mean they don't exhibit depth. The idea is to introduce students to the vast panoply of topics addressed in the school curriculum and to entice those who never knew a thing about Dante, Shakespeare, Neitzsche, or Einstein to maybe take a course in which students can learn more about the things they thought and wrote about.

Tensions involved in maintaining some semblance of broad learning in college curricula have increased with time. College president George O'Brien cites three major obstacles that stand in the way of the pursuit of wholeness in such curricula.[13] First, it becomes more and more difficult to recruit new college teachers who are willing to get involved in coursework outside their specialty. (On the contrary, lately I have noted a trend in the opposite direction among junior faculty, who seem more interested and involved than their predecessors in interdisciplinary research and teaching when they arrive at Colgate.) Second, the more the faculty tends to be composed of specialists, the more diminished the concept of the "Renaissance person" becomes. Finally, students never did and still don't like being told to eat their spinach. They despise requirements, or at best they treat Core-distribution as items on their negative bucket list that they need to "get out of the way," as my advisees frequently express it, as early as possible. At Colgate there's a long history of this curricular tension that I have found applies to other institutions of higher learning as well.

The earliest version of Core in my university was fabricated just after World War II, about two decades after the Colgate Academy, an institution dedicated to training Baptist missionaries, was detached from the university. (Oddly, the label "university" has stuck, even though now we're really a college.) Its seven-course menu—all taught by staffs composed of teachers from various academic departments—included offerings in the sciences, public affairs, fine arts, literature, foreign studies and, above all, philosophy and religion, the latter pair comprising two semesters of the freshman year. Methodologically, Core was built around the "problem method," that is, putting students in contact with "transcripts of experience" that confront us everywhere, not as economists, scientists, or philosophers but rather "as citizens and responsible human beings."[14]

In the late 1960s the basic seven was reduced to five: scientific inquiry, creative arts, problems of contemporary society, the study of a culture other than one's own, and philosophical and religious knowledge. Allowing area requirements to be satisfied through election from among a host of courses taught in various departments further diminished the notion of Core courses being special, different, and, above all, beyond select academic departmental interests.

By the time I happened on the scene, the rigid Colgate curriculum of the early twentieth century, which had been directed almost solely toward training men destined for clerical pursuits, had become more flexible. Still, the Core, which had also begun to evolve noticeably in the direction of dealing with secular issues, permeated all four years of the degree-granting program. At that time, the justification for Core in most colleges was pretty straightforward. First, it was intended to prevent premature specialization by insisting that its constituent courses *not* be taught from a single disciplinary perspective. Second, it was styled to offer a measure of coherence to the student's course program by stressing interrelationships among disciplines. One of its unifying advantages was that students would be reading and discussing common texts and dialoguing on the same issues—it was hoped, outside as well as in class. Third and finally, the program sought to ensure that those who graduated would be suited to be members of the "community of culture." This goal would be achieved by guiding students in becoming more reflective and critical about their own beliefs and values, as well as those that exist in the societies in which they live. This ethically based goal of making good citizens has always been the most controversial. For example, the education historian W. B. Carnochan points out that civic responsibility and promotion of ethical awareness run counter to the ideals of liberal education, which "aspires to disinterest, however much it valorizes" experiences of the past.[15]

Colgate's Core program of the early 1960s accounted for about one-sixth of the total curriculum (today it has declined further, to one-eighth). The major comprised another quarter, slightly more in the sciences. After distribution requirements, students could fill the remaining 40 percent of their course schedule with free electives. Most of the Core was administered in the freshman year. It consisted of two terms each of natural science, rhetoric and literature, and philosophy and religion. The last included a fair dose of New Testament readings (the Book of Hosea and the Gospel of St. Mark, as I recall), fallout from our bygone Baptist educational leanings.

Another quaint religious remnant at Colgate consisted of required daily attendance at chapel. This took place during a specially designated "chapel period" that ran from 10:00 to 10:20 a.m. The short sermon fractured the every-hour-on-the-hour class start-time sequence. Demands of the social revolution of the 1960s, together with the increasing religious diversity of the student body, reduced mandatory attendance to three days a week and truncated religious services to two days a week only; so, if nonreligious students chose wisely, they could avoid sermonization altogether. The other three days of the school week were taken up with announcements and selected secular presentations.

The only Core requirement in the sophomore year, by the end of which students were required to declare a concentration, was a term of "Music and the Visual Arts." Third-year students took an intensive course in foreign "Area Studies." The term *foreign* in those days included the British Commonwealth, China, France, Germany, the Mediterranean, Mexico, Argentina, Brazil, and the Soviet Union. Taught by specialists in anthropology, economics, geography, and history, as well as language professors, this largely social science–based Core sought to equip students to explore other cultures realistically, receptively, and sympathetically.

"American Ideals and Institutions," a historically based, two-semester course on values inherent in the national life, and "America in the World Community" (one semester), largely an analysis of foreign policy, made up the rest of the Core requirements. The idea here was to build on the Area Studies and American Ideals Core by applying what had already been learned so students might understand the international tensions of the day, which at the time comprised the Cold War, the population crisis, and the fate of underdeveloped countries, such as Communist China and India.

All university curricula reflect the perceived needs of the times—"the prevalent habit of thought," as the economist-sociologist Thorstein Veblen once characterized it.[16] This is why building sound moral values and preparing students for good citizenship, not only in their own cultural environment but also in the world at large, loomed as a distinctively novel aspect in college catalogs of the early 1960s; it was not so prominent in the old catalogs of the early 1900s. Between printings, two world wars had taken place. So, too, did the introduction into the college curriculum of "Civics" or "Problems of Citizenship," as it was first called at Stanford when a member of that university installed it in the early twentieth century. By the time I attended Boston University as an undergraduate (between 1956 and 1960), that course had evolved into the ubiquitous "Western Civ," a combination of political science, economics, and sociology—all framed in a historical context and beginning with the French Enlightenment. (Had we become civilized so recently?)

It was only after I became immersed in its content that I began to understand what really drove Core liberal arts. Content aside, the philosophy behind a liberal arts curriculum is to teach students to think for themselves, to be skeptical and to question—the ultimate stage of the "breathing process" (p. 19). This attitude runs counter to the idea of accepting beliefs imposed by consensus and tradition, and it is often not viewed in a positive light in American common culture; neither are its purveyors. During a recent political campaign, a candidate for national office confronted a person holding an alternative point of view who carried a sign advertising her opposition. When the candidate addressed her and inquired into the foundation behind her orientation by asking "what do you do for a living," back came the response "I'm a teacher." The office seeker rolled her eyes and replied "ah, I see." Makes you wonder whether the popular conception of teacher as rabble-rouser stems from the ideal of not blindly accepting traditionally held beliefs arrived at by consensus.

Questioning isn't all there is to it. The liberal arts also aspires to develop tolerance for different perspectives and to cultivate how to reason through them so that students can judge the value and practical applicability of a wide range of ideas. If you're to achieve the latter goal in any meaningful way, you need to immerse yourself in the Classical world of Greece and Rome, the great books, and the history of Western civilization—our tradition. You also need to acquire some depth of understanding in other ways of knowing—the values and institutions tied to other cultures. How else can you form notions of the common good in a changing world that evolves out of the merging and mixing together of these views? As Veblen would have predicted back in the 1920s, how to deal with this complex set of diverse goals would change with the times.

So, how do I answer the "what can she do with a degree in the liberal arts" question parents often ask me? Well, it won't direct her toward a high-paying job faster, but it might make a difference when it comes to how she'll deal with the job market later in life. Whatever job she chooses—if she's typical she'll choose many—the liberal arts will help her be better at it. Why? Because, to draw on Trinity College historian Cheryl Greenburg's response, the liberal arts not only help you discover what you're really good for but also to learn how to raise questions about what *anything's* good for.[17] Many of my former students recount how they were merrily matriculating along at Colgate in their pre-engineering or music majors when suddenly they encountered Freud or Faulkner in their Core courses and how that chance meeting drove them to the psych or English department with a huge thirst in need of quenching. These encounters took them along paths they never knew existed, into unfamiliar territory they sought to explore fearlessly. Even if they didn't end up as psychologists or literary critics, my students' experiences helped them round out their approach to life.

The liberal arts, especially the core of it, are not so much about the knowledge itself as about what you do with it. Immersed in the liberal arts, you acquire the habit of how to reflect on things that give meaning to your life. The liberal arts demonstrate how it is possible for you to reflect openly (yes, *disinterestedly*) on the multiplicity of points of view you can acquire. Leslie Epstein, creative writing director at Boston University, points to the increasing lack of beauty that permeates our everyday lives, coerces our sensibility, shrinks our imaginations, and desensitizes us to realizing what might be possible in the world. It reduces our empathy.[18] I believe, with her, that the liberal arts—especially its humanistic component—combats that trend.

Tradition vs. Change, or How to Move a Graveyard

Earlier I mentioned one academic truism: changing a college's curriculum is about as difficult as moving a graveyard. Here's another: once you get established in the academy, sooner or later the administrators try to make you into one of them.

It was 1979. I'd been teaching at Colgate for sixteen years. I had achieved some success in the classroom. My commitment to engaging my students in fieldwork in Mexico and Central America was well developed (more about my disciplinary hybridization later). In the eyes of Colgate's newly appointed dean of faculty, philosopher John Morris, my crossover from the sciences to anthropology made me a prime candidate to head a major overhaul of the Core general education program.

The basic idea behind the program still rested on the premise that all students should be exposed to great books of the Western world; as we have seen, exposure implied a heavy dose of Old and New Testament literature. Common texts still served as the hallmark of Core. If all students read the same books, they'd have something they all shared to discuss outside of class—in addition to belonging to clubs and participating in intramural sports. But choosing common texts was becoming harder to implement.

The 1970s had been a decade of rapid change in American colleges and universities. It was a time when educational values and norms were challenged. There was bound to be a conservative backlash against proposed curricular changes. The assault on the American professoriate by traditionalists set off a wave of accusations that we profs weren't doing our jobs, especially when it came to teaching dispassionately. Allan Bloom's *Closing of the American Mind* is still the most widely read and discussed book on the topic.[19] Critics charged that colleges had allowed liberal arts curricula to be taken over by advocacy-oriented courses and programs, such as women's studies, peace studies, black, Chicano, and Native American studies, and the like—subjects that appealed to socially fashionable issues. The liberal arts ought to be the antidote to mass culture, not its promoter, they argued.

More personal attacks on the professoriate and how they spend their time would follow. Among the best-known was Charles Sykes's 1988 *ProfScam*.[20] Sykes condemned the publication of useless research in obscure journals that nobody reads and the communication of results in incomprehensible jargon. He complained of teachers being totally indifferent to teaching and accused them of working less than sixteen hours a week. Maybe I'm confusing dream time with work time, but I wonder, as I lie in bed semi-awake at night pondering how to approach the discussion of Plato's idea of forms in tomorrow's Core class or thinking about what I can do to help Harry recover from his barely passing performance on yesterday's exam, where Sykes got his data and how he managed to conjure up such an image of how the vast majority of college professors spend their time. Not at my jobsite! Yet many ordinary citizens continue to view the professoriate from afar as members of a leisure class. I recall cousins, uncles, and aunts in my largely working-class family who, when they see me during the summer months, ask, with no malice intended, "So, how's your summer vacation going?" The teachers I hang with are constantly engaged in discussions about curricula and classroom pedagogy.

Negative outlooks about what really goes on in the research segment of academia were even stronger. Wisconsin senator William Proxmire famously derided academic research when he established the Golden Fleece Awards in 1975. His prime concern was to make the public aware of wasteful government spending. The fact that so many of Proxmire's citations were directed toward government financing of scientific research tells us something about popular culture's perceptions of science. Prime examples of irrelevant academic activity cited by Proxmire included NASA's SETI program (the Search for Extraterrestrial Intelligence), a psychological study of the encoding of facial expressions, and using penis probes and pornographic films to measure the effect of marijuana smoking on sexual arousal. In 1991 the scientific humor magazine *Annals of Improbable Research* began issuing annual Ig Nobel Awards (after the word "ignoble," meaning base, even contemptible) to scientific projects deemed trivial or worthless. "Termination of Intractable Hiccups with Digital Rectal Massage" won the Iggy in 2006. Runner-ups: "The First Case of Homosexual Necrophilia in the Mallard Anas [Duck]," "The Effect of Country Music on Suicide," and "Ovulatory Cycle Effects on Tip Earnings by Lap Dancers."

Okay, Proxmire had a point: it *is* difficult to imagine any practical application coming out of a study on why cookies crumble (I'm not making that one up), and it's humorous for a magazine to poke fun at what sounds like silly science. What's missing in the critique, though, is an apparent lack of appreciation of the value of pure research driven by sheer curiosity in favor of the desire to squash ideas and approaches that aren't motivated by *anticipated* practical ends. I'm thinking of the discoveries of penicillin by Alexander Fleming and of one of the genes for cell division that led to understanding the growth of cancer cells by Paul Nurse. The first happened by analyzing mold on a piece of discarded bread, the second by experimenting with yeast for no particular reason. Both discoveries came too early for an Iggy, but each earned a Nobel Prize. It's also worth remembering that space medicine, though never proposed for study in any of the early NASA space programs, became one of its heralded achievements—contributing to our understanding of immune system functioning, sleep disorders, cardiac arrhythmia, effects of fatigue, and bone density and muscle mass loss.

I think the cold slap in the face of the professoriate struck by Bloom, and later by Sykes's largely uninformed diatribe, has had a healthy effect on the academic community. It brought to the surface a serious debate about the nature of the liberal arts. The idea that political conflict finds its roots in the clash between cultural values advocated by tradition-bound conservatives and the progressive ideas of liberals traces its most recent roots to the campus activism of the 1960s.

The battle lines in the great "culture wars," as they have come to be called, were most sharply drawn in the 1970s. Argued the *critical objectivists*: surely we cannot erase from the curriculum the ideas that lie at the foundation of the Western canon—the writings of the Old and New Testament that comprise the base of Judeo-Christian religion, the grandeur of Greece and Rome, the fluorescence of the arts and sciences in the Renaissance, the industrial revolution, the establishment of the European nation-state, and so on.

Retorted the *relativistic constructivists*: we also need to read about how the ideas immersed in these studies that lay the foundation of our culture have been reinterpreted over the ages; furthermore, we need to incorporate new ideas into the curriculum as well—ideas that apply more directly to the modern world. The culture wars created new challenges about what—and what else—needed to be included in a curriculum that bore some relevance to ongoing issues and problems in a rapidly evolving American culture.

As the world changes, so too does the university and its academic programs. In many universities, including my own, some of the biggest curricular changes happened in the aftermath of the late 1960s and early 1970s, a time of deep public questioning of America's moral values. The Vietnam conflict raised the question: Under what conditions and to what extent is American involvement in foreign conflict justified? Many of my students were more than academically involved in the issues of the times. I recall sitting nervously with a group of advisees in front of the communal black-and-white TV set in a dorm lounge, intently watching the nationally televised drawing of draft lottery numbers. The lower the number (from 1 to 365, each assigned to a date of the year), the greater the chance you'd be called upon to serve if that number matched your birth date in the random shuffle. Antiwar advocate Ken Trevett (today CEO of San Antonio's Texas Biomedical Research Institute) wept in relief when his date of birth matched the number 323; but young Porter Rathmell, whose number was 12, was not so lucky—he ended up a Vietnam casualty.

I remember, too, a few years later, talking with my students out of class about the ongoing Watergate scandal. I have the distinct impression that Watergate had a greater impact on the contemporary American distrust of government institutions than did all the violence and turmoil that attended the 1968 Democratic Convention. That period also witnessed violence in the American cities many of my students came from. Clearly, the racial tensions manifested in the South during the 1950s were still seething in Newark, Cincinnati, Los Angeles, and a host of other urban areas, including my hometown of New Haven, where "the projects" (cheap housing constructed for blacks) were set ablaze. I participated in student-organized sit-ins at Colgate related to one or another of the paramount social issues in 1968, 1969, and 1970—demands for revocation of a fraternity's charter following a racial incident on campus, a protest against the bombing of Cambodia, and another over the shooting incident at Kent State. Why should what happens in the classroom bear no relation to the world outside the ivory tower? Why have we been reading about dead poets and philosophers when we ought to be inquiring why such terrible things are happening all around us in our society? What can we do about it? These were some of the difficult questions my students put to me. I had a hard time offering them convincing, reasoned responses, though our extended discussions led us to realize how difficult it is to answer the big questions. All of these circumstances played a role in my commitment to reform the curriculum.

Back in the late 1950s when I attended college, educators seemed less concerned about the relevance of the curriculum to daily life. The idea was that if students are exposed to a broad range of knowledge in the sciences, social sciences, and especially the humanities, then the encounter with all that American society deems good—proper values and an honorable code of ethics—will automatically become rooted and grow within them. "We are here to cultivate the life of the mind, not to advocate a particular sort of moral behavior," argued a number of the senior faculty as we sat outside Colgate's Administration Building after the 1968 sit-in was settled. (The Board of Directors revoked the charter of the offending fraternity.) I don't recall any general electives on ethics listed in the Boston University catalog when I was an undergraduate, and I never chose to take the philosophy department's offering on moral reasoning. Indeed, Wittgenstein once argued that there was no such inquiry in the entire domain of that discipline.

After the revolutionary 1960s, things were bound to change big time in university curricula. The emphasis on requiring exposure to the big ideas and basic questions that are part of the legacy of Western tradition slowly began to diminish. The slack was taken up by courses that raised questions about who we are, both as individuals and as part of a culture compared to the rest of the world, as well as what are the consequences of our individual and social actions. We contemplated a new, more activist-oriented curriculum, one advocating that each of us must define and interpret our own set of moral values. This seemed to chart the preferred pathway to the pursuit of our personal moral freedom.[21]

Today not all academics agree, though circumstances have changed; for example, English prof Mark Bauerlein is among those who advocate that we need *less*, not more, relevance in our classrooms.[22] Students need to learn about ideas that resist the influence of pop culture and the relatively narrow, self-focused youth perspective. Tradition is good. Our deep past is filled with bigger and better stories about the human condition than those that flood Internet websites. The tension over the issue of relevance in the academy is still with us.

Add to the problem of revising the curriculum the increased diversity in college admissions, which blossomed in the 1970s. When I arrived in the early 1960s, Colgate was an all-male institution, with 85 percent of the 97 percent white male student body made up of high-school graduates from New York, New Jersey, Pennsylvania, Massachusetts, and Connecticut. Two percent of the student body was black, and there were no women. Today the student population has doubled: 53 percent are women, 8 percent Hispanic, 4 percent Asian, and 5 percent black. Every state and two dozen foreign countries are represented. In part because of our rural, far northern location, this is still not considered a strong record at diversifying the campus population.

Incidentally, coeducation on the American campus actually goes back a long way.

> She doesn't think.
> She doesn't pet.
> She hasn't been to college yet.[23]

It's an old college joke from the 1920s, when campuses first started admitting women—up to 47 percent attendance on some campuses by the end of that decade. The archetypal female was "Betty Co-ed," a skinny flapper (the open-top galoshes she wore were said to make a flapping sound) with a shingle hairdo that would give way to a bob in the 1930s.[24] She lived in a dorm, far from her parents; like her gender counterpart, she was there to party and climb the social ladder. She drank and smoked.

Our Core revision was inspired by a late 1970s response to increasing specialization in college curricula. Harvard economist and Dean of Arts and Sciences Henry Rosovsky spearheaded an effort to overturn Harvard's "Chinese menu" approach to gen ed and introduce a Core program based on common experience, common discourse, and shared values.[25] So-called educated people,

Rosovsky argued, no longer shared in enough intellectual experience to enable them to communicate with one another or to acquire any sympathy for understanding how another's mind worked. The Harvard program included eight courses in five academic areas: literature and art, math and science, history, and philosophical and social analysis—about one-quarter of the total curriculum regardless of concentration.

When I was invited to head the Core curricular reconstruction process at Colgate, I was pressed to include more material on non-Western culture; specifically, we should pay more attention to gender issues, colonialism, and perspectives on race relations. Also, basic skills in the quantitative sciences, in reading, writing, and language skills, needed to be shored up. At a time when generalized liberal learning in small colleges was starting to give way to vocationalism and when hiring specialists to set up research programs was seen as beginning to encroach on the traditional mission of teaching-oriented institutions such as my own, assuming a leadership role in curricular revision would prove a more difficult task than I had imagined.

I had been aware of many of these developments from my continued participation in Colgate's general education core program; yet I also sensed a feeling of wanting to reciprocate an institution that had given me plenty of leeway to develop a new scientific concentration program and acquire first-rate instrumentation to put it into operation, and I accepted the dean's appointment as director of the Division of University Studies. Duties attending the three-year term of office included supervising general education and its core component of required out-of-department courses for all students as well as overseeing programs the college was just beginning to develop that did not fit the standard disciplinary structure, such as women's studies and environmental studies. How to manage changing a college curriculum at the end of a fast-moving decade? The graveyard analogy loomed in my mind.

When it comes to the question of identifying what knowledge is truly vital, the academic crowd can be very opinionated. Many of my colleagues, particularly the old guard, were suspicious of anything novel. Some felt threatened that their special interest might be excluded from the revised program. Others, especially some scientists, didn't take disciplines other than their own very seriously. I recall one of our math professors vocally responding to a poster the anthropology department had put up advertising a guest lecturer's topic "Andean Counting Devices and Inca Mathematics" with an exclamatory

"Hah! Aren't they dead?" And a geologist suggesting over coffee with a group of peers that "once we straighten out the course numbering system in the science division, we ought to trot over to humanities and show them how to do it." (He had a hard time understanding how any department could allow a student to take a 300-level course without 200- and 100-level prerequisites.)

In May 1959, Sir Charles Percy (later Lord) Snow—chemist, civil servant, and novelist—delivered a controversial lecture at Cambridge University, the contents of which were published that same year.[26] In the 1960s it would become required reading in Core programs in many American universities, including my own. The lecture was titled "The Two Cultures." Later, a second part of the written version of Snow's remarks carried the title "The Scientific Revolution." Like me and others trained in the early post–World War II period, Snow viewed his scientific profession as the answer to the world's problems and looked with disdain upon those engaged in any academic field of inquiry other than his own until he realized that there is a great divide between two different kinds of intellectual inquiry that live side by side in the academy—the literary and the scientific. He identified "between the two a gulf of mutual incomprehension . . . hostility and dislike, but most of all lack of understanding."[27] Non-scientists, he continued, have the impression that scientists believe literary intellectuals care only about restricting art and thought to the existential moment. Snow's twofold contribution laid bare the increasing polarization of the disciplines that had begun to emerge out of intense specialization and the disastrous results that might ensue should we continue to educate our students as we do. An ever rarified vacuum is developing out of the diminishing dialogue between the two cultures. The cultural impact of the increasing specialization of knowledge leaves no room for assimilation, no synthesis, no connection between the intellectual engagements that confront the educated mind. Oddly, Lord Snow was lambasting the British university as he looked to America, where the liberal arts still thrived, for solutions.

I think Snow had it right. Science, social science, and the humanities *are* a lot like islands in a sea of mutual incomprehensibility. How could I possibly begin to get our faculty to agree to any conceivable form of a revised program? The path toward a solution came to me in a flash. I would allow *every* member of the faculty to express his or her (by 1979 there were more than a handful of women on the Colgate faculty) opinions about what ought to comprise a sound Core program. To circumvent the "why wasn't I consulted?" response to any program that might ultimately be proposed in university-wide faculty meetings, I would patiently and systematically interview every member of the faculty, one or two or three at a time. So I spent a good chunk of my budget on a top-tier espresso machine!

Dialogue lies at the root of all intellectual progress. And what better way to conduct serious eyeball-to-eyeball discourse than over a good coffee? Greeks do it most mornings at little round tables outside their taverns. Middle Eastern businessmen sip tea from transparent glasses in the bazaar; truck drivers have a beer at a little hole-in-the-wall truck stop or diner (I should know; my father owned one across from a big overseas transport company adjacent to New Haven Harbor.)

I set up my machine in the chapel basement daily from 10:00 to 10:20 a.m., the vestigial remnant of Chapel Period. Figuring I could run the table in one semester, I had my administrative assistant set up invitations, two or three to a time slot, to all 175+ members of the faculty. I paired economist with biologist, historian with poet, neuroscientist with sociologist—anything to elicit contrasting points of view. Regular or espresso? Cappuccino or latte? Diversity all around. In return for my hospitality, I was barraged with all sorts of unanticipated advice: make history a required course; make physics a required course; make anthropology a required course; make students take four years of linguistics; stick with the program as it is; lose the entire program, and so on.

Most memorable of the suggestions was a highly imaginative concept offered by a professor in the music department. Bill Skelton was an old Colgate don, a member of the faculty since the early 1950s. He'd served as an aircraft tail-gunner in World War II and had entered the halls of academia under the postwar GI Bill. Bill was an inspiring teacher and a great innovator—he started our off-campus India study group and ran it for nearly forty years and created Indian music courses on campus. Bill was one of the first American academics to bring Ravi Shankar to a college campus. He conducted the Colgate Symphony Orchestra with the flair of a Leonard Bernstein, and he had an ego to match. When it was Bill's turn at coffee he chose—what else?—a double espresso. As the conversation began, he leaned past the disinterested chemist I'd paired him with and whispered "Tony, I've got a big idea. No time to lay it out here. Take you to lunch tomorrow at the Inn."

Eager for any novel Core spin, I showed up promptly at Hamilton's elite dining spot, just across from the green on the corner that housed our town's only traffic light. After a ten-minute wait, I spotted my luncheon host at the door. We ordered Bloody Marys, made small talk, then moved on to lunch. When our sandwiches arrived fifteen minutes later and I had yet to hear anything remotely related to education, much less a big idea from his side of the table, I zeroed in on the question. "So, what's your big idea about Core, Bill?" "Yeah"—long pause, self-confident smile—"let's make it an opera" he gestured with his hands, as if perched on the conductor's platform. "What do you mean 'it'?" I retorted. "We'll make the whole Core program into an opera. It'll take four years," his eyes widened as his face took on a slightly mad-looking, eureka gaze that penetrated my very soul. "The freshmen will be the stagehands, the sophomores will do the libretto, the juniors will write the music, and the seniors will perform it." I noticed a large blue vein bulging in his right temple as Professor Skelton gesticulated and breathlessly fleshed out the details in an impassioned voice. As he paused and eagerly awaited my reaction, I noticed that I was having trouble moving my mouth and holding on to my fork. Bill's emphatic conclusion to the plan broke the protracted silence: "and, and . . . I will conduct!"

I honestly can't remember what happened next. I may have been afflicted with momentary blindness, deafness, and loss of speech, but I recall that when I finally became conscious of any ongoing discourse, we seemed to be sharing thoughts about how difficult it is to push through curricular change and especially how hard it can be for some of our colleagues to open themselves up to new ideas, regardless of how novel they may be. He was right about that. The waiter delivered the check, which sat untouched for a few minutes. As the conversation dissipated into generality, I reached out and said "I've got it. I have a budget for these things."

If you want to reform a curriculum, you need to deal with the big questions: What does it really mean to be educated? Is it just about acquiring a body of knowledge, or does it have as much to do with experiencing the process of how one comes to know? Or is it a combination of both? Experience taught me that there are two camps here: the *product* camp and the *process* camp. Surely you need to become familiar with *some* basic knowledge to understand how to think, how to reason, how to work with ideas, how to *argue* a case. You can't comprehend the rational bonds that join diverse ways of knowing in the absence of an organized body of knowledge to debate and question. So says the product, or *content,* camp. Extremists in this camp argue that we should teach *only* the canon of the West, each expert in his/her field attending to her own appointed task; for example, specialists in Greek philosophy should lead the encounter with Plato and art historians should engage Rembrandt. The *process* camp, on the other hand, tends to be populated by those who seek a curriculum that tries to bring the disciplines and their teacher-experts into individual courses. Learning is more about process than product, they say. Those in the process camp believe students learn better when they enter into dialogue with teachers who are *not* experts on the subject matter they confront together in the classroom because the teacher is then forced to become an active learner along with the students. And who knows better *how* to learn than a teacher?

One of the problems with the non-process-minded faction is the distaste for immersing themselves in an enterprise that requires them to tread on foreign turf. Even the most skilled and secure educator can squirm at the prospect of facing a classroom filled with bright inquiring minds, aware that even though she has the advantage of experience and mental skills when it comes to dealing with texts and problems, the level of her knowledge of the basic stuff that makes up the subject often barely exceeds that of her pupils. That was certainly the way I felt when I was first thrust into Core science and asked to deal with those unfamiliar heroes of chemistry—Dalton, Cannizzaro, and Lavoisier—alongside the familiar icons in my own discipline of astronomy: Galileo, Copernicus, and Kepler. How could I fault novice teachers a couple of decades later for reacting as they did when they encountered my attempts to recruit them into a new Core program with processual leanings?

There were other difficulties with the Core revision process. Departments were commencing a "more-is-better" curricular phase as they sought to increase the number of required courses, especially in the sciences. Part of the motivation was derived from the increased effort to place more majors in graduate schools. Getting scientists to participate was especially difficult. Highly specialized, they were among the most reticent to embrace the importance of studying issues that connected science and society, especially when asked to do so with colleagues from outside their home in the Division of Natural Sciences and Mathematics. In addition, a new era of student freedom had increased their demands for more free electives. Finally, wresting Core from the domain of an earlier Colgate era, when the goal of many small colleges was centered on educating Christian missionaries, would also prove problematic. Put simply, there was a lot of old-time religion in our existing Core program.

As the brief caffeine-fueled discussions developed into lengthier group meetings, the humanists and social scientists became embroiled in a huge debate over whether *text* should take precedent over *context*. "How can you possibly teach Jane Austen without thoroughly understanding the history of the place of women in nineteenth-century America?" posed one sociology professor. "We need to teach the text itself, not just *about* the text," responded a young recruit from the English department. When it came to *which* text, opposing factions offered their own *sine qua non* choices: How can anybody really understand the rise of modernity without reading Charles Darwin's *On the Origin of Species*? Not if you exclude Sigmund Freud or Adam Smith or Karl Marx, argued other proponents. When an art historian suggested that the architecture and stained glass of Chartres Cathedral, all rendered in the form of 35-mm slides, serve as a text in one of the Core courses, a philosopher protested, "How can that be a text? It has no words!"

The humanities served as the principal battleground during the reform-minded late 1970s when I took over general education at Colgate. Most agreed that an educated person needed to acquire some familiarity with the great works of philosophy, religion, and literature, as well as an appreciation of art and music, along with some understanding of the methods of interpreting these works. But once again, there was little agreement on precisely which great works ought to constitute the new curriculum. Which are truly the timeless classics, the "must reads" that best engage the big questions and the most meaningful issues expressing the human condition? Even the objectivists who believed in a Western canon couldn't agree, though most felt it must include select Old Testament readings, a Greek classic or two (but which ones—Hesiod's *Theogony*, the *Odyssey*, surely something of Plato and Socrates?), and how can you leave out Shakespeare?

Opponents charged that such deep immersion in the Western tradition smacked of a kind of elitism that goes with the patriarchal, imperialistic attitude that has led our culture to place the West above all the rest. Extreme relativists proposed abolishing the canon altogether. A more moderate faction, well aware that all the canonic texts were authored by upper-class, white, European males, offered a more flexible list of required basic texts (nicknamed the "usual suspects"). That list was supplemented by additional readings that dealt with gender, race, and class issues, which had made their dramatic appearance as contemporary social issues on campus in the decade leading up to the advent of curricular reform. The new idea here operated on the principle of creating opportunities for interdisciplinary learning through a set of courses built around "Ideas," "Institutions," "Cultures," and "Values"—all without diminishing the importance of the Western canon. Treading the line between teaching the intellectual tradition of the West while still giving credence to a vast underrepresented segment of human society would require lengthy dialogue.

Getting faculty to team-teach was probably the most difficult obstacle to emerge out of the multidisciplinary revision we contemplated. Here, I'm not referring to tag-team teaching, where you split a course chronologically into sausage link–type units taught, in turn, by a lineup of faculty experts. I'm talking about a more intellectually and economically costly enterprise, wherein faculty actually commit themselves to engage one another—and their students—on a regular basis in the classroom throughout the semester. To serve as an example, a few of my colleagues and I designed and taught a pilot version of such a course. It turned out to be one of the most illuminating experiences in my teaching career.

The course was titled "Evolution," and my co-teachers were a biologist and a social historian. The biologist would teach Darwinian theory, and the historian would deal with the controversy of its sociobiological implications. As an astronomer, my assignment would be to deal with how Darwin's view of life influenced the way physical scientists came to understand the inanimate world (e.g., the big bang, or so-called evolutionary cosmology). Early in the course the biologist, Bill Oostenink, a giant of a man who delivered his message clearly in a booming voice, was holding forth at the front of the classroom on the subject of DNA. (We had been reading Watson and Crick's The Double Helix, which detailed the discovery of DNA.) Backed by abstract-looking blackboard diagrams, the language of his presentation was heavily laced with scientific jargon: "And then the messenger RNA . . ."; "Along the network of neurons . . ."; "The coding segments of the gene . . ." As the lecture continued, I noticed the historian Curtis Hinsley, a passionate man noted for his candor (often shared openly and without the slightest provocation), beginning to grimace and squirm in his seat.

Continued the biologist: "Once this information is received . . ." and "If the switch is turned on . . ." The historian's grimace changed to red-faced apoplexy, his squirm to uncomfortable bodily writhing. Suddenly, Hinsley lurched out of his back-row seat and shouted over his pointing finger: "Wait a minute! Wait a minute!" Startled, the biologist dropped his chalk and wheeled his large frame around like a radar dish attempting to hone in on the direction of a booming signal. "You're talking about DNA as if it were a computer!" hollered the historian. After a long pause the life scientist retorted, "Well, it is" (another long pause), "isn't it?" The several dozen young minds in attendance, mouths agape, swiveled back and forth attempting to follow the impassioned dialogue. "The words you're using— network, receptor—you're telling your audience that a molecule is a computer," protested the historian. Countered the biologist, "Well, if it walks like a duck and quacks like a duck, then it is a duck." The two professors argued passionately tit-for-tat for the remainder of the period and beyond as I witnessed one of the great unanticipated, unrehearsed—and, I would argue, most important—events in my classroom experience.

Initially, much of what went on had a negative impact on some of our students. They complained that their professors couldn't agree on what they were teaching. They weren't sure who to side with—the expert historian or the expert biologist— until our small group discussions helped elevate them a notch in the learning-breathing process.

My anecdote about interactive team-teaching cuts to the heart of a central question about the way we think science works—or doesn't. Are the models we create approximations of unattainable truths—mere extensions of our intellect—or do they unmask a real hidden truth? Do our explanations reveal the real thing, or are they only metaphors—the cobbling together of tangible, familiar, and contemporary shapes, sights, and sounds that offer tantalizing tastes of the unreachable underlying essences that constitute the real world? Our interdisciplinary team-taught course really got us to the big questions that are very often passed over in content-packed survey courses in the individual disciplines.

University of Illinois Chicago professor of education and English Gerald Graff has written eloquently on cross-disciplinary teaching.[28] He points out that when we are required to bring together materials from disciplines other than our own, we are forced to reassess how our area of study connects with other fields. I agree with him that students learn better when they are put in the same position, especially when they see experts in conflict, as our students experienced in our team-taught course on evolution. Years later I still hear from them about the surprising, novel way they apprehended the confrontation between truth and metaphor. I wish more deliberately confrontational courses were part of our Core curriculum.

Sadly, "Evolution," along with the interdisciplinary "capstone" courses that made up the revised program we proposed and implemented back in the early 1980s, evaporated from the Core curriculum in the mid-1990s, largely as a result of our inability to staff them. Requiring three faculty members to be active participants for a full term in a single course proved too costly, even with the advent of a new generation of teachers more willing to participate in the enterprise of interdisciplinary learning, which by then had begun to achieve credibility in the halls of academia.

By the late 1980s the "I-word" had officially entered the Colgate Core program. Its most distinctive element was a sequence of four courses, each organized to encourage students to think across the boundaries that divide the traditional disciplines. This goal would be achieved by combining methods of inquiry from the humanities, sciences, and social sciences in ways not limited strictly to any one of them and applying such inquiry to persistent fundamental questions posed in classical texts that one confronts as current issues, such as the relationship of the temporal to the eternal and the definition of the individual within society. As we described it, *"Interdisciplinary* inquiry is designed not to seek agreement on issues, rather to demonstrate their complexity when considered from various perspectives."[29]

Diversity, Modernity, and Globalization: New Cores for New Generations

Major curricular revisions in general education programs at all universities, particularly those with Core components, happen every decade or so. Colgate's most recent version, implemented in 2010, is a typical hybrid model that shares a number of aspects with programs developed by other liberal arts colleges. It's worth a closer look so we can see how it compares with what was done a generation ago. The idea that Core should consist of specially designed courses struggles to remain intact. Moreover, the number of

Core requirements has been reduced, while the intended coverage of areas and issues has expanded. There are simply more constituents to satisfy today than a generation ago. In my view this creates a significantly diluted curriculum, with fewer concrete interconnections among Core courses than in the earlier program. Straining to satisfy demands from many quarters, today's common experience Core at Colgate "takes seriously classic texts as well as multiculturalism and globalization, the importance of the past as well as the contemporary moment, the relevance of modern science and technology, as well as the humanities." It asks students to approach problems in "integrative cross-disciplinary ways about their world and themselves."[30]

"Legacies of the Ancient World" is now the only staff-taught course. Basically, it's the old "Western Traditions" humanities class—the one that deals with the virtues, the good life, the true, the just, and the beautiful. A vestige of the common text requirement is still there: all students read Homer, Plato, and parts of the Old and New Testament. "Legacies" is the first course our freshman students take, and it remains largely in the provenience of the humanities. Those who teach it are rewarded with the freedom to choose one or two complementary texts they feel are applicable in their particular section.

Personally, I'm not terribly fond of the "teach the West first" approach because there's an inherent risk of conveying the notion that Western ways of knowing are somehow superior to others. In addition, the increasing ethnic and racial diversity in the student body makes the case for giving priority to the legacies of Western philosophy, politics, art, religion, literature, and science seem less appealing. As a teacher of science with a specialty in ethnoscience, I am very sensitive to attitudes expressed by peers in my root discipline, who believe the Western scientific approach to understanding nature is the only way to arrive at the *real* truth about things—understanding the natural world "such as it is," as they term it. I think we need to concentrate not on comparing Indian music, Chinese science, and African religion with their Western counterparts in a value-laden framework; rather, we ought to confront each of them *in their own context*. We must place ourselves in front of a mirror surrounded by the faces of the other. What better way to understand our own systems of thought than by dealing with those of another?

"Challenges of Modernity" introduced another new term into the curriculum that burst into prominence on college campuses in the 1980s. Modernity is a complex and controversial topic, even down to its very definition. Most historians apply the Western concept of modernity to developments rooted in the aftermath of the Middle Ages: the move from feudalism and agrarianism to capitalism, the rise of industrialization, the creation of a more secular world based on rational thinking, and the development of the nation-state. On the other hand, many sociologists think of modernity as the set of social conditions that respond to the Enlightenment. Still others regard modernity as a social force, the force of progress that liberates us from ignorance. Political scientists usually define modernity by the tenets of the modern liberal political system, while in the artistic realm the necessity of innovation becomes the requisite paragon. So you can see why the term carries obvious topical appeal in a liberal arts curriculum. It offers multiple definitions of who we are in the present so that everyone can relate to it from a different perspective. Historically, Colgate's version of "Challenges of Modernity" covers only the period since around 1990 in any depth. Urbanization, techno-development, imperialism, gender and sexual identity, and racism are among the issues that stretch the intellectual membrane that covers it. On the other hand, much of the common experience that used to be central to Core gets lost because we allow our instructors to select most of the texts they use in their sections. How else can they be enticed to participate in the program? Since students aren't reading the same texts campus-wide, there's little incentive to talk about issues outside class, much less walk the common ground they cover.

How do scientists think? That's the main topic of the science-based courses in the contemporary Core program. To avoid the purely discipline-based science survey aspect that often permeates elective courses in the sciences for non-science majors, the goal of "Scientific Perspectives" is to broaden a student's understanding of scientific analysis and explanation by placing method in the context of a broad range of social issues. Course titles include "Viruses: Enemies and Tools," "Eye, Brain, and Visual Perception," "Ecology, Ethics, and Wilderness," "Critical Analysis in Health: AIDS," "How the Web Works," "Global Sustainability: Energy and the Environment," "Drugs, Brain, and Behavior," "The Nature-Nurture Debate," "Earth Resources," "Magic, Science, and Religion," "Science and Democracy," and "The Advent of the Atom Bomb." Again, by appealing to a contributor's specialty, the topical approach makes it easier to recruit faculty. It also encourages teachers to branch out a bit from their own specialized sphere of inquiry. The flip side is that the science Core loses much of the efficacy of the interdisciplinary sense of the earlier program, which strongly encouraged team-teaching (though a few of the offerings are team-taught, such as the "Atom Bomb" and "Sustainability" courses). The idea behind Core immersion in "Legacies," "Modernity," and "Science" is to direct students to think about broader questions, such as, what is the difference between acquiring knowledge through faith vs. reason, and how are different kinds of belief justified?

Since American foreign policy is shaped by public opinion, colleges need to prepare all their students in international relations. Today, we are citizens of the world. The last two courses in the current version of the Core curriculum attempt to take up the challenge. "Communities and Identities" is a revised version of the old "Core Cultures" course of the 1980s, which had updated the area studies requirement of the 1950s and early 1960s—the one that stressed "being aware of, and sympathetically sensitive" to, other cultures. How better to question your own values than to study a culture other than your own, a culture in which morality might take on a different meaning or where different codes of justice might operate? What social principles are transcultural? Students spend an entire semester focusing on one society, such as Argentina, China, Ethiopia, Russia, Liberia, Mexico, Peru, or the Dominican Republic, depending again on the instructor's area of specialty. One obstacle in teaching such courses is that American college students have less knowledge of geography and international issues than their counterparts in most other First World countries. Further, we are the only country in which eighteen- to twenty-four-year-olds score lower than their elders in that area.[31]

Today, no self-respecting undergraduate Core is without a course that addresses globalization. "Global Engagements" is Colgate's latest novel contribution to its Core program. A consequence of modernity, globalization refers to the varied processes of international human connectedness that have arisen from the interchange of ideas, products, and worldviews. It moves once-isolated cultures toward a common world consciousness. The course deals with questions such as: How do we make sense of an increasingly interconnected world? What do students need to know to live responsibly in contexts that require an understanding of the complexity of human beings, whether in the United States or in the broader world? Among the global issues considered are disease, natural disasters, loss of biological species, global warming, economic development, social justice concerns, and issues related to cross-cultural interaction. Judging from this diverse list, some critics regard the course agenda as too inclusive. As with the science and culture cores, "Global Engagements" is clearly designed to draw upon teachers of every disciplinary stripe. Sorting out big questions from trendy issues that demand popular entry into the curriculum has become a delicate balancing act, almost as difficult to engage as posing the big questions themselves.

Add to the demands of most contemporary Core programs the mandate to teach students how to be creative, think critically, and demonstrate a capacity to write and speak with a measure of skill in a world of ever-increasing specialization. My own view is that such skills ought to be required in both concentration programs and electives. With so many constituents to please, how can any group of educators, even if passionately devoted to the task, create a working program, especially in a time of increased vocationally oriented education? In addition to our own, the Core programs I have surveyed at other universities labor intensively to stretch the bounds of the course descriptions in an effort to attract new faculty to teach in the program. After all, how can we possibly fulfill the goals we've set for a program if we can't staff its courses?

One of the most difficult tasks in creating a sound core general education program lies in convincing your colleagues that it is part of their responsibility as educators to join in the conversation, to place the shared mission of liberal learning alongside their own disciplinary self-interests. *What* I teach has changed since I was a young, more narrowly focused faculty member. Decisions about what courses I select, devise, and team-teach now range far beyond my earlier sphere of inquiry, thanks mostly to the education I received as a result of embracing the Core program. Now a deep believer in the liberal arts, I admire those who persist in the demanding task of managing the core of it. So many of these well-intentioned, expansive teachers still experience, as I did, difficulty in raising their colleagues up to their level of enthusiasm.

Be-all and end-all course innovations enter and leave the academy with undiminished frequency. The late 1960s and early 1970s were rife with "Transcendental Meditation" and "Depth Psychology," while "Postmodernist Theory" ruled the 1980s. "General Systems Theory" was another of the educational fads somewhere in between. Leo Elison, a professor of economics, was one of my Colgate colleagues who got caught up in it. A passionate academic, Leo never embarked on any educational venture less than wholeheartedly. In faculty meetings he would sputter and spit, often tripping over his words in his highly charged haste to articulate his message, his jugular throbbing in unison with his tongue. Late one morning I spotted Leo's head popping around the corner of my open office door. Before I could invite him in, he was hovering excitedly over the front of my desk, an overhead projector in one hand, a fistful of printed transparencies in the other. "Tony," his eyes widening, "we've got to teach a Core course together. I think we can work out a way to bring your interdisciplinary studies into General Systems Theory."

Realizing that I still had to go over some notes before my afternoon class and not wanting to be rude, I responded with a friendly "how's that," hoping for a brief reply. Scarcely had my words reached his tympani than he was plugging in his projector and directing my view toward the lighted blank cream-colored wall that faced my desk. "Let me explain General Systems to you first," he responded, laying down the first in the sizable sheaf of plastic sheets. At the top of the single-spaced page appeared the title "General[1] Systems[2] Theory,[3]" each word footnoted as indicated. "Now, by general, I mean something that covers all existing situations, and a system is a set of things that work together to make a complex whole. That takes us to theory. A theory is a set of principles or ideas intended to explain something; therefore I'm talking about a study of aggregates in general so as to cover the principles that can be applied to all types of systems—in other words, universal principles that apply to all systems in general."

Leo had gone on for fifteen minutes (I have given an extremely abridged version of our encounter to this point), and we were only at the third word on page 1 in what, to judge by the untouched pile of plastic sheets at the edge of my desk, would be sure to amount to a ten-hour presentation. Worse still, I could not imagine how anything dear Leo was telling me might have the vaguest connection to a team-taught course. All attempts to interrupt his monologue, which became more and more tedious even before we had reached the bottom of page 1, failed. Still, I patiently persisted. I tried to ask a question and he waved me off. I raised my hand. I squirmed in my chair. "But wait. I don't understand," all to no avail. Leo was so caught up in his presentation that he had no realization, at the forty-five-minute mark, that his audience of one, now drowning in incomprehension, had been forced to tune out. At one point I thought of saying "shut up, Leo," but how could I be rude to a man so passionate about an idea that he would take the trouble to walk all the way across campus to share it with a colleague? Finally, out of sheer desperation I clutched my stomach, doubled over, and groaned. "Oh Leo, my stomach. I have this terrible pain. I can't . . . gasp!" I staggered out of my chair toward the door and disappeared down the hall, abandoning Leo and his loaded projector. I bolted out the door of the building, took a walk around the Quad, killed another ten minutes by grabbing a Coke at the Co-op, then snuck into my building through the back door. As I stealthily approached my office I sensed no sign of life behind the still-open door. Leo had left. I felt bad, but what could I do under the circumstances but fake stomach cramps? Leo called me that night to ask if I was feeling better. I apologized, studiously avoiding his attempts to reschedule. Maybe he'd forget about team-teaching with me and move on. True to form, there was Leo and his projector in the office of a history department colleague two weeks later when I happened by on the way to a meeting.

As I had learned by participating in a handful of efforts at curricular reform and having supervised one of them, installing an educational program everyone can agree on involves extraordinary compromise. This same kind of accommodation to diverse interests (call it intellectual appeasement) is evident in Core curricula at universities other than my own. For example, Harvard undergrads are required to choose one course from each of eight categories: Aesthetic and Interpretive Understanding, Culture and Belief, Empirical and Mathematical Reasoning, Ethical Reasoning, Science of Living Systems, Science of the Physical Universe, Societies of the World, and United States in the World.

To balance Core requirements and freedom of choice, most general education programs opt for adding a distribution requirement, sort of a Chinese menu approach in which students elect a certain number of courses from three major areas: social science, science, and humanities. Most schools in the United States offer no Core program, only a distribution requirement consisting of a sampling of courses taught in the individual disciplines. Often the divisional requirements are further subdivided; for example, the humanities bill of fare often consists of one required course in the arts and another in literature, while the sciences are usually partitioned into physical and biological. Here's one problem: studies show that students enrolled in colleges and universities that offer such programs tend to select the more vocationally oriented courses, as well as those that carry the lightest writing requirement—

the well-trod collegiate path of least resistance. To counter, some programs add a small number of special Core-like courses outside departmental aegis that all students must take. For example, Lafayette College offers "Values and Scientific Technology" and "Writing" (English 101); Columbia College adds "Contemporary Civilization" and a tag-team–taught science course; Claremont College requires a trio of courses in interdisciplinary Core humanities that includes writing and critical analysis.

The expansion across disciplinary lines has led to the creation of cross-listed courses often taught in partnership with contiguous disciplines. Core requirements vary between the "Chinese buffet" of all electives to a highly structured set of courses. St. John's College is the extreme with nine core courses, compared to Brown's no requirements and Yale's straight distribution. That would be two courses each from the humanities, sciences, and social sciences, in addition to one course on quantitative reasoning and one language course. Along the requirement spectrum lies the minimalist Vassar, which insists on one course stressing quantitative analysis, a language, and a freshman seminar. Lafayette has its writing course taught by the English department, as well as "Values and Scientific Technology," accompanied by a distributive requirement consisting of three (total) courses from the humanities and social sciences plus two from the sciences. At Claremont College there's "Interdisciplinary Core Humanities," "Writing and Critical Analysis," and one elective from each of the following: science, social science, race and ethnic studies, gender studies, math, language, the arts, and letters.

And so, America's colleges continue to re-make up their minds about the best way to achieve the lofty goals they assign to their concept of well-roundedness. Distribution or Core? Or both? To use the analogy of the appreciation of a good meal, it is as if we would take our students through a test kitchen and have them sample the tips of myriad spoonfuls among a vast array of flavors or sit them down to experience the depth and range of a well-planned full-course meal. Like good chefs, good educators need to decide what they want to serve up to their students that they will savor and that will leave a meaningful lasting impression that penetrates beyond their taste buds. Some iconic dishes may not make it to the table, but diners whose tastes linger might become motivated to go on and try a bit of cooking on their own, even if they don't use every ingredient in the kitchen. After all, few can afford both the galley tour and the sit-down dinner.

Perhaps there is currently so much specialization and
so many movements and fissures in higher education, that the important questions have been lost.
—*David Edmonds and John Eidenow*[1]

Teaching as Storytelling and Showing

Everybody loves a good story, and I think being a good teacher begins with
being a good storyteller. By telling stories you can hook your students into
appreciating the human quest to understand the world by reflecting on how
it has been perceived through different eyes—those of the poet, the artist,
and the naturalist—throughout history.

*"Remember when you invited your former student, David Carballo, to come back
to Colgate and give a guest lecture on his archaeological excavations in Mexico?
I was a freshman, and that talk was one of the most unforgettable events in*

my college career," Josh, now a senior and one of my most engaging students throughout our four years of unbroken contact, told me. Josh is the sort of guy who drops by the office occasionally for wide-ranging conversation—not the kind of student who pops in, asks how I'm doing, and follows with "by the way, I was thinking of applying to business school and I wonder whether you could write me a recommendation."

"What stuck in your mind about that?" I asked. "Well, I remember when you announced his visit you said 'Now, you may not catch everything our visitor is going to talk about. He's a specialist with a PhD in Mexican archaeology who has done some very important work since he graduated from Colgate fifteen years ago. But I want you to know that when he was here he majored in political science and had virtually no experience in archaeology and anthropology. That all came later. He didn't have a hint of his true calling until he was a senior.' Then you proceeded to tell the story of David's career shift." "Well," he went on, "even though I got lost in the detailed data and didn't follow every piece of his reasoning, listening to him made me realize, when I was a worried freshman, that it's never too late to get turned on by something completely new and follow a completely different path. Anyway, that incomprehensible lecture made me loosen up about my options. So here I am about to graduate in a few months, and I've moved all the way to environmental geology. Amazing!"

In an interview, the writer, historian, and teacher David McCullough told how he reignites an interest in history in the classroom:

> It isn't as though we have to trick them into taking some vile medicine that no one would want to swallow. An interest in history is the most natural thing in the world. I fell in love with history when I realized it was like doing the work of a detective to discover the story of what happened. If you give students assignments whereby they make their own discoveries, do their own research, go to the physical place where things happened, and interview people about it—once they get on the case—they can do spectacular work. At Cornell I taught a lecture course where I gave each student a historic photograph. I gave them the minimum of information about the picture. The assignment was to research the photograph, and write a paper about its subject.[2]

I refuse to think of science as just a stockpile of facts; it's a wondrous story about humanity's journey into the unknown. I begin my introductory astronomy course with "star stories." I start with the lost legacy created by urban electrification that turned night into day. It happened when Thomas Edison threw a switch connecting a long string of incandescent lamps along lower Broadway in 1880—the Great White Way. Then I take the class outdoors under our dark rural skies and show them how the stars move across the sky. As I narrate, we follow the stars from east to west, noticing that they pass slowly along broad arcs; stars in the south trek along shallow curves that don't get very high in the sky. When we turn and face north, we see stars traveling in circles around a fixed point where the Pole Star is located. Those closest to the pole never set; the ones farther from the pole barely scrape the horizon at their lowest point of descent.

As time passes and the stars change position, I tell the Kiowa Indian story about eight kids—seven sisters and a brother, represented by the stars of the Big Dipper and Arcturus, respectively—who were playing a game. The boy was pretending to be a bear. You can see him chasing the girls, who act as if they are frightened, in circles through the woods. Suddenly, the brother turns into a real bear, which causes the girls to run for their lives. As they flee they pass a tree stump (which turns out to be Devil's Tower, Wyoming, of *Close Encounters* fame). The stump says to them, "Climb on me and I will save you." When they do, they are swiftly transported to the sky. They become the stars of the Big Dipper. Today, we can still see them running around in a circle.[3] Then I tell them the local Iroquois version of the story: this time the bowl of the Big Dipper is a bear being chased by three hunters (the Dipper's handle) armed with bow and arrow. In the autumn, when the Dipper reaches its low point in the sky just after sunset and grazes the horizon at tree level, they say that the arrow has just penetrated the bear's body. The blood he sheds makes the leaves on the trees turn red. As I tell the story, I ask them to sketch the star motions in the clear star-studded autumn sky.

Former students who visit years after they graduated remark about how these and similar stories have been unforgettably engraved in their minds. They tell me that every time they look up, the stories remind them of how the sky turns. Because we also discuss sky narratives in a Native American context, students learn that skywatching isn't just a Western preoccupation. The relationship between people and the sky plays different roles in diverse cultures of the world. There is power in the story. To put it in Native American storyteller Scott Momaday's words, the story *humanizes* us; it offers greater meaning to our existence.

The word *teach* comes from the Old English verb *techen,* which means "to demonstrate." In a demonstration you act out a story. Like good acting, good showing requires practice. Done well, there is nothing quite like a live demo to convey how nature behaves. Done poorly, as with my badly executed "drop-ball" experiment (p. 33), it can be even more memorable to those who witness it. Maybe that's because a failed demo reveals defects in a category of exalted beings looked upon by their young charges as flawless and unerring.

True story: there I was watching the professor at the base of the upward-sloping lecture hall—its bleachers packed with eager student spectators—astride the lectern amid a panoply of chains and pulleys, a frictionless air track, an inclined plane, and, at the center of the hall, a long silken rope attached to the 16-foot-high ceiling. At the base of the rope was suspended a bowling ball, weighing 10 pounds, which the professor nudged ever so gently to set his lecture on the pendulum into motion.

"The period of swing of a pendulum, as I will demonstrate this morning," he began, "depends solely on its length. And no matter from where I release it," he continued, "it will return precisely to that point. It will never violate the principle of the conservation of energy as it moves unimpeded along its arc." Having thus focused attention on the hanging ball, he then walked along with rope and ball, all the way to the blackboard 15 feet away at the front of the room. He positioned himself with his back to the board, his head touching its surface, then pinned his head in that position by holding the bowling ball tightly against his chin. Next he told the story of what was about to unfold. "Now, when I release this pendulum bob you will note that its speed will increase as it descends along its arc. It will approach the bottom of its swing position at maximum speed, thanks to the pull of gravity; but then, like all law-abiding pendula in the universe, it will lose the energy it had acquired in its descent and, as it moves to its maximum amplitude over there" he reasoned as he pointed up the aisle toward a wall at the back of the lecture hall, "it will halt [pause] and then it will retrace its steps right back to here [pointing his index finger at his chin], traveling no more, no less—for its energy must always be conserved." And then, with the bob of the pendulum still held tightly to his chin and the back of his head still pinned to the blackboard, he set the 10-pound missile free.

Fifty pairs of eyes watched the ponderous ball descend. It picked up speed, slowly at first as it passed the lectern, then faster and faster still as it raced past its low point directly under the pivot fastened to the ceiling at the center of the room. Then it shot up the aisle precisely where the professor had aimed it. You could almost hear the whooshing sound and feel the breeze the ball exuded as it traveled up-up-up the aisle to the top of its course just a few feet short of the window at the other side of the hall. There the sphere halted momentarily. The mere six seconds that had passed seemed almost an eternity. Then, as the weight began its return descent, the student body took on a worried look. Here was a 10-pound bowling ball hurtling toward a defenseless professor standing with the back of his head pressed against the board. There was no escape route. Should physics fail him, his fragile skull would shatter like a coconut struck with a sledgehammer. But the professor didn't flinch. The smile that broke over his face as his young charges looked on in horror radiated with confidence; for the wise man knew that even though the pendulum bob was racing toward his cranium at colossal speed, it had yet to make its taxing final climb. Newton would then compel it to slow its speed. It must halt precisely at the tip of his whiskers. Nature commanded it. "Oooh, gasp," the audience held its breath nervously as the last second of the full swing period was completed. Then a relaxed "aaah" when the pendulum stopped a millimeter short of the professor's whiskers. "Amazing, wow, yeah," and other such gesticulations, too punctuated with erratically exhaled breath to be discernible, followed as the pendulum, accompanied by a round of applause, began a repeat, far less attention-getting round-trip.

"Now let's take a look at the equation of motion of that pendulum," said the professor, his audience now in the palm of his hand, as he picked up a piece of chalk from the tray and turned to face the blackboard. Meanwhile, the unwatched pendulum coursed to a halt on the other side of the hall and commenced its scheduled return to the front of the room. "Uh-oh"—then a chorus of gasps as the weight smote the professor a glancing blow at the base of the skull, sending him flying, arms and legs flailing, across the lectern and onto the floor. No, he wasn't seriously hurt. But he was a laughing stock, as teachers often are who run afoul in the classroom. Moral? It takes a lot of savvy if you're going to mess with nature. Or, wait until the experiment is over before you draw conclusions.

Basically, I'm a science teacher. I think that as a representative of my chosen field, my principal goal ought to be to show my students how a scientist's brain works. That translates to introducing them to the skills of my craft by immersing them in quantitative reasoning and experimental methods. The latter ought to include some direct experience observing nature. I think one of the fun parts of astronomy lies in learning to use a telescope and how to keep a notebook that details a series of each student's precise, regular observations of the sky. Equally important broader goals include an understanding of the historical background of how the science of astronomy developed; for example, I devote an entire class to explaining how astronomy's birth mother was astrology, and I spend quite a bit of time dealing with how the fruits of my discipline impact society: Should the Hubble Space Telescope be replaced and the space program continued, even in the face of a downturned economy? What is the value of pure research in astronomy—or in any scientific discipline, for that matter?

"He who can, does. He who cannot, teaches." That old saying captures the attitude of many institutions with PhD programs. In some of them the "terminal master's degree" is viewed as the gateway out of a program you can't cut. It's a negative sign along the highway that leads to that alternative career: teaching. The same superior attitude can permeate undergraduate programs, especially in the sciences; for example, some students who begin to pursue concentrations in physics, chemistry, biology, or geology often end up with a general science major, which consists of a battery of courses from each discipline. This is advertised as the spawning ground for future teachers and popularly regarded in the halls of academia as the alternative to the preparatory programs for graduate school in each of the disciplines. Some students elect to take a fifth year to complete a Master of Arts in Teaching.

Our teachers, and the programs designed to train them, are separated out from the more highly regarded (and generally higher-paying) professional careers. Responding to the timeworn "he who can" slogan, the publisher of a textbook I recently adopted sent me a coffee mug that reads "He who can teaches. He who cannot seeks a less challenging line of work." Those of us who teach college-level science can become deeply immersed in, even intoxicated by, the wonders of our specialties. Often we don't take the trouble to cultivate the complex, challenging craft of effective teaching.

I think the most difficult impediment for the science teacher is audience receptivity; to put it bluntly: kids hate science. Weighty textbooks inculcate fear in the hearts of young initiates. Worse still, before our students encounter us, they have often been confronted with a mass of mindless memorization and needless jargon in middle and high school, all of it directed toward passing proficiency tests. No wonder the kids who enter my classroom are predisposed to think that whatever I'm about to dish out is sure to be boring and irrelevant to their lives. I agree with scientist Robert Hazen[4] that good science can be taught and learned without jargon and complex mathematics and that "you don't have to be a scientist to appreciate the overarching scientific principles that influence every action of our lives."[5] If we worked more on conveying *why* we love what we do, learning science might actually be fun.

To give an example, one of the most confusing concepts in astronomy has to do with trying to figure out what-goes-around-what. To resolve the motion of the stars, sun, moon, and earth, I assign each celestial body to a member of the class, and we act out "a year in the life" in front of the group. One person is the moon (Diana) who attaches herself to the earth (Gaia), each by grasping opposite ends of a meter stick. I label the characters with special handmade signs (a silver crescent moon and a green rotating earth, respectively) that I pin to the backs of their shirts. The sun is represented by a third student at the back of the room. In addition to the identifying label (Apollo) that I stick, along with a cardboard yellow sun disk, on his shirt, I give him a powerful flashlight to shine down the aisle of the darkened lecture hall to illuminate the pair of celestial denizens at the front of the room. Then I ask Diana and Gaia to duplicate the movement of earth and moon (our month) by revolving about the balance point between the earth-moon seesaw, which I mark by suspending a weight from a point on the meter stick 1/80 of the way between them. After they practice this relatively simple step, the silvery moon character doing most of the dancing, I enhance the choreography by asking Gaia and Diana to trace part of a seasonal year; that's the time it takes the balance point between them to revolve around the sun. To execute this movement, I ask the pair to move together, keeping the balance point on track over a broad arc about 25 feet long, centered on Apollo. I make a dotted line out of a chain of 4- × 6-inch index cards to trace out the intended course on the lecture room floor.

This stage of the demo proves difficult for two reasons. First, the two moving student bodies must keep the tip of the suspended bob over the line of index cards *and* revolve about each other at the same time. Second, they must time their movement to fit the actual rhythm defined by the period of the month (around one another) *and* a portion of the year (along the index card track). Needless to say, this maneuver requires a few practice runs. Meanwhile the stars, represented by the remainder of the class, sit fixed in their seats, except that they are imagined to lie a relatively large distance from Gaia, Diana, and Apollo. Next, Gaia's dance steps become even more taxing. I instruct her: "Gaia, there are about 30 days in a month; so you need to spin on your axis 30 times between when you leave your starting point and arrive over there at the end of the month" (pointing to the termination point of the arc of index cards 25 feet away). Diana has it relatively easy: she can face Gaia straight on. That's because the moon rotates on its axis in the same period that it revolves around the earth. By the end of the dizzying exercise, my students are far less confused about the concatenation of complex motions of earth, moon, and sun than they appear to be when I only diagram the situation on the board geometrically (I deal with that, too, with a simple handout). They never forget the real "dancing with the stars."

I also rely on class participation to act out the vastness of the astronomical distance scale and the puny sizes of the celestial bodies that occupy it. I introduce the "Tony Aveni Fruit and Vegetable Model of the Solar System, patent pending." I begin by focusing attention on a foot-wide pumpkin placed on the table at the front of the classroom. That's the sun. Then I open a series of small containers housing an orange, an apple, a radish, a pea, a peppercorn, and various smaller spice seeds tucked into a tiny envelope (other seasonal fruits and veggies are optional substitutes). Next, I hand a meter stick to a student in the front row and ask him to measure off 30 feet toward the back of the classroom. I then hand the occupant of a seat in that region a coriander seed. "That's Mercury, the planet closest to the sun," I tell her. Venus and Earth become peas at 55 feet and 85 feet, respectively, from the table. Moments after their attendants put them in position, I place a mustard seed alongside the second pea, an inch away from it. "That's the moon." Then the fun begins. Mars, a peppercorn, needs to end up 125 feet away; that's just outside the door of the lecture hall in my scale model. Jupiter, a small plum, belongs across the Quad at the doorway of West Hall dormitory, 145 yards from the pumpkin. I hand these objects to volunteers and ask them to place them at the proper distances after class. Because Saturn, represented by a large radish, belongs at the base of the hill toward town, just beyond the Administration Building at a distance of 280 yards, I look for a volunteer headed that way, and so on: Uranus and Neptune become a pair of olives at 550 yards and 840 yards, respectively. Placing Pluto, the tiniest seed I can find in my spice cabinet (sorry, but in my heart I still can't deny Pluto its traditional planetary status), requires a dependable student who either runs cross-country or owns a car. It belongs in the Pizza Hut parking lot 1,160 yards away at the edge of town. (Trust is necessary if the solar system is to be represented correctly!) I end the lesson by pulling out a slightly larger pumpkin from beneath the desk. It represents the nearest star. "Now, who's headed for LA?" I ask. One of my film studies majors was so affected by this live demo that she made a video project out of it. Denied travel expenses, she traveled no further than the local Pizza Hut.

Showy? Certainly. Juvenile? College students don't think so. What about all the time spent going through such communal exercises? Test results verify that the time we spend acting out these demos is well worth it. Student comprehension of material subjected to a story they act out sticks; and to judge from conversations with former students, the sticking power lasts longer. There's an added bonus that comes with classroom activities of this kind: they bring teacher and student closer to the same level. And that facilitates learning, too.

Learning by Experience

One of the hallmarks of imaginative teaching lies in a willingness to experiment, to innovate, to escape from the nest you were hatched in. For me, the academy in the late 1960s and early 1970s was one of the most opportune places and times to do so. Never were students more tuned in to social issues; never were they more involved in world politics—the peace movement, the protests, feminism, the challenges posed by racism and urban blight. And their teachers, who grew up in a more restrictive generation, seemed ready for change. More innovative curricular programs emerged out of that counterculture decade than during any other period since World War II; for example, at Colgate we went co-ed; we developed an achievement-oriented degree, offering our students the opportunity to matriculate by attaining successive levels of increased knowledge and skills. We also created a Freshman Seminar program, a host of off-campus study offerings, and, perhaps most innovative of all, the January term.

J-term was a one-month term wedged in between the fall and spring semesters. You took one course with one professor in a small seminar-type setting, and its subject matter was often pretty unorthodox. There was "How to Write a Novel," "Tropical Ecology and Parasitology," "Chess Theory," "Alchemy and Chemistry," "Cryptanalysis," and "Psychophysics of Hi-Fi and Stereo" (sounds a bit dated for older readers and meaningless for younger ones). Many of these courses were conducted off campus: we offered "Geology of Jamaica," "Bats of the Caribbean Islands," and a host of medical and business internships. What's more, the experience was un-graded, just pass-fail. This offered the advantage that a science student who wondered what it would be like to write a novel or a humanities student with a desire to learn what goes on in a chemistry lab could indulge in their curiosities without fear of penalty.

J-term also had the potential to become rather free-wheeling, especially in the liberal-minded atmosphere of that era. Among the questionable courses was "Oenology"—yes, wine tasting. The instructor conducted some of the classes while seated on the branch of a tree, his class sipping beneath it. (The drinking age was eighteen in our state at the time.) I recall one of my ultra-liberal colleagues approving every off-campus study independent project any student proposed to him, such as "I want to travel around the country on a motorcycle and keep a diary." A pair of roommates requested that I oversee their proposal for an exchange of skills: "I know how to play guitar and Jeff doesn't, but he is excellent at racquetball and I'm not. What we were thinking is . . ." I stopped them dead in their tracks and sent them in search of another mentor. Suddenly realizing that he was shy one credit for graduation, a senior dropped by my office in early February and inquired, "I spent the entire break reading *The Brothers Karamazov*, and I was wondering, could you maybe see your way to giving me a *retroactive* J-term independent?" These abuses of liberal, independent learning opportunities were more than counteracted by serious enterprises, such as NASA and museum internships, telescope making, darkroom photography, and poetry and music workshops.

Today, the curricular penchant for so-called contact learning continues in many small colleges, with short-term topical courses like "Public Speaking," "The Prozac Culture," and "The Politics of Food." To judge from the more recent selections listed in course catalogs, though, many of these intensive learning experiences serve other interests than interdisciplinary inquiry, such as making up for lost ground; for example, there are offerings in intensive Spanish or Calculus 101 and the currently indispensable "Stats."

In 1964, the first year of the J-term at Colgate, I concocted a course called "Astronomy at the Telescope." I'd attract my students to the wonders of the cosmos by having them spend extended time peering through Colgate's new 16-inch telescope, the one Dean Storing had provoked me to acquire (p. 37). Together we'd learn hands-on ways to collect data with a real research instrument by acquiring skills in astronomical photography, spectroscopy, and photoelectric photometry. My idea was that students would become engaged and curious by seeing things for themselves instead of only reading about them in dry textbooks. That would open up a natural pathway to the library. Again, you learn best by doing things for yourself. At least that was the theory.

Sadly, my educational experiment failed miserably. I lay blame less on a lack of student motivation and more on the vagaries of the upstate New York climate. January is the coldest and snowiest month of the year in Hamilton. How snowy is it? We average 130 inches of white stuff a year (about a third of it in January), accompanied by a mean temperature of 26°F. And when it isn't snowing, it's cloudy. (Did you know that, next to northwest Washington State, central New York holds the distinction of being *the* most cloud-bound territory in the contiguous 48 states?) As you can imagine, under these circumstances, not much got done in "Astronomy at the Telescope." Even when my students did get to use the scope, there were often near-fatal consequences: three cases of frostbite and one instance in which I needed to pour warm water on a student's cheek to unstick his face from the side of the telescope to which it had frozen—his fault for breathing during a critical moment of data collection.

After consecutive Januaries of near-death experiences by exposure, I was forced to abandon my experiment in experiential learning. At the next turn of the year I offered a new course titled "Reenacting Ancient Scientific Measurements." Still operating in the vein of contact learning, this class would set out to replicate some of the ancient Greek foundational methods for determining the distance scale of the universe. My pupils would use the same tools and techniques written down by the natural philosophers. For example, I devised what I felt was an ingenious plan to replicate Eratosthenes's experiment for measuring the size of the earth. He did it in the third century BC by marking the length of his shadow at noon on the same date of the year at two different locations. From these measurements he worked out the difference in the sun's altitude above the horizon, which is the same as the angle between the two locales as viewed from the center of the earth. (To calculate the diameter of the earth, you need to know the distance between the two locales, which for Eratosthenes were the cities of Alexandria and Syene, today Aswan. They are about 500 miles apart, or $7°$ measured over the earth's surface. Unable to wait a year to arrive at the same date for the second measurement, we improvised.) To replicate the experiment, I would send half the class, or six students, to each of two places a considerable known distance apart and have them set up surveying equipment on which I would previously train them. By phone contact they would simultaneously measure the position of the sun in the sky.

Getting half my students to go to Montreal, one of my chosen sites, in the middle of winter was like asking them to volunteer for dental work. For the other site, Miami, I had no trouble putting together a research team. But there were problems with this experiment in contact learning as well. Setting up the phone hookup for recording data simultaneously was easy enough. We chose sites conveniently positioned near telephone booths (remember them?) on major highways in each of the two cities. Then, with watches synchronized and just as we had focused on the sun and were about to take our instrument readings between intermittent clouds at both stations, the operation in Montreal was suddenly aborted when a huge snowplow pitched a ton of dense white powder on our measuring equipment. My northern research team had positioned the instrument too close to the road. This episode was followed by two days of totally overcast weather in Canada. You needn't ask how the Miami team waited out this period.

Such are the travails of experiential learning in the field. In the end, things actually worked out quite well. My students learned firsthand that precise knowledge isn't acquired as easily as the way you read about it in most textbooks. But then, I wonder how many textbook authors actually venture out into the real do-it-yourself world? After we worked over the data back in the classroom, we ended up with a result for the diameter of the earth that was off by only 20 percent from the currently accepted value. To judge from our historical readings, that's about as close as the ancient Greeks ever got it.

For the next two years of J-term I played it cool by running a little seminar titled "Theories of Cosmology." In daily two-hour meetings we'd read and talk about the origin of the universe, from the Greeks to Einstein. One day, while discussing one of the readings on Egyptian cosmology, we came across a section on the precise layout and orientation of the famous pyramids. They were all aligned with their sides pointing to the North Star because it marked the pivot of all sky motion. The Egyptians called it the "nail of the sky," the fixed point you could always rely on to orient yourself. By analogy, the pharaoh was the "nail of the earth," the great stabilizer of social forces, the one all Egyptians could depend on for stability, the great ruler they would follow to seek their identity and destiny. Culture structures nature. What a neat celestial metaphor, I thought. Perhaps, the text went on to speculate, pyramid builders in other civilizations also aligned their major works of architecture in harmony with cosmic phenomena. We talked about that idea and then I gave an assignment: What were the other pyramid-building cultures of the world, and what do we know about the ways they might have aligned their pyramids? Back came the reports from China, Sumeria, Mexico. Surprisingly, very little had been written about building orientations, especially in ancient Mexico.

The idea of cosmically oriented architecture stuck in my head. It also became embedded in the clever conniving minds of a few of my more adventurous acolytes. Mexican pyramids were accessible in a mere five days on the new high-speed US interstate highway system. Gas was cheap (only 31 cents a gallon in the late 1960s). And the climate? There would be no snowplows to thwart our efforts at setting up surveying equipment. So I appointed a committee to do a deeper survey of the literature: find out whether any researchers had actually measured the orientation of Mexican pyramids and, if so, what they had found. To our surprise, there was just a single publication of any substance on this problem in a reputable journal—a research paper by two Mexican archaeologists dated 1932. They had concluded that some of the larger pyramids in the Valley of Mexico—Teotihuacan, Tenayuca, and Tepozteco among them—were similarly oriented in space, but they gave no reasons why. I thought it odd that no one had followed up on what seemed a rich topic. What a perfectly valid justification for a J-term course based on experiential learning! Joint undergraduate student-faculty research? There wasn't much of that going on in the 1960s, but it sounded like a good idea. My students could learn by doing things for themselves, and as a bonus we could maybe make a tiny contribution to the pyramid of knowledge (sorry!).

So it began on the cold, crisp, and, oddly, sunlit morning of January 2, 1970. Ten of us—fellow (geology) professor Bob Linsley, his fifteen-year old son, David, four Colgate students, three female students from neighboring Skidmore, and I—set out from Hamilton, New York, in a pair of station wagons for Mexico City, Oaxaca, and the Yucatan. With overnight stops in Richmond, Indiana; Muskogee, Oklahoma; Laredo, Texas; and Monterrey, Mexico, on the fifth day, having covered 3,000 miles, we reached Mexico's capital city.

A friend recommended we stay at the Mayaland on Calle Antonio Caso. It was a grade B-minus hotel, which translates to thin mattresses and occasional luke-warm water, but I was told I'd be able to bargain them down to five dollars per student in triples: twin beds and a rollout. The food wasn't bad, and they had an indoor garage. When the appropriate street came up, I circled the glorieta (rotary) and, staying to the right, luckily caught the exit, the other vehicle following. We unloaded the bags and surveying equipment and I went in to register the group, leaving a pair of student drivers to park the wagons in the garage beneath the hotel. Later I learned that the roof of one of the wagons fell a few millimeters short of the height of the entryway ceiling and consequently scraped its way into the chamber.

The lobby was small and, like the city, dimly lit. An old three-seat sofa and a cou-ple of non-matching hard-back chairs (one of them occupied by an elderly man in a rumpled suit and beat-up fedora), along with an old soft drink dispenser, nearly filled the space. The sound of a ceiling fan ticked away the seconds. The front desk was scarcely a yard wide, and the attendant behind it greeted me with a close-up smile. We exchanged pleasantries, reached final accord on the cost of a three-night stay, and commenced several trips in the elevator—which was so small it could have served in mine rescue operations—up to our rooms.

"Okay, 304 [my room] is mission control; see you there for a meeting at seven," I instructed my knowledge-hungry crew. This would give them half an hour to tidy up prior to the brief orientation session, when I'd lay out the plan for the next few days: one full day at Mexico City's National Museum of Anthropology and History, a day trip to the pyramids of Teotihuacan about an hour northeast of downtown, then half a day at the Aztec Templo Mayor (Great Temple), a fifteen-minute sub-way ride away. The rest of the day would be left open for exploration on their own. After the meeting we'd all go out for the nightly communal dinner. I could sense the excitement of young people in a new place, most of them independent of their

families for the first time. They were eager to explore, to see things, and to encounter new experiences for themselves.

No sooner had I finished showering than the first few arrivals, burgeoning with questions, came knocking: "What time are we leaving tomorrow?" "Where can I buy a serape for my dad?" "How much?" "Can we climb the pyramids?" "Does this hotel take Mexican pesos?" "Is Yucatan in Peru?" One young charge burst through the half-open door and exclaimed excitedly, "Hey professor, I just met a Mexican man from Cleveland. That's my hometown!" "Cleveland?" I retorted. "How do you know he's from Cleveland?" "Well," he replied, "I went to the lobby to buy a Coke and there was this guy sitting next to the Coke machine. He asked me where I was from and then told me 'I'm from Cleveland, too. My mother still lives there. She's very ill, has to use a wheelchair, and there's nobody there to take care of her. I'm saving my pesos so I can go to visit her; maybe you can help me out?' So I gave him a dollar." "John," I scolded. "I'm afraid you've just fallen victim to one of the oldest tourist scams in the world. That guy is no more from Cleveland than I am from . . ." As I thought about naming some faraway place to test his geographic knowledge, a second student came flying through the door and announced, "Hey, you'll never believe it, I just met a Mexican man from Buffalo."

"Why do you put up with it?" friends ask. "Can't you do something more rewarding for a living?" Whether they are referring to dealing on a daily basis with inquisitive young people with the same degree of naïveté we all once possessed or they mean I might consider earning a higher wage than the modest salary of most academics, my answer is the same: I enjoy being with young people. They are open and easy; they are tolerant, flexible, questioning, and, yes, naive. But they haven't yet traded away their youthful enthusiasm and idealism for the harsh realities of the hard-edged world. My job is to keep them that way even as I endeavor to guide them toward acquiring new skills and responsibilities.

Having seen the museum, our next order of business turned to visiting the great pyramids of Teotihuacan. Once home to 100,000 people, the city's earliest building phases date before 200 BC. This great city served as the cultural pacesetter in what anthropologists call Mesoamerica, an area encompassing all of Mexico and parts of northern Central America, until its decline in the sixth century AD. Seven hundred years after that the Aztecs, who conducted sacrificial rites at its ruins, came to regard Teotihuacan as the place where time began, where the gods sacrificed themselves to set the sun in motion. When we had studied the archaeological site map in class, we noticed Teotihuacan's oddly skewed axis, 15°—so out of line with true north-south. The Teotihuacanos seem to have constructed all their buildings on a grid fixed about this axis. To judge from the plan, the original architects even went to the trouble of changing the natural course of the San Juan River, which flowed through the great city from northeast to southwest, to force it to fit the grid. Apparently, the lesser cities that surrounded it faithfully copied the Teotihuacan design. What especially attracted us to Teotihuacan was that archaeologists who had excavated the site in the 1960s mentioned certain "architects' benchmarks" the founders might have used to lay out the grid. Maybe we could find these benchmarks, make some measurements, and see what they pointed to.

We made the two-hour drive northeast from downtown Mexico City, arriving at the site late in the afternoon. We had a quick look at the small rundown museum at the southern entrance to the site, then we sprinted northward half a mile up the so-called Street of the Dead toward the looming shadow of the great Pyramid of the Sun, our surveying equipment in tow. If we hurried to the top, we might get a glimpse of the setting sun so we could make an orientation measurement. Climbing up 250 steep steps at an altitude of 6,500 feet with heavy equipment in tow wasn't easy.

Once we ascended the five flights of steps on the multi-tier 230-foot-high pyramid, we caught our collective breath and planted the tripod at the center of the summit, marveling all the while at the commanding view of the vast ruined metropolis below. Unfortunately, the sun was too low to get a fix, so we thought: let's wait a while and get a bearing to measure the building's orientation by shooting the North Star. (You can't use a magnetic compass because magnetic readings wander—and besides, compasses don't generally point to true north anyway.) As darkness set in, Polaris made its appearance over the Pyramid of the Moon half a mile away. The site's grid axis may have been skewed from the north, but the two big pyramids seemed to line up almost due north-south from one another. Strange!

It was dark now; we had just finished leveling the instrument and were about to take readings when our attention was diverted by a pair of flashlights bobbing their way up the steps to the summit where we stood. Two men in gray uniforms with identical caps and badges, torches in hand, approached us. "Sus permisos, por favor" (Let's see your permits). We pigeon-Spanished our way through the ensuing dialogue with the better English-skilled of them. Neither looked pleased with our inability to produce a scrap of documentation that would permit us to use measuring equipment, much less to gain access to the site after closing hours. We were promptly placed under arrest, marched down the steps of the pyramid to a makeshift paddy-wagon, and trucked off to the office of Ernesto Taboada, superintendent of the Teotihuacan ruins in the neighboring town of San Juan. Taboada, like most Mexican officials, was a cordial man, though not beyond administering a stern scolding on the necessity of following protocol when we sought to work on the great treasures of the cultures of ancient Mexico. Of course, he was correct. We were not exemplary visitors. "You must go to the office of Dr. Bernal in Mexico City to get your permits," he concluded, writing down the appropriate address. Then he freed us.

The next day we paid a visit to the office of Ignacio Bernal, eminent archae-ologist specializing in the Olmec culture, supervisor of all archaeological ruins in Mexico, and—of greatest import in the present context—bestower of permits. "Nacho," as we later acquired the privilege of addressing him by his nickname, was an expansive, charismatic, outgoing character. The lim-ited extent of my knowledge of ancient Mexico that he was able to extract from our conversation may not have impressed him, but, recognizing that I was a well-meaning, if vastly uninformed, novice, he generously gave me a sufficient length of rope. Bernal told us that measuring the alignments of pyramids to see whether they were celestially oriented might actually be a worthwhile task. He explained that none of this sort of research had been done before. Then he told us of an unusually shaped ancient Zapotec building in the city of Oaxaca that we might want to check out. Finally, he wrote me a permit in cursive longhand: "This will introduce to—list of sites and their superintendents—Anthony Aveni and his students from Colgate University, who have permission to set up a surveyor's transit, etc." We were off to Oaxaca, a long day's drive south through the Sierra Madres. (We'd revisit Teotihuacan on the way back.)

Our target was Monte Alban, specifically Building J, an oddly skewed struc-ture in the shape of a pentagon. Viewed from above, it looked like home plate on a baseball diamond. A 1950 guidebook we purchased in the museum indicated that the point of the arrow-shaped structure might have been delib-erately aligned to the stars—an ancient observatory!

As you approach Oaxaca City, Monte Alban, like all the other ancient hill-top ruins that flank the Y-shaped valley in which it is situated, clearly makes its presence known. Profiles of grass-covered pyramids jut out starkly along the mountainous skyline. Getting to each of them would necessitate some arduous climbing, but the pyramids of Monte Alban—biggest of all the archaeological sites in the area and made famous in the 1940s by the celebrated Mexican archaeologist Alfonso Caso's excavation of its jade- and jewel-bedecked Tomb 7—were accessible by a paved road. A small museum adjoined the parking lot just outside the ruins. The visitors' area has been vastly enlarged since. The ruins were overseen by a single official and a couple of guards who tended to the 2-square-mile plaza, which was surrounded by smaller pyramids. Most structures were unexcavated, but the hundred-or-so tourists a day who ventured to Monte Alban were permitted to climb them, walk the plaza and the ball court, and visit the museum—all of it doable in a few hours.

But *we* were here on a mission. "Can you take us to Building J?" we asked the chief of the museum, confidently flashing our permits. "Ah, you mean this one," responded the accommodating official, pointing to an aerial photo on the wall in which it stood out even more starkly than it appeared on the map in the guidebook. J was situated in the middle of the south end of the main plaza. It easily caught our eyes because the "home plate" axis was twisted 45° out of line with all of the other structures, which lined up pretty close to north-south. "It is a strange one, isn't it," he went on. "Yes, it is. We want to measure it and find out what it points to," I said. "Oh, it points to where the sun sets on the first day of winter," the guardian retorted confidently as he pulled a badly tattered rag bond publication in Spanish that I hadn't seen off the shelf. He pointed to a sketch and caption. "Look here." It occurred to me that the date, January 10, isn't so distant from the solstice. Because the setting position of the sun changes very little around its December 21 standstill, we might be able to witness the event. A small *mordida* (a tip for extra favors) of just a few pesos was enough to garner permission from the guardian for us to spend the entire night at the ruins.

We set up our sleeping gear at the base of Building J and ascended the platform at the top, equipment in tow. As the sun began to drop out of the late afternoon sky, it became clear that something wasn't right. The sun seemed positioned way too far to the right. At the steep angle of descent in this latitude (17°N), the sun didn't stand a chance of reaching the point of the arrow. We watched it go down, noticing that sunset happened much faster than it does in our high northern home latitude, where all things celestial are angled as much to the right as in the downward direction; but still there was no chance that the setting sun could come even close to the point of the horizon that lay in the direction where the arrow pointed. Finally, the solar disk glanced off the side of a distant hill. Last gleam occurred at 5:45—more than 20°, or 40 widths of the sun's disk, west of the arrow point.

The next morning we arose early, still perplexed by what we'd witnessed. Gleaming Apollo, having popped up on the opposite side of the ruins, shown brightly in our faces. We sought out some strong coffee from a small *tienda* (snack bar) near the site entrance. At that moment, up the hill came the guardian in his late-model sedan to commence his daily appointed task. We met him in the parking lot, and I told him that the solstice alignment explanation for the peculiar orientation of Building J couldn't possibly be correct. "Well, that's what it says in the book," he retorted, shrugging his shoulders. "*Quien sabe?*" (Who knows?) We would need to come back next year to measure and map the building. While we were chatting, a well-tanned, middle-aged American in a broad-brimmed hat, who we'd seen in the museum the previous day, approached us. He introduced himself as John Paddock, a Stanford University archaeologist who had worked in Oaxaca for years. "So, what are you mapping?" he inquired. We explained and, after questioning us further about our methodology, he responded: "I've got a building over in the next valley that I've been excavating. It looks like a miniature version of J. How'd you like to come over and measure it?" Clearly, there was work to be done.

I didn't realize it at the time, but that brief encounter following a night out at Monte Alban, Mexico, with my students would alter the course of my professional life. When we got back home, my students and I searched the literature for the origin of the Monte Alban "solstice hoax." We learned that the so-called facts about J's orientation had simply appeared in print out of nowhere. Nobody had challenged them. As far as we could determine, no one had actually measured J, not even the great Alfonso Caso, though Caso had referred to a narrow horizontal passage in the building that might have been used to sight the stars. Maybe his statement fueled the orientation myth. Quien sabe?

What about J's peculiar shape? Well, it *could* have had something to do with the stars. But no one had measured the building with a view toward trying to determine what it might have pointed to. This would be our task. We resolved the next year to take up a thorough study of the building, mapping every excavated layer. My new career in the interdisciplinary field of "archaeoastronomy," a word we would later help define, was born.

Postscript (intended solely for readers who relish excruciating detail): Which way *does* Building J point? We discovered that the arrow marks the average setting point of five of the brightest stars in the southern sky, including the stars of the Southern Cross and Alpha and Beta Centauri. But the so-called arrow may not be the only peculiarity associated with J. When we looked more closely at the Monte Alban map, we noticed that the arrow point forms nearly a right angle and is neatly squared off with the three other structures in the plaza: Structures G, H, and I. I think J's strangeness may lie more in the way the axis of its doorway and front (northeast) stairway are twisted out of line from the site's main axis. When we measured the orientation of the skewed doorway, we found that it aligned with the rising position of Capella, the sixth-brightest star in the sky. But Capella was no ordinary star in this place and time, for in 250 BC, when Building J was erected, Capella's first annual appearance in the sky (its so-called heliacal rise) occurred on the same day of the year that the sun passed the zenith, or overhead point. Colonial documents tell of the widespread tradition of celebrating the new year on the day the sun crossed the zenith. Evidently, the people of Monte Alban made their city so it would be in tune with their sky gods, who signaled the appropriate time when the sun would arrive at the zenith through Capella's seasonal reappearance. When we later returned to Teotihuacan, this time with permits in hand, we would discover a similar relationship among pyramid, sun, and star. That city's skewed axis, marked by the architect's benchmarks—a pair of petroglyphs in the shape of a double circle centered on a cross—lined up perfectly with the place where the Pleiades set. Now, the Pleiades at Teotihuacan bore the same relationship to the sun as did Capella at the more southerly location of Monte Alban. Their heliacal rise marked the new year as well, the day when the sun passed their zenith.

When one of my students during our next field season at Monte Alban began asking questions about how the sun changes its position through the

seasons, I realized that if I were going to continue to take students on experiential learning expeditions, it would be a good idea to equip them with not
only the skills and techniques of astronomical measurement but also a knowledge of the history of the ancient cultures they would confront. So I devised
a course titled "Astroarchaeology." I later changed it to "Archaeoastronomy,"
after the new interdiscipline that would grow up around our work and that
of others. I installed the course as a prerequisite to enrollment in my J-term
field-based course. This offered a double advantage; first, it weeded out students who possessed only a passing interest in the program (as I said earlier,
Mexico isn't a bad alternative to four weeks of winter in the frigid north).
Second, the course created a small cadre of serious, highly motivated students. Ten years later it led to an interdisciplinary textbook.

I ran my archaeoastronomy program for twenty years, until J-term fell
by the wayside in 1989, a casualty of the curricular reform in the 1980s I
spoke about earlier (p. 56). Critics on the faculty claimed it was difficult for
attention-deficient students to focus on a single topic for a full month (not
true). Students, for their part, complained that there weren't enough interesting off-campus offerings—too many remedial math-language catch-up–type
courses. Clearly, I would need to circumvent the curricular rules if I wanted
to continue the program. So I decided to reinvent archaeoastronomy in the
context of my own mini-curriculum. I would offer a spring-term course titled
"Field Studies in Archaeoastronomy." It would begin just after Christmas,
three weeks before the start of the spring term. The first segment of the
course would meet in Guatemala, Mexico, Peru, or wherever the necessity
to conduct field studies dictated. The new version of the program would
amount to a year-long experience—the old fall-term "Archaeoastronomy"
prerequisite course followed by a second segment of "Field Studies," beginning with a month's experience surveying at the archaeological sites. The
rest of the spring semester would be devoted to analysis of the data and fol-
low-up. When we returned to campus from the field portion of the course,
students would work on research topics of their own choosing, provided
they bore some relevance to the experiences engaged in the field.

There was one obvious drawback: those who wished to enroll would need
to sacrifice a significant chunk of their winter break, which had now filled in
the extinct J-term "mini-semester." At first business slowed, but soon I began
to acquire dedicated, high-caliber students who were willing to commit more

time and effort to the whole experience. Over the twenty or so years since its inception, mother necessity's child, "Field Studies," has produced some of my best students and some of my fondest memories.

Lima, Peru, was, in the 1980s as it is today, the pickpocket capital of the Americas. It's where I first encountered the mustard squeeze dispenser ruse: a guy comes up to you and squirts mustard all over your shirt; then, as you instinctively try to cleanse yourself, his partner sneaks up from behind and filches your billfold. Or the coin-drop trick: a man trips and, as he falls to the ground, a dozen or so coins fly out of his hands. You put down your pack, help him gather the lost loot, and his co-perp makes off with your stuff.

We'd just arrived on Lan Chile Airlines, a day before the dozen students who would accompany us on a surveying project in Cuzco, the ancient Inca capital, an hour flight out of Lima. I was carrying $8,000 in cash, my budget for the entire month. Lorraine and I checked into the Claridge (another grade B-minus) Hotel in downtown Lima. My plan was to take a cab to the upper-middle-class Miraflores district to visit Juan Ossio, a good friend who was just beginning his career as a professor of anthropology at the Catolica, Peru's most prestigious academic institution. Juan could be depended on to give us the best exchange rate during the habitually up-and-down periods of currency fluctuation—far better than the national banks.

We arrived at Juan's modest home well before dinner; still, he insisted that we stay. As a result, we didn't get around to any financial transacting until well after 10 p.m. "I can offer you 960,000 soles to the dollar," said Juan. The best I'd seen on signs outside exchange booths in Lima was 825,000 soles, so it sounded like a pretty good deal. I counted out my $8,000 and laid it on the kitchen table while Juan did the computation; we agreed that I was due just under 9 billion soles in the then-vastly inflated currency. (This was just a year before the Peruvian government decided to move the decimal point three places to the left.) By the time Juan had finished counting out all the colorful bills, Lorraine and I were confronted with a stack that reached above my knees from the floor. "How will I carry it?" I worried as I cast an eye toward the dimly lit street, wishing I'd had the foresight to bring along my briefcase. "Don't worry. I have something," answered Juan. He disappeared into the laundry room adjacent to the kitchen and returned with a pink plastic bag. We stuffed the money inside, rolled up the bag, and, exchanging departure pleasantries, went out to meet the cab Juan had called to take us back to the hotel. As we headed *downtown, I clutched the money bag tightly to my chest, thinking of what perfect prey we'd be for the cadre of street thieves awaiting us with their condiment dispensers (ketchup is a common alternative) when we exited the vehicle. We made it back safely, and I exhaled my first full breath of the late evening when we locked the door and flopped, still dry-mouthed, on the bed. I clutched my source of sustenance for the month tightly against my chest. We slept that night with the money under our pillow.*

Scheduled for a noon flight the next day, we woke up late and hungry. Then it dawned on us: What to do with the money when we went to breakfast? Can we hide it in the room? We tried the underneath-the-mattress locale and found that the corner of the bed where we tried stuffing the loot was elevated a foot above the other corners. I tried standing on a chair and loosening one of the ceiling panels, but there wasn't sufficient space to accommodate the bulky mother lode. Finally, we settled on breakfasting separately. I'd take the first guard shift and stay in the room with the cash while Lorraine went down to breakfast, then we'd trade assignments. By morning's end we'd made ready for the most dangerous leg of the trip: the ride to the airport, me tightly clasping the pink plastic laundry bag and Lorraine serving as sentinel. After experiencing an uneventful flight and short cab ride to the Hotel Del Sol, located on Cuzco's main drag, we gave the package to the hotel manager, a person we knew we could trust. We instructed him to lock it in the hotel safe. Breathing a sigh of relief, we dropped in at the café adjacent to the hotel and I drank coca tea, an excellent deterrent to the headachy feeling that always accompanies the sudden encounter with an environment 11,500 feet above sea level.

After a well-deserved afternoon nap we awoke a few hours later, thoroughly revitalized. By then the first of my students had begun to arrive, eager to explore and filled with the usual student queries: "So, where are we going tomorrow?" "How can I call home?" "Can you drink the water here?" "Is the street food okay?" "What time's dinner?" I laid out the evening plan: a short orientation session and then a three-block walk to the Café Roma on the Plaza de Armas, with a little tour of historic sites along the way. Realizing I had not a sol on me, I went to draw some cash out of the cache in the safe. When I arrived at the desk I found the night manager on duty—a dashing young man with slicked-down hair, a bit tall for a native Peruvian. He greeted me, and especially Lorraine, with the same smile he had just worn for two of my female students. I told him I'd like to pull a few million soles out of our stash for the evening meal. He responded with a head shake and delivered the bad news, "Only the jefe, Don Rosario, has the combination. He is the only one who can open the safe, and he does not come back until tomorrow." So there I was, leader of the expedition, without the wherewithal to take its first step, a locked iron door standing between me and a billion soles in hard cash. Humbled and disgraced, I was forced to borrow money from my students.

About midnight on the fifth day of surveying and mapping the orientation of Inca shrines in ancient Cuzco, I was awakened by a knock on the door. One of my least traveled and youngest students stood there in tears. "Professor, I have a problem," she confided. I invited her to sit, get control of herself, and tell me what was wrong. Was it something she ate? Was she a victim of the leger-de-main of the ubiquitous pickpocket? She looked unmolested. "What's the matter?" "I've fallen in love with the night manager," she replied. "He wants to marry me . . . next week-end." "What? Wait! But you hardly . . . I mean, how do you know? That's crazy!" I was clearly far less composed than she. I felt totally incapable of responding to the situation, so I played my trump card and woke Lorraine. She succeeded in calming both of us and managed to convince my student that it might be a good idea before proceeding too far too fast to get to know Geraldo a bit better, maybe go out on a few dates, meet his family. At least this seemed a viable way to quench the flame of passion that enveloped the poor smitten young woman, who declared over and over how madly in love she was with this attractive lad. Lorraine succeeded a day later in getting her to promise not to tie the knot on this trip to Peru. Instead, she'd invite him to the States.

He actually visited, and she visited his family in Lima. They dated and became romantic pen pals. Ten years passed before we saw her again, at a national meeting. She had finished a PhD in astronomy and had a tenure-track position at a large university, where she was doing research in astrophysics. Later, she became department chair. When I inquired about whatever happened to Geraldo, she smiled the smile of one who has ably trod the road of experiential learning: "We're still friends." A few years later she served as a surrogate mom, bearing the child of her sister, who was unable to deliver because of medical complications. How quickly they grow, I often think to myself—and what a joy it is for a teacher to be a part of that growing process.

I never set out to fashion my students into cardboard cutouts of myself. Think of a world filled with archaeoastronomers roaming the ancient land-scape, pointing their instruments down to survey the ruins and upward to gaze at the sky! Neither can I—and they—imagine where they might end up as a result of an encounter in my interdisciplinary class. As I was writing this manuscript, Lesley (Class of '89) wrote to me. She'd just listened to NPR's *Science Friday* program about how going to college and career paths cross:

> By my junior year I was desperately trying to figure out my major. Being introduced to your field of archaeoastronomy tied together my interest in Spanish and in astronomy and helped me realize that my seemingly inconsistent studies had actually been all tied together by an interest in Latin America. I eventually studied in the Dominican Republic and was one of the first graduates in Latin American Studies before there was such a program. Your having helped define the diverse field of archaeoastronomy opened my eyes to how combining fields of learning can take you on lifelong paths of exploration. My professional life has taken me on many different paths (working with immigrant populations in Washington, DC; arranging international exchange programs in Central and Eastern Europe; working with refugees in Hungary; and founding an environmental nonprofit with my husband), but they have all been challenging and caused me to want to continue to learn.[6]

I attribute a good part of the success of the full-year archaeoastronomy program centered on experiential learning to focusing each annual field experience on a specific research topic: solar-aligned buildings in the Maya zone, round structures of east Yucatan, calendrically related Aztec sculpture in the adornment of colonial church facades, the Nazca ground drawings of Peru's southern coastal desert. Born out of educational innovation and especially the attempt to promote active learning, as the hybrid discipline of archaeoastronomy became established as a legitimate interdiscipline, each field trip was enriched by the addition to the group of invited Mexican, Guatemalan, and Peruvian anthropologists and archaeologists interested in our specific research problems, as well as teachers and graduate students from other universities who wanted to develop and participate in programs of their own.

You never know what students involved in interdisciplinary learning might engage. Take Samantha Newmark, an English major at Colgate with a passion for Medieval and Renaissance poetry. After she completed a year of archaeoastronomy with me, she enrolled in my seminar "Aztec Thought and Culture." She chose to write a paper on Aztec poetry. Now, it happens that Aztec poetry bears little relation, either in verse form or content, to any sort of poetry known in Western literature. What made Sam's paper so special was the independent, unique way she was able to expose and articulate in the passages she analyzed thoughts that informed the vast gulf between these diverse forms of expression, a task she never could have accomplished without being well acquainted with relevant material from both cultures.

All the while, my focus has never veered from the students; they will always be at the center of the learning experience. When they were with me, they seemed to know they were part of something new and special. I may have been an expert astronomer in their eyes, but in this context they could co-experience my struggle as I attempted to shape a work in progress. They were immersed in it just a few steps behind me as we held hands and I, if unsteadily at times, led them on a journey into the unknown. We were, quite literally, making much of it up as we went along—a far cry from the formal classroom experiences of lecture and discussion.

My excursion into helping found the interdiscipline of archaeoastronomy, later called cultural astronomy, began on a whim developed in an on-campus class on a snowy winter afternoon. Though it turned into a serious research project at Monte Alban, I never had in mind to sway from my own professional track. Things just happened and I continued to embrace the spirit of trying something new. Even as I was getting away with curricular bending in the aftermath of J-term, fellow rule breakers at the college also offered short field projects of their own—a three-week experience in a kibbutz in Israel following a course in Jewish studies or a week in the field (usually spring break) in the middle of a geology course. "Extended Study" is now a mainstay in our curriculum; call it an improvised cut-and-paste version of the defunct "January Term." Curricular reform works best, I think, when it remains open to meaningful experimentation.

Am I the Sage on the Stage: What Makes for a Good Lecture?

Know thy audience! That's the cardinal rule of sound lecturing in any arena. As I began my foray into the world of interdisciplinary learning and especially once I started writing trade texts in the 1980s on cross-disciplinary topics such as the history of clocks and timekeeping, the relationship between astrology and astronomy, and the fascinating history of the moving interface between science and the occult, I also began to receive invitations to speak before a variety of general audiences—at universities, societies, private clubs, and the like. In addition to serving the broader community, these lectures can be valuable experiences that help teachers think of new ways to express themselves—even if things may go awry in unfamiliar situations.

The Century Club is a nationwide social organization consisting largely of people at the extreme end of the longevity spectrum (not surprisingly, 90% of them are women). The local chapter nearest my college got wind of the fact that I'm a fairly engaging speaker who has managed to develop a capacity to speak to a lay audience on a range of topics of broad interest. So they invited me to their headquarters—a charming, early 1900s brownstone in nearby Utica, New York—to give an illustrated lunchtime talk on the Nazca lines, the giant ground drawings consisting of animal effigies, trapezoids, spirals, and other figures etched a thousand years or more ago on the coastal deserts of southern Peru. I had spent the previous decade working there with my students, and my British Museum book on Nazca, with lots of color pictures, had just been published.

On a sunny autumn Monday noon, Lorraine and I made the forty-five-minute drive to the lecture venue. We were greeted at the door by the club president, a sprightly, azure-coiffed, octogenarian woman. She ushered us into a large, well-lit dining room where another dozen and a half ladies of similar ilk (and one old guy hunched over a walker) barraged me with questions about the college, my wife's artistic pursuits (she's a photographer . . .black-and-white photograms), and, of course, the Nazca lines. They had prepared a sumptuous lunch: meatloaf, peas, mashed potatoes, and different hues of Jello for dessert. Homey and delightful!

After lunch we adjourned to a parlor filled with antique furniture, where three or four rows each of half a dozen chairs were squeezed close to a small podium and screen; a slide projector (no PowerPoint then) was stationed on a table at the middle of the room. I had planned a short and sweet, jargon-free half-hour version of my Nazca talk, with no more than two dozen colorful illustrations. I had removed all the graphs containing scientific data about radiocarbon dating and ceramic sequences that my professional collaborators had been collecting on the Nazca figures over several seasons. Despite all the interest generated through lively discussion at the table, this was, after all, a post-prandial event for a group likely endowed with a short attention span. I knew my audience.

Following a generous, well-informed introduction by the club president, I carefully worked my way to the lectern. The overheated environs were decidedly cramped and the front row of chairs so close to the screen that I could have reached out and touched my nearest listener. Five minutes into the talk, out of the corner of my eye I caught a woman in the front row. Her body was listing forward 10°, 30°, then 45° degrees, accompanied by an increased lowering of the cranium. Having reached her tipping point, she pitched forward and free-fell just to the side of me on the carpet. As she slowly rolled over on her side, I leaped back in horror, dropped my extendable metal pointer (no laser pointers either), and took the single step forward that separated us, all the while mentally reviewing my scant knowledge of resuscitative rescue methodology. In a flash, the helmet-haired elder seated next to her intervened. "Oh, don't worry, professor," uttered the white-haired, wizened woman on the other side of the fallen victim, who by now had braced herself up on one knee. "That's just Gertrude falling asleep during lecture again. She's okay, does it all the time; please continue with your speech."

There are other lessons to be learned in the life of the lecturer, especially when doing a gig in a strange place: make sure you know how things work. Test your media in advance for compatibility with the local electronics—and, above all, be aware of which buttons you're pushing at the podium. I once witnessed a nervous graduate student at a national meeting of the American Astronomical Society who ascended the dais to present a ten-minute version of her young life's work. The huge lecture hall at the state mega-versity that hosted the sessions had just undergone a makeover, and the new control panel next to the lectern was equipped with every state-of-the-art, high-tech device a presenter could wish for—dimmer switches, back lights, and an ultra-wide screen for double projection.

Hands trembling, the terrified novice opened her folder and proceeded to read very carefully. You don't want to leave out a single important citation when you're a graduate student. You never know who might be present in the audience to scold you afterward. I could barely see the top of the dark frames of her thick glasses as she bent over her paper and carefully enunciated every word, avoiding the slightest look out toward her vast, intimidating audience. Then she pushed what she thought was the correct button and continued, "My first slide shows the spectrum of one of these supergiant stars . . ." A half dozen words into the sentence, the entire platform carrying speaker, podium, control panel, and American flag slowly began to descend into the floor. We sat there transfixed while the poor student, her eyes still riveted to her text, read on, unaware of the changing scene surrounding her. Slowly, she began to disappear into the floor—first her feet, then her legs, hips, waist, chest, neck . . . Suddenly she looked up and confronted a sea of occupied footwear at eye level. The poor student let out a blood-curdling shriek, whereupon a brave inhabitant of the first row dove into the pit, hit the appropriate button, and returned her to the surface of the earth.

Whether a member of your audience spontaneously falling at your feet or your own self-inflicted descent into the abyss, sometimes it's difficult to anticipate glitches that might occur during a presentation. I once showed up at a small Midwest college, only to discover that no screen was available for projecting my images. Minutes before he was to introduce me, my worried host hastily huddled with his students. He dispatched two of them to run across campus to their dorm and snatch a bed sheet and a few thumbtacks with which to stick the sheet to the wall of the seminar room, thereby saving the day.

Of all the unusual experiences I've encountered on the circuit, none was more bizarre than the sequence of events that transpired in the fall of 1983, when I accepted an invitation from a one-man science department to speak at a tiny college in the southern Appalachians. My host, Charley, and his wife plucked me off a Cessna at the local airport and whisked me through a quick lunch at the only place in town, the mini–Holiday Inn where I'd be housed for the night. During lunch my host told me about the six courses he was teaching that term and the labs he needed to set up for each of them. He also ran the school's observatory and meteorological station, and he did a weekly science column for the local newspaper. Charley's wife was equally busy in local civic affairs. She did a lot of community volunteer work— the library and childcare center (then called "the nursery school").

After lunch we raced to the small lecture hall venue to get set up. My host needed to procure the screen and the projector from audiovisual storage. I followed him around, struggling to keep up with his lightning pace. As we maneuvered, he told me about some of the lab improvs he'd made in the machine and carpenter's shop. Evidently, there was no tech support at this tiny institution, but he still loved his job.

By mid-afternoon things were all in place. A respectable audience began to dot the fifty-seat room, while my host struggled and sweated as he tried to get the jammed portable screen to open up. When all was in order he stepped to the podium, pulled a 4 × 6 index card from his pocket, and did the introduction. Faintly applauded, I walked to the lectern. As I composed myself for my provocative opener—"What makes both the Egyptians and the Maya so mysterious"—I noticed a drop of claret at the side of the lectern. Blood! There was blood trickling down the side of the podium. From where was I bleeding? I felt my face and quickly inspected both sides of my hands (casually, of course). Not a trace. Couldn't be me. I had just arrived *at the podium. I glanced over at Charley, who had seated himself in the front row, and noticed blood dripping from his right pinkie. Evidently he had cut his finger while struggling to open the screen. I casually sidled over to him and smuggled him my handkerchief, subtly pointing to the wound, of which he seemed unaware—all the while distracting my audience with a few opening thoughts about what makes things "mysterious" in general. Charley gripped the handkerchief and tightly wrapped it around his finger, a look of gratitude spreading over his countenance. Forty-five minutes (plus fifteen minutes of Q&A) later, the bloody episode ended. As he ushered me back to the Holiday Inn in his beat-up station wagon, Charley apologized. He regretted that he couldn't take me to dinner because he had yet more work to do that day, but he would launder my handkerchief (which was still wrapped around his pinkie) and get it back to me. "No problem; keep it." It was the least I could do to comfort my overextended, wounded host.*

Following a light supper, I returned to my room, showered, grabbed my pajamas and robe, and flopped in the easy chair. I snapped open the gratis copy of USA Today *and flicked on the TV (there was just one station) and prepared to duo-task on what had happened in the world that day while I had been busy giving my presentation. There I sat listening to the local news and browsing the sports section, periodically looking up over the page at the screen, then casting my eyes back down toward the print. I can do the full cycle in about 30 seconds, not including commercials—that's when the paper stays up. Following the baseball scores I heard the announcer say, "And now here's Charley Smith with a look at your local weather." Out to the weather map strode none other than my dear host, pointer clutched in wounded hand: "Hi folks. Tonight we can expect a low pressure area to arrive from the west."*

Live informative entertainment—the big public lecture offered at colleges for the surrounding community has become a casualty of TV and the Internet, not to mention academic busy-ness. There was a time when such events were actually run by the communities themselves, with varying degrees of connection to formal educational systems. Devised by Yale graduate Josiah Holbrook in the early nineteenth century, the community lyceum's main purpose was to dispense the latest scientific knowledge to middle-class New England laypeople in a large assembly hall. (The word *lyceum* comes from the neighborhood Temple of Apollo [the wolf slayer] and later came to mean a neighborhood apartment appropriate for lectures.) The biggest towns invited public lectures by inspiring notables like Emerson, Thoreau, and Webster. Today one can hardly imagine a Huxley or Pasteur speaking *live* to, much less writing for, a public audience (I'll have more to say on this topic when I deal with techno-learning on p. 121). Today, scientific knowledge is disseminated to the masses through YouTube and Wikipedia entries, or it flows from the pens of science journalists, many of whom are not well acquainted with the subject matter they write about. The purveyors of the scientific corpus in my field usually choose to report dazzlers like "new planet," "maverick asteroid," or "black hole" discovered. There's much more going on in solar system research than the debate over whether Pluto is a planet or water exists on Mars.

On campus and in the academy, lectures prevail. A 1987 survey revealed that lecturing was the mode of instruction in 89 percent of science and math classes, 81 percent in the social sciences, and 61 percent in the humanities (though 81% of art historians and 90% of philosophers used the lecture mode).[7] Now, this was *before* lecturing to students came under criticism by a new pedagogy in the 1980s and 1990s, which called for ramping up active and interactive learning as an antidote to student passivity. More recent surveys indicate some movement toward non-lecture teaching methods; for example, data from a 1999 survey of four-year institutions indicated that 56.5 percent of male and 32.3 percent of female instructors lectured extensively. A 2002 survey revealed that slightly less than 50 percent of classroom time focused on instructor-centered learning.[8]

My own view is that the lecture—a presentation clearly organized, well researched, and fluently delivered, one that begins with a statement of the goals of the lesson and moves toward a closure that harkens back to these goals—is a most efficient way of conveying a body of knowledge. More important, the well-crafted lecture ought to *inspire* students to explore further on their own. Lectures need not include pyrotechnics and histrionics, and they shouldn't be punctuated with *irrelevant* quips and distracting asides. Whether paced off in front of the room and delivered with a variety of vocal inflections or conveyed as a soft-spoken, measured oral narrative in front of a lectern, the good lecture should exude passion in the heart of the teacher; but to become truly effective, the desire to know needs to be transferred to the student.

Communicating passion through enthusiasm seems to work for me; it's what underlies my appreciation of Caleb Wroe Wolfe, my old geology professor who unabashedly acted out his love affair with the rocks he brought into the classroom and lab (see p. 12). His hand-waving gestures and the wide range of modulation of his voice, his bigger-than-life persona, might seem part of a circus act were my adult mind to confront them today, but old Caleb's tactics grabbed my attention when I was a freshman. And once he got hold of me, a wave of inspiration to geologize entered my young mind and heart. His carefully timed utterances drove me to the lab, to the library, and out into the landscape. Every time I look down from the window of an airplane or drive past them, I still recognize all the glacial geological formations—eskers, moraines, and kettle ponds—Professor Wolfe romanced in his class.

A common justification for teaching by the instructor-centered method is that, to use a gas-station analogy, it's the only way to pump the vast amount of knowledge that needs to be transmitted in any course of study (I find this especially true in the sciences). This assumes that the mind of the student is an empty vessel that needs to be filled. By extolling the structured lecture, I don't mean to put down the en vogue pedagogical mode of student-centered learning that advocates breaking down the class into small interactive groups. If it isn't dominated by a single individual or two, as some of my students complain, interactive group learning can have a positive outcome, as I'll show in the next section. As my readers may by now be aware, I employ that style of pedagogy in most of my smaller classes.

Learning is a two-way street, so good listening is as much a part of the lecture environment as is good lecturing. There's a big difference between *hearing* and *listening*. According to auditory neuroscientist Seth Horowitz, hearing is an automatic, adaptive sort of alarm system. It's always turned on, even when you're sleeping. To select and allow what you hear to become the focus of your mind requires attention. You need to concentrate on the words, the inflections, the emotional undertones to acquire the meaning of the vibrations that enter your mind by setting your eardrum to vibrate in harmony with them—that's listening. It's a cognitive process and it requires your attention. We don't listen! And that's a problem, according to Horowitz, "an epidemic in a world that is exchanging convenience for content, speed for meaning. The richness of life doesn't lie in the loudness and the beat, but in the timbres and the vibrations that you can discern if you simply pay attention."[9]

Intelligent listening precludes intelligent conversation. I got perturbed reading MIT clinical psychologist Sherry Turkle's *Alone Together*.[10] She explores the effects of replacing face-to-face social discourse with media-assisted communication. Turkle tells the story of Audrey, a sixteen-year old Facebook addict, who thinks of her profile as her avatar. She creates her own person, posting select pictures of herself while editing away others that don't suit the cyber-person she wishes to construct. On MySpace she has face-to-face conversations with young foreign men who flirt with her image-twin. Sounds like harmless adolescent play, but think of the consequences. Going to school has become, for Audrey, an exercise in professional training to get into college. Real life is the Internet, the virtual Audrey.

Cell phones, likewise, allow us to communicate our lives to a vast array of people in tiny snippets while simultaneously living them. Twittering, blogging, texting—to anyone habituated to this high-speed, clipped mode of discourse, the idea of live, eye-to-eye listening and conversing would be too exhausting, says Turkle. There's no time for it. It requires too much attention.

So, how do I teach my students to listen? Some of them have developed the curious skill of looking directly at me while they write or type the words that fall from my lips. I say to them, "Now put your pens down because here comes a very important point, so listen." Then I tell them, "Okay, *this* you *really* need to write down because it's more important than the earlier stuff I told you about." Sometimes I'll summarize a lecture in two or three bullets (no more) on a PowerPoint slide. I also distribute paper handouts of my outline, usually in the form of a few questions, that I ask students to answer on their own after the lecture is over. And yes, I forbid all electronic devices in my classroom, except for the laptop/iPad by permission only if they *must* use it to take notes (not to surf, text, or tweet). In addition, I do not allow students to leave and re-enter the class room during lectures. I think these rules make for developing good listening skills.

There's a need in the academy for serious discussions about what constitutes good pedagogy, the sort of dialogue I experienced with my mentors when I first came to Colgate and that seems to have disappeared in the busy workaday stream of activity at American colleges and universities. The agenda at most department meetings focuses on who will teach what course, which textbooks, rooms, time slots we'll use—business that could easily be conducted by e-mail. We seem to share our classroom successes and failures, how we tried to employ a novel technique, or how we behaved when encountering a bizarre situation—all important considerations that can inform pedagogy—during informal discussion over lunch, if we dare take time to leave the office even for that, or in rare one-on-one discussions in confidence with those we trust.

Even though I encourage questions, there is no getting away from the fact that in a lecture course I am doing most of the talking and my students are largely listeners. In recent years, listening time has been reduced substantially. The age of the Internet, though it promotes interaction, also vastly reduces attention spans. (Fact: total media exposure among eight- to eighteen-year-olds increased by 50 percent from 1999 [7½ hours] to 2009 [10¾ hours].)[11] To make matters worse, modern culture finds it necessary to engage in the impossible human task of directing attention along multiple mental pathways simultaneously. Hardly a lecturer alive three decades ago will disagree with the premise that stand-up learning is much more difficult to pull off than the talk show mode. And it doesn't help if you simply deal out bullet point info-nuggets on a PowerPoint presentation followed by broad conclusions that usually end with "it turns out that . . ." or that popular expression (cueing students to close their notebooks) extolling the onset of nightfall: "What happens at the end of the day is . . ."

At the risk of sacrificing coverage and the orderly exposition of my lesson, when I lecture I like to make an argument, then recast it in as many different ways as I can. I pose questions for my listeners as I go along or, better, I try to present the argument in such a way that it might invite questions. For example, when I talk about the timing of the harvest festival celebrated by the Ngas of western Nigeria through the sighting of a particular tilt of the first crescent moon they observe in the west at dusk, I point out that the idea of crop fertility is also coincident with the coming-of-age ceremony of young male members of that society. "Can you imagine celebrating that?" I ask rhetorically. And I usually get a response or an end-of-class query from one of my Jewish males, like "well, what do you think a Bar Mitzvah is?" That usually leads to more questions, like "so, where are their parents" or "they look a lot younger than thirteen." When I lecture on the Aztec practice of human sacrifice to keep the Sun God on his celestial course, I begin by referring to a quote from Johannes Kepler engraved on a plaque outside the entrance to our interdisciplinary science building: "Why are things as they are and not otherwise?" At the outset I ask the class to consider how an Aztec scholar would have answered that question.

Breaks in my narrative to set up responses to questions are deliberate, and I spend time thinking them out well in advance. If class time doesn't permit, my course website includes an option for virtual discussion groups, where students are invited to talk with me or with one another. Of course I still hold office hours, about six hours a week, but in recent years visits during office hours have become vastly diminished because of busier student schedules and an increasing distaste, even a fear, among them to engage in face-to-face dialogue.

An air of sanctity always seems to permeate any discussion about what goes on in the classroom: "I'm the teacher; this is *my* domain, and no one should invade the privacy of my actions. Besides, we all know what we're doing, don't we?" But this can be problematic, especially at colleges where peer review is at least as important as student evaluation of teaching. A few years ago I attended (as required in our mentoring program) the big lecture class of one of my younger colleagues. I sat at the back of the room overlooking fifty open laptops. (The rest of the group took notes the less conventional way, with pen and notebook.) I found the lecture pretty informative, if a bit disorganized. When I looked over his shoulder, I noticed that the laptop operated by the student immediately in front of me was tuned in to replays of last night's Yankee game. An adjacent tablet displayed action scenes of dolphins frolicking in the Caribbean. A young woman at the end of the row was deeply immersed in purchasing shoes online. In the midst of the lecture she got up and left. Ten minutes later she returned, a latte in hand, and continued to make her selections.

During that class I witnessed about a dozen other students leave the room, half of them returning after lengthy absences. Had an epidemic of bladder inflammation invaded our campus? My eyes couldn't probe the content of the forest of electronic devices, but to judge from the quick stats I compiled, a sizable minority was engaged with the outside world. Many were texting and tweeting. A bit rattled by this inattentive student behavior, I sat in my chair after the class was dismissed. I felt embarrassed for my fellow teacher, who had invested quite a bit of effort in his presentation unaware of what was going on. After fielding questions from a fair number of serious listeners at the front of the room, he asked how I thought it all went. I couldn't help but retort, "You've got a problem here that needs attention." Perhaps he was so engrossed in lecturing that he was not tuned in to what was happening. As time passed the situation improved, thanks to the stern warning the instructor gave at the start of next semester's class about what *would* and would *not* be tolerated in his classroom. When I tell this story to follow professors I usually get the resigned response: "Happens all the time."

Discipline is important, and students need to know who's in charge of the class. In 1974 I accepted a visiting appointment at a large state university in a pleasant maritime climate. I was teaching an intro astronomy course to a very large audience. We weren't three weeks into the term when suddenly, from the middle of the lecture hall, a loud snort resounded. In the midst of the crowded hall I spied the source of the atmospheric disturbance. It had emanated from the gaping mouth of a rather large student sprawled out over three seats. Head back, mouth open, and deeply cradled in the arms of Morpheus, he was snoring loudly.

Nothing bothers a teacher who carefully prepares a lecture more than a student who falls asleep during it (tweeting is a close second). Impulsively, I took action by quietly dismissing each member of the class around him, leaving no one but me and the still unconscious noisemaker in the hall. Then I turned to the board, banged my pointing stick (still no laser pointers) on the table, and began speaking in a booming voice. From the corner of my eye I spotted the hulk coming back to life. Reflexively, he pawed around his pockets for his pen, picked up the notebook that had spilled off his lap during his sojourn to the Land of Nod, and halfheartedly began transferring the words issuing from my mouth onto his blank pages. As I turned to confront him, I caught him glancing at the vacated spaces to his left, then to his right. In a double-take of historic magnitude, the now-wide-awake student leaped out of his seat as if it were a live electric chair and scrambled over the rows of seats behind him two at a time, his belongings trailing in his wake. Out the back door he flew, as if in a nightmare. He may still be running, for I never saw him again.

Stories like this one characterize the difficulty of engaging students who are not tuned in or turned on, especially when it comes to academic matters (a topic I'll deal with further in chapter 5).

I think good lecturing is, at least in part, instinctive. Early in my career, one of Colgate's legendary lecturers, Douglas Reading, who dazzled his European history classes with gesture-enhanced verbal accounts of World War I battles and studied imitations of speeches by Churchill and Roosevelt, pinned me against the wall of the faculty lounge (he was extremely near-sighted). He looked at me through his thick "shotglasses" and said in typical basso rattle, "Look, Aveni; teaching is like pitching. Either you know how to do it or you don't." Jane Hannaway, who directs the Educational Policy Center of Washington, DC's, Urban Institute, echoes Reading's assessment: "Successful teaching depends in part on a certain inimitable 'voodoo.' You either have it or you don't. I think there is an innate drive or innate ability for teaching."[12]

Sound data back up the Reading-Hannaway theory. Educational researchers who examined test results in the No Child Left Behind program concluded that one impact factor that stood out above all others had to do with which teacher had been assigned to the student. Students associated with weak teachers—those who lacked control of classroom discipline or wandered from the lesson plan and in general failed to inspire a passion for learning in their students—consistently scored lower on tests.

In his advocacy of teacher- over student-oriented learning, Mark Bauerlein thinks it's better to be the "sage on the stage" than the "guide on the side."[13] If I resign my authority by disavowing my expertise in the classroom in favor of equalizing student opinions on issues in which they are clearly less informed than I, then how can I expect them to learn on their own, to enhance their expertise in my field? Can I merely assume that they'll know how to grapple with the big questions? Can I expect my students to seek knowledge and truth on their own simply by assuring them of the integrity of whatever they say in class or write in a paper? Bauerlein thinks many mentors have abandoned their posts, and survey data on "learner-centered" classrooms appear to back him up. The National Survey of Student Engagement reports that, in such situations, contact time with teachers outside class is no different from instructor-dominated classes that place the student in a more passive mode.[14]

The magic touch alone doesn't guarantee an effective teacher. We know what *doesn't* necessarily yield success in the classroom: an advanced degree, high SATs and GREs, confidence, warmth, even enthusiasm. Some educational researchers feel that what we characterize as success as a result of natural-born genius may really be underlain by good technique and deliberate and careful practice; these are mechanical efforts you can be trained to cultivate. For example: don't move around when you give directions. This simple advice has been shown to be successful in capturing student attention, a real plus in classroom management. "Cold calling," or picking out a student to answer the teacher's question, seems to work better than asking for a simple show of hands.[15]

Recently, I was invited to co-chair a first-year faculty workshop called "The Art of the Lecture." I began with the stats on the decline of the lecture mode in the college classroom I quoted earlier and added my own thoughts about how marketing might have contributed in part to that decline. To attract students, the college needs to stress the one-on-oneness of the product it offers. There's no place on a college's website for a photo depicting an instructor at a classroom blackboard in front of a room full of students. A much more effective sell might show two or three students seated with their instructor at a round table, each accompanied by a laptop.

When I finished my presentation and opened the floor for discussion, one of the novice teachers responded, "You seem a bit defensive about preserving the lecture, and I don't think you should be. I was inspired by great lecturing, and I'm not afraid of using it in my classroom." Another thanked me for making her feel less guilty about teaching the way she did (by lecturing). "I guess I believe there are just times when students ought to listen," a third participant e-mailed me. I was genuinely surprised by such reactions coming from a group of thirty-year-old pedagogues who, I thought, would have been thoroughly immersed in the student-centered learning mode educators have been missionizing about for the past generation.

Getting students' attention is only part of the picture, and having them take notes seems not a problem for most of them. Knowing how to sort the information they collect is a more formidable task. They need to learn that while they acquire the information, they must not do so in the usual multi-task mode in the midst of it all. But one of my advisees confided: "Lectures are so-o-o boring. I spend most of my time texting, but if I hear something interesting I'll switch over and take a few notes." Like fellow teacher Greg Graham, I insist that students "pay attention to where you pay attention."[16] I try to exemplify this by retraining my students to single-task, for example, by immersing them in cultivating the art of conversation or by giving them a few silent moments to contemplate what just went down before picking things up again—and, of course, without texting, tweeting, or checking out frolicking dolphins on YouTube.

Again, don't get us wrong. Everyone in the workshop agreed that in a class of twenty-five or fewer, discussion, punctuated by mini-lectures, is a very effective way to teach. The problem is that most course enrollments in American university classrooms exceed that number. Colgate is one of a small percentage of exceptions: 64 percent of our students are enrolled in classes of fewer than twenty, and our student-to-faculty ratio is nine to one—a luxury.

A flurry—I'd say even a "squall"—of Twitter and e-mail dialogue followed in my teacher workshop's wake. "Sure, we all use Twitter, YouTube videos, and electronic discussion boards and PowerPoint when it's appropriate," responded one of my young colleagues, "but let's not *replace* lecturing with interactive learning tools because if we do we're in danger of losing one way to enable the sense of purpose in the classroom, the bond between the professor and the student." Said another, "It isn't about imparting facts as much as it is about selling the product, being the excited messenger convincing the student that this stuff is really worth thinking about even late into the night with your roommate." So true! I remember, after listening to an inspiring lecture "What Are Photons?" in my introductory freshman physics class, Matt Goldfarb (my roommate) and I were reviewing the material. (In the old days you could actually study in your dorm room!) Exhausted, we hopped into our bunks and switched off the ceiling light. Then he queried in the darkness, "Hey Tony, what exactly happened to those photons?" We lay awake pondering until the wee hours of dawn. Okay: you can inspire, drive people to the library or into the lab, but learning is an activity of the mind. It's a reciprocal process.

I think a lot of the real learning begins out of class, after class, and especially during office hours. This is where I can really begin to understand the variety of minds I encounter, and that helps me to better serve my students' needs. Getting them to come in is the hardest part of the operation, especially in the contemporary college scene where everyone is doing everything—from sports to clubs to attending extracurricular events. I can tell who is having trouble by looking over the quiz and written assignment grades. I can see it in their eyes when we're together in the classroom. I single out some students—I have their pictures and I've memorized their names. Yesterday I sought out J.P., a Latino student who seems a bit out of his social element in our not-as-diverse-as-we'd-like-it liberal arts college. "How's it going?" When he shrugged, I added, "I see you had a little trouble on that last test. Why don't you drop by the office and let me go over it with you?" Many students who do come initiate the discourse with "I know this is a dumb question, but," a sign of their lack of self-confidence. Another student admitted she didn't want to come in because she was too embarrassed by her poor performance. I tried to persuade her that we needed to put the results of that last exam aside after we focused together on where she erred and how our discussion might help her deal with the material for the next exam. Even pre-class small talk can render you more approachable in the eyes of one who might think you are too busy to see him outside class. Admittedly, it takes a while to bolster student confidence, but to be effective a teacher must be patient and persistent and, like a good doctor, practice a caring bedside manner. So much of teaching depends on your personality and your desire to interact; if you don't really care, then you're in the wrong racket.

For a long time I thought Douglas Reading's postulate regarding the "born teacher" meant that teaching is more art than craft. But as time passed and I acquired more classroom experience, I began to realize that the "how to" part of his message carried a deeper meaning: when you teach, you have to be yourself; your style of teaching will always reflect your personality, your attitudes, and your behavior outside of class. As teacher Jay Parini phrases it, you should never try to teach from outside your "natural range of intellect or emotions, or outside the circle of [your] sensibility."[17] So, teaching is not acting. If you're aware that you're acting, something's wrong. I sense the truth of Parini's words every time I lose myself in class, when I find that I am less self-aware and more engaged in openly sharing thoughts and ideas with my students. Only after such a class do I feel I've really gotten to them. I witness it in the expressions on their faces. It's an almost magical kind of transcendence, and I'm not satisfied that I get there as often as I wish.

So here I am, unabashedly confessing that my affair in the classroom is an ego trip. Did Pasteur, Huxley, and all the other celebrated lecturers of the past get that same high? Having the students in my grasp, wielding the awesome power to influence them—teaching can border on being a dangerous profession!

Late Friday afternoon, same class with the somnolent student, and the topic was the origin and evolution of galaxies. Big slide show, dozens and dozens of denizens of deep space of every conceivable size and shape—spiral, barred spiral, tightly wound, loosely wound, each an island universe unto itself made up of hundreds of billions of stars. I fixed on an image of Stephan's Quintet. (No, that's not a musical ensemble; it's five galaxies a hundred million light years out in deep space tangled in a gravitationally induced embrace.) "Can you imagine?" I exclaimed. Then I raised my eyes and beheld that my cosmic ardor evidently was not shared by a sizable segment of the youthful conclave. More than a handful of my disconnected charges were doing their own imitations of the sleeping hulk. True, Thursday had been "party night," but I was still furious (remember, sleeping in class is my pet peeve). My first impulse was to yell at them; but then I remembered the sage advice from my respected colleague Flora Clancy, an art department colleague: "Tony, when my kids doze off in class, I drop a little anecdote centered around a subject that appeals to them, like sex. That always brings them back to life."

I decided to apply Flora's formula to the task of recovering lost minds. Pointing to the quintuplets on the screen, I remarked: "Now here we have proof about where galaxies really come from. They reproduce sexually. See how tangled together they are. This one's a male; that's a female. They're having sex! After 9 million years she'll swell up to hundreds of times her normal size. Then she'll spew forth thousands of tiny baby galaxies into the intergalactic realm."

It worked! Suddenly, the class came alive. All over the hall, students took up their pens and began writing it all down. Encouraged, I went on with the improv: "See these irregular galaxies? They were born out of the union of two barred spirals; the ellipticals over here are the result of shorter gestation periods . . ." until the bell rang, ending my celestial fairy tale. The kids dutifully closed their notebooks and headed out the exits. There I stood at the podium pondering the falsehoods I'd disseminated. Ah, the power of the teacher!

As the weekend unfolded, I began puzzling, somewhat guiltily, over my conspiracy of words. "I'm telling you," I told Lorraine," they believed every word of it. They wrote it all down." She raised a skeptical eyebrow in my direction; still, as much as I didn't want to believe I'd hoodwinked the class with so much bio-astronomical nonsense, it had happened.

I couldn't wait for the Monday following, when I would confess my sin openly before the house. The last thing a teacher wants to do is mislead his students. I began the class by re-projecting the slide of Stephan's Quintet. "Remember these galaxies I talked about on Friday [how could they not?]. When I said they were reproducing sexually, I was just kidding. They're really tangled together like that because of gravity. There are no mother and father galaxies and no babies either. They're just galaxies. Get it? It was all a joke."

For a moment, silence, a few cocked heads and frowns of bewilderment. Then, almost as if they were wired in series, my students began to erase or scratch over what they had written down three days before. I recall glimpsing one message writ large on the pad of a diligent note taker seated in the front row: "PLEASE DISREGARD THESE NOTES. THE PROFESSOR MADE A JOKE."

I have told that silly little birth-of-galaxies story to my classes at Colgate many times. It serves as a way of showing them that I am aware of the problem of boredom in the classroom and that I am willing to go to any length to alleviate it. I'll admit, too, that it's a way to make them feel superior because, as one of them remarked, "we aren't as dumb as those other students of yours—we'd never do that."

Teaching a big lecture class may be economical, and its goal, like that of all teaching, to ignite the fire in students' souls to wish to go beyond the professor's teachings on their own, may seem unattainable; but I am convinced that there are ways of maximizing a lecture's effectiveness. So even though I prefer narratives to lists, let me summarize them. First, focus the subject around a few broad questions designed to relate the arguments presented to areas of inquiry that might matter to the audience you're addressing. Second, begin with an overview of the itinerary you'll be leading your students through, being sure to incorporate where the reading or written assignment due that day fits in. Third, as you tell your story, engage your students with the important questions, some of which you'll show a willingness to open up—even if only on a preliminary basis—during the class. Be modest when it comes to the number of topics/questions you can cover in an hour or so. If the density of material is too high, this will get in the way of improvising as well as attaining closure. Fourth, end by recapitulating some of the major highlights you've explored or discovered along the way. Fifth, end your ending with a coda that offers questions for further discussion. Finally, give a clear indication of where we'll be headed the next time we get together. And—just another reminder—if you're not excited or enthusiastic about it all, get another life.

Or the Guide on the Side: Is Techno-learning the Answer?

"I am your resource. I will not lecture. Now, what shall we talk about today?" I've heard this before, and I think it can often be a sign that a teacher is too busy to prepare for class. The Socratic method, engaged thoughtfully, necessitates an attentive teacher-listener, one who is able to generate and direct discussion, anticipate questions, and know how to redirect them as opposed to simply doling out answers. Socrates practiced it as a *dialectic*, or critical inquiry, between individuals centered around asking and answering questions, the goal being to eliminate contradictory ideas to arrive at greater consistency. The label that came down to us as a way of debating issues to promote critical thinking, literally to enable you to recognize your own ignorance, as Socrates put it, has now come to stand for classroom discussion in general. Teaching in discussion mode requires frequent pauses to recollect, to summarize, before moving ahead. Over- or under-controlling dialogue is another problem. You don't want to force your students to arrive at a conclusion without understanding why. Digression is a problem in interactive learning, so you need to stay on point. Socratic teaching can also be a humbling experience, especially when the time inevitably arrives when the honest teacher, seated in the circle and looking eyeball to eyeball at her students, is forced to admit "I don't know."

Despite my praise of the well-tempered lecture, student-centered learning remains my primary mode of teaching, especially in classes that enroll twenty-five or fewer students. I can't work effectively in that mode with more than that number. Teachers who conduct discussion classes are well aware that evening out student participation isn't easy. A few talkative individuals (I call them the "front-row crowd"), who raise their hands regularly to ask a question or make a point, tend to dominate at the expense of well-prepared, thoughtful, but more reticent students in the classroom. Cold calling, either in lecture or discussion, can be effective, if threatening, because it requires that all students be prepared to respond.

I recall noticing Kayla's saucer eyes flashing a signal that told me she wanted to contribute to discussion, but something seemed to inhibit her urge to speak out. I didn't want to thwart her innate curiosity so, out of concern over her repeated silence, I invited her into the office for a one-on-one conversation about the readings. Once we got to know each other, Kayla began to confide in me. She admitted that she was embarrassed to speak because she was afraid she might say the wrong thing. She confessed to having experienced a lifelong difficulty with oral communication, especially when it came to choosing the correct words.

Kayla's first oral presentation of her essay in my seminar was a disaster. She punctuated every sentence with multiple "likes" and delivered her speech in a slumped-over posture, her sleeves pulled down over her knuckles like some turtle retreating into its shell. When I politely pointed out these off-putting verbal and physical affectations, Kayla at first felt hurt. Later she admitted she hadn't been aware of them. Cultivating skills necessitates repetition. I invited her to practice short verbal passages in the office. "Try doing this, Kayla; try not doing that, Kayla." I offered praise when she progressed and constructively criticized when she slacked off. I got the feeling that she disliked my constant harping. That was how I felt about Ray Weymann when I was his student (p. 12), but I also get the sense that she appreciates the attention I've devoted to making an innately bright person a better communicator. At semester's end, I continued to call on her; though she had not completely overcome her communication problem, she made some progress. My time with her was well spent.

Sometimes we aren't aware of the lengthy germination period required of the seeds we sow. Working with Kayla reminded me a lot of Candice, who preceded her in my classroom by about eight years. She, too, really wanted to engage—again, you could see it in the eyes—but she had little self-confidence. She never uttered a word in class until I started calling on her. A few months ago, out of the blue I received a letter from her. Candice thanked me, as she had done before she graduated, for the extra help I gave her. Then she recollected: "You know, I still have vivid memories of our seminar during the fall of my sophomore year. I was still in the 'hesitant' stage, as far as contributing to class discussions, however, you provided everyone with a comfortable, inviting environment and showed me that everyone's voice should have a chance to be heard. (Now you can't shut me up if you try!)" Candice practices law.

I take interactive teaching seriously, and I constantly worry over it. Even though I invest two hours or more of preparation for every one I spend in class, I still find myself pacing around the office prior to class, going over my thoughts. Even after all these years I'm never quite sure I've got it right. What questions might I anticipate from my students? What are the most important points and connections to be sure to get to in the discussion? Often, I find myself getting to class early. It eases the tension and helps translate any doubts I have into useful energy. I enjoy greeting my students at the door and getting to know their names. You can't carry on a dialogue with a sea of nameless faces. I'll take my printout of the roster of pictures of those enrolled in my class, then try to fit names to faces as they get seated: "Are you Charlie? Didn't recognize you with that different haircut," showing him the picture. "Don't you play basketball?" "Meg, is that a break or a sprain in your knee?" "Kennelley—I went to school with a Kennelley. Where are you from?" On opening day one of my colleagues projects a picture of her family on the screen as she introduces herself, ending with "and this is our dog, Mitch." Teaching requires person-to-person interaction, and I believe these little one-on-one social icebreakers (as opposed to the formally organized departmental mass conventions that take place on Parents' Weekend) move me a little closer to knowing something about what's going on in my students' minds. Small talk is no substitute for learning, but small efforts on a teacher's part can go a long way toward facilitating the learning process by encouraging us to get familiar with one another on a social level; and that fosters openness. Student and teacher—we are *all* people.

Another way to get my students to work interactively is to improvise and experiment. Creating opportunities for students to work together is one strategy. I'm fond of assigning group projects. For example, in my ancient astronomy course I try to give students a feel for what low-tech science was like in practice. I divide the class into teams of three or four and ask them to create a rudimentary seasonal calendar by going outdoors at sunset over the course of a month to chart the course of the setting sun along the horizon. I allow them to use only sticks and strings, no pre-calibrated measuring equipment. The exercise is repetitive and creates havoc with their busy schedules. I get complaints about which delinquent in the group is not showing up or contributing to writing the final report. Still, in these little task-oriented collaborations, students learn to develop social skills and to appreciate the advantages as well as the pitfalls of cooperative learning applied to problem solving.

The assignment also requires that students pay close attention to the natural environment; for example, they notice that the sun sets at a different time every day, often during dinner hour. "You need to be there," I encourage them, "just as the ancient skywatchers charged with the important task of charting the god of time knew when to go to work." There are occasions when I think it would be much easier to simply show a series of pretty pictures of setting suns and discuss what happens; but then the reports come in, and I find that a significant number of students prove that not only do they "get it" but also that they know how to go on from there. They come back to class with deeper questions: How long would it really have taken low-tech people to create a calendar in the environment? First, there's the problem of the weather interrupting their observations, as it did ours. How could they find the spare time to do this if they needed to hunt and gather? Did they have specialists? Members of that class who visit or correspond with me years later remark, "Every time I watch the sun go down, I remember when you made the class go out on that hill and stake out sunset after sunset. Now I know the date of the year by memorizing points on the horizon I can see from my living room window."

Interdisciplinary classes like ancient astronomy also turn out to be excellent media for revealing student biases. Can the modern mind look objectively at an ancient artifact like 5,000-year-old Stonehenge or the Maya pyramids and really know the intent of the culture that built it? Some of the literature we read in my course focuses on the possibility, still controversial today, that Great Britain's famous monument might have been a precise astronomical observatory, possibly even a computer for tracking eclipses. I ask my students to write a short essay that answers the question, are the modern astronomers and engineers who offer these scientific interpretations of Stonehenge guilty of erecting cardboard ancestors of themselves? The goal is transformed from a scientific inquiry about the uses of ancient architecture to a deeper socio-logical question about modern ethnocentric behavior.

I haven't the space to lay out a primer for interactive learning, but I can recommend a good source developed by a group of educators, headed by Terry Doyle of Ferris State University, who have put a lot more effort than I into developing one.[18] Doyle views learner-centered teaching as a means of subjecting every activity in the classroom to this question: Given the context of my students, course, and classroom, will this teaching action optimize my students' opportunity to learn? Urging students to speak in class, to defend a point of view, to accept criticism, and, most difficult of all, to rethink or change a position are among the key selling points the instructor must get across to her class. One must learn to experience a genuine pleasure in sharing, defending, or arguing a point. These skills, asserts Doyle, can come only from repeated engagement in a given group. This cultivates the notion that we are all engaged in an activity that elevates us by examining different points of view. It's okay to disagree, and we're not to blame ourselves for not knowing something. Even though the presentation is a bit didactic, I like the supportive, sensitive tone to the real world model Doyle and his group advocate.

Once I get to know my students, especially in small-group interaction, I marvel at the diversity of their reactions to what they experience. I learn that all the minds I encounter are not the same. One memorable experience illustrates. One of the most persistent common curiosities among students of astronomy has to do with UFOs. "I know you think there's no evidence for them, professor, but wouldn't it be neat if they were real" is a question frequently posed. Interestingly, UFO sightings wax in hard times and wane in good. During the Vietnam War era, for example, there were many sightings. At one such peak period, a couple of psych majors approached me to gain approval for an experiment they wanted to conduct using my class. They would perpetrate a hoax by building their own homemade UFO. They made it out of a plastic bag, a pair of balsa wood sticks, and a candle. Basically, their device was a simple convection balloon, the sticks nailed crosswise with the candle mounted at the center and the entire apparatus fixed to the open end of the bag. Light the candle, the air in the bag gets hot, and up goes the balloon. They would set off their device on a piece of property adjacent to the observatory, where I conducted nightly sky-observing sessions with students enrolled in my introductory astronomy class. The experimenters planned to aim the craft so it would float over the space where the students were busily peeping at telescopic celestial wonders. Their idea was to test the notion of "seeing is believing." How do different people respond to something they witness with their own eyes?

Always a proponent of scientific experimentation, I enthusiastically endorsed the project. And so, on a mid-September evening, the budding scientists set to their task. I could faintly hear the crackling noise their feet made as they stepped on dry twigs in the adjacent woods upwind of the observatory. They had some trouble lighting matches in the damp ambience, but finally they got the candle lit. Up-up-up the craft rose, then it moved toward the driveway of the observatory beside which our half-dozen, evenly spaced 6-inch reflecting telescopes, each attended by three or four students, were positioned. As the light breeze took hold of it, the faux UFO passed over the driveway at an altitude of about 100 feet. Few caught sight of the missile until one student looked up. Open-mouthed, he let out a yell: "Oh my God!" (Yes, OMG was a popular phrase then as well.) "It's a UFO!" As the luminous ball gained altitude and passed over the campus in the direction of the golf course, the excited young man chased after it, waving his arms and screaming wildly. "Hey, stop; we're earthlings, we won't hurt you"; then they both disappeared over the horizon. I stood next to the alien persuer's lab partner who responded calmly, "Bet it's some silly balloon someone made out of old laundry bags." The next day, members of the class chided the unwitting dupe, who admitted to spending most of the night out on the course searching for the elusive interstellar interloper—in vain.

Before the UFO incident, I hadn't thought much about how different the perception of a visual phenomenon might be to two of my students—two different people, each conditioned to respond to what they sense in a different way. The incident reminds me that all minds are not necessarily the same. So why should I expect uniformity in the way they interpret our in-class dialogue and the questions we pose to one another?

Today, it's called the flipped classroom, the inverted classroom, or student-centered teaching—brought to you by MOOCs (Massive Open Online Courses). Educators seem to have a penchant for reinventing the wheel. A colleague recently told me, "You know, Tony, I'm tired of people discovering interactive learning as if it's never existed before." While the philosophy of interactive learning began with Socrates, it goes back, at least in the modern era, to John Dewey, who championed it in the early twentieth century—the notion that real knowledge is meaning based on what we acquire from previous experience. He called it *constructivism*. Dewey emphasized hands-on, task-oriented, project-based learning.

To facilitate interaction in the contemporary classroom, any number of grants are available for installing digital learning media. These include fully equipping classrooms with built-in laptops, mandating direct access to the computer to solve problems, videoconferencing, and so on. My opinion is that none of this substitutes for eyeball-to-eyeball dialogue. Nor does computerized learning do much to solve the problem of the lack of curiosity and the unwillingness to engage deeply rooted complex problems I find in many of my students. Conditioned by "yes-no" digital responses, students can acquire the impression that getting to *the answer* is easy if you make the correct choices. The fact that they communicate by tweeting in bits and bites offers a further deterrent to formulating and articulating a rational, complex argument. Non–face-to-face communication in little snippets doesn't help. In the digital world of simultaneous noise, pictures, and few words—all hastily expressed in fewer than 140 characters—communication with and among my students gravitates toward brief, instantaneous encounters. All of this is not conducive to thinking rationally and creatively, goals to which we aspire in an academic environment.

"Death knell for the lecture?" reads one headline. "Is new technology a valid, affordable passport to personalized education?" Many promoters of online teaching answer yes to both questions. Consider the advantages: the video content they use engages the new generation of YouTubers. The content of such courses, doled out in bite-sized bits, fits reduced student attention spans and incorporates a flexible way of directing instruction to the individual student; it's more like tutoring. Like the Keller Plan of the 1960s, also called the Personalized System of Instruction, you get tested when you think you're ready to move ahead. As administered, for example, by the Stanford University Artificial Intelligence Laboratory, such courses include an interactive forum in which students can vote on questions and answers to sort out the most important inquiries, which can then be answered by a staff member, usually a graduate student. Statistics show that this works just fine for subjects like computer science and math and maybe even for some basic physical science courses; but can interactive computerized learning teach creative problem solving? Can it help students think critically? The Stanford Lab makes no elaborate claims, beyond regarding online education as a first step toward a deeper understanding of concepts and ideas. At least at this writing, interactive learning using online resources has become a fad.

It makes sense, argues proponent Nathan Heller. "Actors, musicians, and even standup comedians record their best performances for broadcast and posterity. Why shouldn't college teachers do the same?"[19] The Internet is the obvious place to do it. It's a tailor-made delivery system to individuals and institutions for packaged courses from the best in the discipline. As in the old lyceum (p. 108) lectures, the great guru can dole out his wisdom to the unwashed masses. But unlike the lyceum, audience opportunity for interaction happens only through response to electronically graded true-false questions.

CAI (Computer Assisted Instruction) brings with it self-paced and self-directed learning, which means the student gets to decide what he wants to learn and in what order. Moreover, the computer can exercise various senses in the presentation of information. Being impersonal, unlike the authoritarian figure in front of the classroom, the computer allows you to make mistakes and not feel bad about it, especially if you're shy and sensitive. Some CAI programs incorporate an entertaining "game" element, where the student is confronted with a real-world simulation and invited to compete with other students—who gets the most correct responses the fastest or who wins a race on a game board. Again, few advocate CAI as a substitute for traditional in-class learning, whether in a student- or teacher-centered curriculum; rather, teachers can use information technology to enhance their role in the education process.

MOOCs, like Open University, Wiki U, and I-Tune U, offer Internet lectures and courseware on line, much of it free of charge. Open U, based in England, was downloaded 16 million times in 2012, 89 percent of the time outside the United Kingdom. In January 2012, I-Tune U surpassed 100 million downloads. Celebrity lecturers, like eighty-three-year-old biologist Marian Diamond of UC Berkeley and Ramamurti Shankar, who teaches physics at Yale, pull more than a million viewers on YouTube with their dynamic classroom performances. In addition, top institutions like MIT, Harvard, and Stanford are basically bottling their product and offering it as an act of largesse to teach an educated-minded public that can't afford to pay for the high-price academic diet. Independent learners make up half the audience. Of course, you don't get course credit watching a brilliant physics teacher fly around the room demonstrating (correctly; see p. 82) how a pendulum swings, but it might motivate you to enroll in a course or maybe even a degree program at a local community college. If you're already enrolled in Physics 101, you can enhance your coursework—maybe even acquire the inspiration you feel you're lacking in your current learning environment—by tuning in.

Self-enrichment is a noble human goal, especially in the dummied-down culture America has become. But how can self-motivated, high-quality education truly be rewarded? A next step might involve building full semester e-courses so accredited colleges and universities could consider open courses as part of the accreditation system at community colleges. Carnegie Mellon's program in the Open Learning Institute, which is currently developing a series of such courses, has determined that student users can cut their learning time in half and that they are more inclined to stick with a class in which they are having difficulty rather than drop it. But other leading academic institutions are picking up the slack. For example, at this writing, Harvard's Division of Continuing Education offers sixty-five courses for degree credit in evening and online mode.

Still more recently Coursera, a for-profit company founded by Stanford computer scientists, is offering more than a thousand MOOCs enrolling nearly 3 million students.[20] It consists of a consortium of twelve major universities, including Stanford, Michigan, Princeton, Penn, Illinois, Virginia, and Johns Hopkins. Worldwide MOOC enrollments stand at 5 million.[21] Some courses are for credit, but most carry only a statement of accomplishment and a grade. Cheating is a problem, however, and to remedy it, Coursera proposes setting up test centers. Most MOOCs offer computer science, math, and engineering, but the company—which has enrolled nearly 1.5 million students, mostly from abroad—has plans to set up history and poetry offerings as well. Similar non-profits like UDACITY, with half a million enrolled, and EDS, with 400,000, offer a dozen courses each. At this stage no money is exchanged, but for performative professors attracted by the prospect of disseminating their knowledge to a vast audience, the teaching assignment compels the ego. And for companies recruiting future prospects, selecting from a pool of students whose quality of learning is sanctified by America's top universities is a big draw.

Is techno-learning a panacea? The jury is still out on the future of online higher education. The debate remains loud and widespread. Hardly a day goes by without a new op-ed piece. But I sense a backlash brewing. Recently, Amherst rejected MOOC programs, citing the deleterious effect they would have on small discussion classes at its residential campus. Worried that the university might end up offering fewer courses, Duke withdrew from Semester Online, an education consortium that offers online courses for credit.[22] While San Jose State University remains committed to online courses as a way to reduce costs and bring in more students, its philosophy department objected to employing materials taught by the Harvard superstar lecturer licensed by the MOOC with which it has contracted.

There isn't much regarding efficacy. One study conducted by Ithaka, the non-profit parent company of the digital library website JSTOR, showed no significant difference in educational outcomes between online and in-class learning; however, the course involved was basic statistics.[23] In contrast, Columbia University's Community College Research Center has produced a larger study showing that community college students who enroll in online courses are significantly more likely to fail or withdraw than their traditionally enrolled counterparts. Also, low-performing students fall even farther behind in online courses.[24] The student attrition rate—about 90 percent— remains a problem. Another is that while most such courses work for skilled and highly motivated students, they don't seem to serve the bulk of the college enrollment, made up of struggling students who need close guidance.

Online instruction in the humanities is a big problem. Like the online courses, I make more frequent use of imagery in my big lectures because I see it as a way to hook my students. But visual imagery matters less in the humanities, where we seek to discover who we are and who we want to be, writes English professor Mark Edmundson; we represent ourselves to ourselves through words: "Words allow for a precision and nuance that images do not seem, for most people, to be able to provide."[25] College is a place where you can "read yourself aright." It's not about becoming more intellectual, never being embarrassed in conversation at a party. You read great works, he says, "to see if their authors know you better than you know yourself."[26] How do you assess online essays? How do you evaluate answers to complex questions that often incorporate subjective elements? How do you quantify feelings evoked by poetry?

In numerous discussions with me about matters educational, my Colgate colleague Bruce Selleck has pointed out that to engage in meaningful learning, students need to acquire a skill set to engage course content. The learning process also involves gratification delay. The commodified nature of online learning exemplified by MOOCs, then, applies only to those fortunate enough to have received sound, early, basic education.

Journalist Amanda Ripley did a personal comparative study of online vs. in-class learning. She enrolled in a MOOC in physics. Then she attended a couple of live physics classes at the private Georgetown University and the public University of the District of Columbia. The first course consisted of three hour-long lectures, punctuated by Q&A, along with a weekly lab. The

Georgetown students also met with a live teaching assistant once a week for a problem-solving session. "The class felt like a luxury car, exquisitely wrought and expensive," she wrote.[27] Even at the lower-tuition UDC, Ripley felt that, unlike the classes the same professor also taught on Udacity, the live experience was more effective. The instructor reviewed the basic math in far more detail than his counterpart on Udacity, and questions from students made it clear that this was necessary. He cold called and by the end of the hour everyone got to share thoughts with him. Ripley added that he "was helping them with many skills beyond physics. He was cultivating discipline and focus, rebuilding confidence and nurturing motivation."[28] These broader skills are much more difficult to teach electronically.

Editor-journalist Arnold Jacobs went further. He signed up for eleven online courses and offered this amusing report card:[29]

Professors: There were a couple of boring clunkers but most seemed knowledgeable, well-informed, and organized. The humor didn't go over all that well: his biology professor used a Charles Darwin bobble-head doll as a prop and the philosophy professor donned steampunk goggles when he lectured on the logic behind time travel. Pop-stars? Not really; but they were all respected in their fields (Grade: B+.)

Convenience: Jacobs watched lectures while walking his treadmill. He just forwarded when things dragged and replayed sections he didn't understand (Grade: A.)

Teacher-Student Interaction: Jacobs entered but failed to draw a winning ticket on an exclusive ten-person Google hangout with one of his professors and failed to master the complex interactive software in another class. He got no responses on discussion boards (Grade: D.)

Student-Student Interaction: Given the luxury of living in a big city, Jacobs tried to meet with his history class study group at a Dunkin' Donuts, but nobody else showed up. On the other hand the message boards were helpful, though they lacked the rapid exchange of ideas that evolves in face-to-face discussion. Video-chatting with a few engaged classmates helped (Grade: B-.)

Assignments: There were a lot of multiple-choice quizzes, most of them stressful. He even discovered a website that gave the correct answers to the quizzes in his Biology class. He wrote a few essays that were graded by his peers. Who died and made you professor?, he wondered at some of their slights (Grade: B-.)

Jacobs gave his overall experience a B. Given all the negatives, he sounds to me like an easy grader. While he felt his retention rate was low and he couldn't think of any way to apply his newly acquired knowledge, he did feel a sense of self-improvement. Maybe MOOCs will help people get jobs or think up new business ideas, opines Jacobs, but they won't live up to their hype. Jacobs completed only two of the eleven courses.

Online education may be all the rage, but will it make universities a thing of the past, as some proponents have claimed? Sebastian Thrun, a Stanford research professor who teaches online computer science classes, predicts that by 2060 only ten institutions of higher education will exist in the world and that degrees will vanish.[30] Careers change so rapidly and frequently, he argues, that the model of spending a fixed time following high school to educate oneself toward a career will become obsolete. Instead, we'll return to college online at various times in our lives to update what we need for the future.

Unless, like Thrun, all you think there is to be gained by going to college is the acquisition of knowledge, I doubt computers will ever put learning by direct contact out of business—any more than Netflix will shut down live theater on Broadway. Whether for engaging people who want to test new waters or for those who have an innate sense of curiosity, informal online learning, at most, might be a viable enterprise for our woefully undereducated populace. *That* would be a good thing.

Summing up the last two chapters, I've become both sage on the stage and guide on the side. I've tried to take advantage of new ideas and new technology to make myself a better teacher. While I think I perform more comfortably in my job using *only* talk and chalk—or even a stick in the sand—I know that I can make myself more effective if I remain open to innovation and experimentation. I remember, in my mid-career days, the advent of the overhead projector. You drew or wrote stuff on a roll of plastic imaged on the screen behind you. At first I resisted it because it hindered walking around and gesticulating. In addition to facing the class, you could overlay graphics, and multiple colors could be more easily added, eliminating constant erasures. But when I realized that its advantages outweighed its disadvantages, I went with the overhead. Well aware of my contemporary students' attraction to imagery over word (largely motivated by the Internet), I've even learned to develop PowerPoint lectures punctuated by interactive exercises. Some of these require me to break up the class into small groups so they can respond to key questions we don't have time to engage in. This dialectic component of my classes is aided by computer discussion groups.

I've been around the classroom long enough to realize that communicating my enthusiasm and getting my students excited about something is no guarantee that they'll buy into it. I need to work more at learning to dialogue the way they do.

What's On the Test? Teaching and Measuring Basic Student Skills

Learning to write, to speak, to think critically: How do our curricula respond to these skills that underlie practically every educational goal statement? When I attended college in the 1950s, all students were required to take "Freshman Comp." I wrote a three- to five-page essay each week. The instructor marked it up with a red pencil, noting errors in grammar and syntax, in addition to pointing out flaws in organization, coherence, and narrative flow. I found it was a lot of hard work, and often the subject matter I was required to deal with was of little interest to me. Basically, I hated it, but it did teach a young person who had scarcely written a word in high school how to begin to communicate through the medium of writing and especially how to mount an argument, take a position. Frequent contact with the instructor, who, like most who taught these small section courses, served in the English department, was a plus. Wish I'd taken greater advantage of his office hours.

Seven years later, when I arrived at Colgate, PhD nearly in hand, our English department was in the midst of a revolt against shouldering the burden of this sort of program. There were no writing departments, not even an organized discipline bearing that label, until the 1970s. Like me, the English professors wanted to teach what they *did*: literary criticism, Renaissance poetry, the American novel, and so on. The effects of the age of specialization that Charles Percy Snow had warned about in the 1950s (p. 63) were in full swing. Unable to staff the course, the college dropped "Freshman Comp" altogether, replacing it with the unenforceable dictum that each of the Core courses take over the writing requirement. This would consist of a certain number of pages of writing, usually fifteen–twenty per semester in each course. The change offered the student two distinct advantages: he could write a paper that related specifically to the subject matter dealt with in the course; and, if he did the readings and attended all the classes, he could learn how to put together a coherent narrative. These pluses were counterbalanced by the distinct possibility of being stuck (or blessed, depending on your attitude) with a professor so absorbed in his profession that he couldn't care less about spending time helping students practice the art of writing.

One of my advisees told me she had received B grade after B grade on her essays from one of her instructors, who habitually added very few red marks on her papers, capping off the bottom of the last page with little more than a hastily scribbled short phrase such as "good work" or "needs more attention to organization." (Today, red comments on a paper are a no-no in most quarters. The color of blood connotes punishment and general negativity. Better to correct with a green pen.) Suspecting that the teacher was not reading what she wrote, on the next assignment, in the middle of a passage on communism and following a sentence that began "The Soviet Union under communism . . ." she inserted the words "had a little lamb, its fleece was white as snow, and everywhere that communists went, the lamb was sure to go"; then she continued "soon began to rival the United States as a world power." When the instructor returned the paper, it bore the anticipated red "B" on the title page and "nice job, but try to be more clear" at the end. She flipped through its pages and encountered no vermilion marginalia. As my advisee had anticipated, her evidently unseen non-sequitur insertion elicited no reaction. Unfortunately, she made the mistake of confronting the professor in his office about the matter, accusing him directly of never having read the paper. Denying the allegation, he responded with a "how dare you" outburst that drove her from the premises. There the matter rested. (She received a B in the course.)

Learning to write well is too basic a skill to leave to instructors who don't care or aren't aware of how to implement it. I think the current trend toward relegating this demanding task to adjunct faculty who, regardless of level of experience, receive a pittance for their services is deplorable.

Recently, one of my students came in for a bi-weekly progress report on his senior thesis. I happened to have on my desk the third draft (so labeled) of a paper I was about to resubmit to one of the journals. As I wheeled around to face him, I instinctively grabbed it and blurted out, "Hey Jeff, take a look at *my* writing assignment here." His eyes fixed on the number "3" and he replied, "You mean you actually go through all those prep stages you make us go through? I thought professors were experts on how to write." "How do you think you get to be an expert?" I responded. Then I added, "Wait'll you see the job the referees are going to do on this," pointing to the handful of pages I held. "There'll be a fourth draft for sure, probably three months from now, if I get it back by then." Jeff reflected for a moment before reacting, "Wouldn't it be neat if you could give us all 'incompletes' in our coursework, then require us to resubmit our revised drafts next term? I'll bet we'd learn a lot more about how to write in the real world, wouldn't we?" Need I point out that Jeff was an unusual student? Before we got to work on his draft, we mused together over what a bureaucratic nightmare such a course of action would pose for the university registrar.

Practice, practice, practice. Revise, revise, revise. Sounds like a no-brainer, but survey studies show that students who write the most, especially under close mentoring, improve the most.[31] Class size matters. In low-enrollment seminars my students and I can experience the luxury of seeing a paper through to completion. Usually I assign a twenty-five-page paper, to be developed in several assignment stages—outline, bibliography, first draft, second draft, final draft, and abstract—during the term. Then my students can experience the *process* of writing, of which the final product is only a part.

Former student Christine Cucciarre, who teaches a course titled "Writing across the Curriculum" to college faculty, agrees. She thinks one way to lessen the heavy burden of grading multiple drafts is to ignore grammar and mechanics at the outset. Writing is thinking; writing is learning. It's a process, not a product; and the more of it you do, the better you get at it. So tackle organization, structure, and clarity of thought first. Deal with grammar later. (Incidentally, Christine was kind enough to comment on an earlier draft of my manuscript.)

I think what applies to the written word ought to apply to word of mouth as well. Rhetoric, or the ability to create and deliver a persuasive argument, used to be a college requirement. Communicating electronically has had a detrimental effect on cultivating the art of discourse in my students. Today's version of oratory and public speaking is largely confined to Debate Club.

To remedy what I feel is a loss vital to a well-rounded education, like many of my colleagues I require each of my students to give class presentations of their written work. I usually assign one of the listeners, in a rotating framework, to lead the discussion that follows each presentation, often by taking an opposing view. The rest of the class submits comment cards to raise questions and indicate what they didn't understand. These go to the presenter, who assesses them in putting together the next draft.

Like most teachers today, I like to get my essayists up in front of the classroom. But keeping the discourse going can be a problem. Betsy was one of my brightest students, though unfortunately she was overworked by the demands of her athletic predilections (she was a field hockey star). Though she usually sat in the back row, often entering late, I could always see whether the whites of her eyes were visible. When she frequently nodded off, I was never reticent to make her aware of her unscheduled somnolence with a "what do you think, Betsy" or "earth to Betsy." When it was her turn in front of the class, she experienced frustration in keeping the class tuned in. Three minutes into launching her presentation, Betsy looked quizzically at one of her teammates who usually occupied the seat next to hers at the back of the room. A frown fell over her face and she intoned: "Heather, how dare you fall asleep during my presentation! Don't you realize how hard I worked to prepare this speech?"

What does it mean to "be creative," and how do our colleges respond to the goal of teaching students how to become creative? I believe it deals with cultivating a capacity to perceive what science philosopher Jacob Bronowski calls *hidden likenesses*.[32] Let me give you an example. One day, while visiting Mexico City's National Museum of Anthropology and History, I spotted a sculpture I hadn't seen before. Tucked away in one corner of the Aztec Room was a jadeite representation of a calabash, or gourd-squash. The piece was about a foot across and had been carved out of a single chunk of stone. No real-life squash could have looked like this. The artist had rendered the mature, ready-to-eat Aztec staple with its attached flower open to full bloom. Now, even a weekend tiller of soil knows that when the flower is fully open and developed, the squash will barely have sprouted; or if the squash has fully matured and it's ready to pick, its flower will long since have withered and dropped off. Clearly, the native sculptor was capable of creating a beautiful work of art, but he must not have been a very keen observer of nature.

I've thought a lot about the artist who made that carving just a few generations before Cortés landed on Mexico's shore half a millennium ago, and I've come to believe he was neither naive nor inattentive. Rather, I think the artist was expressing a knowledge of the world about him in a way unfamiliar to us. He had conflated different stages of plant metamorphosis into a single coherent image. If this bothers us, maybe it's only because, as Darwin's heirs, we live in a world that stresses evolution, development, and change. The story lines we create to explain how nature works follow the passage of all things, animate as well as inanimate, through timed stages—quasar to galaxy, gas cloud to star, streambed to canyon, ape to human. The sculpture I was looking at is as foreign to me as is an image showing the head of an aged woman attached to a lithe young body. I think the Aztec sculptor's intent was to express knowledge about the plant world that was important *to him*. Maybe it was less significant to show a particular growth stage in the life of the plant. Rather, for reasons we may never know, the combination of realities pulled from different time frames and brought together by the human imagination into a composite whole may have held greater significance. It helps if you're an insider, that is, if you know something about how various plants change in appearance as they grow, and if you understand Aztec culture. What might appear nonsensical to the untrained, uninformed eye at a single moment in time suddenly crystallizes into a coherent and meaningful representation of nature in the eye of another beholder.

In my interdisciplinary example of human creativity, the focus of attention resides less in the subject matter and more in the process—the creative process of discovery that comes from finding a hidden likeness between two forms previously thought to be unconnected. This is the way Bronowski explains it when he employs another pair of unlikely images side by side to demonstrate a creative act well-known to all beginning students of physics: an apple hanging in a tree and the silvery moon suspended from the sky.[33] When Sir Isaac Newton witnessed the apple fall, he is supposed to have wondered whether whatever force drew it to the earth might also pull on the moon, thus keeping it in orbit. Newton's discovery was the concept of gravitation. The earth's gravity unites the apple in the garden and the moon in the sky. What unifies them can be expressed in a single mathematical law that describes how each moves. Two dissimilar appearances joined by a universal principle that forever after establishes their underlying sameness: both possess mass and therefore mutually attract every other object in the universe. How do you demonstrate that in the classroom? Students who understand some physics and mathematics, who come to apprehend Newton's laws, and who experiment with falling bodies can re-create in a laboratory the essence of the unity inherent in Newton's discovery. They become the insiders who can share more fully in the discovery process. The creative process is the same, whether you compare a falling apple with the moon, as Newton did, or the composition of a squash plant in a work in stone, as did the Aztec sculptor.

But changing a student's mind may be harder than we think. In one study about what makes things move, even when confronted with evidence to the contrary, students doggedly clung to their preconceived notions about the cause of motion, often arguing that whatever was demonstrated to them had to do with some other principle or that the case didn't apply—anything to avoid confronting the possibility that their understanding of the situation needed to be revised.[34] Oddly, this held true regardless of how students performed on exams. Apparently the way students think cannot be adequately measured by performance on standard tests, researchers concluded.

Critical thinking and creativity go together. Creativity is a kind of controlled power. While it emanates from freedom, it isn't simply "doing as you please," argues Charles Anderson.[35] If you're given the freedom to break rules and cast off inhibitions, you also need to acquire the discipline and depth of knowledge to realize when to exercise that power, especially when (and when not) to go on with the course of action or perspective you've chosen to pursue. A style, an approach, an interpretation is creative, says Anderson, only when it expands the boundaries of a system. In that sense, the anonymous Aztec sculptor was creative; so was Newton. But heed this rule about rule breaking: if you're going to be an iconoclast, you'd better know something about the mold you intend to shatter. As an interdisciplinary scholar, I've seen more than a handful of the sorts of creative insights I just described that light up the minds of my students. I never know when they will happen, but I've learned that most such happenings emerge out of frequent contact and dialogue with others engaged in similar studies, whether instructors or fellow students—in other words, becoming an "insider." Those who have acquired sufficient depth in allied areas of interest, along with an imagination and a sense of daring, are more likely to make the leap of discovery between known and unknown worlds; then they find hidden likenesses of their own.

My role as a teacher is to think along with my students, not just encouraging the flowering of good ideas but also constructively pointing out where they might go astray so they can make their own choices. But criticizing is far more difficult than encouraging. Young students often confuse criticism leveled at their work with criticism of themselves or their character. "How could you give me a C-minus on my paper when we drank a beer together at the pub last week?" Doug was in tears as he confronted me after class. "It wasn't about *you*. It was about the *paper*, Doug," I responded. "I really like you as a person. Now let's go over how we can improve your narrative."

You develop *constructive* criticism out of the habit of questioning. Like the good writing habit, it takes practice. The kind of criticism and questioning I'm thinking of isn't cynical. It's the kind of skepticism that stems from dissatisfaction embedded in a desire to understand things at a deeper level and in a way that tries to connect with one's previously acquired knowledge. (Think of Stage 3 in the breathing process I discussed in chapter I.) Learning, I tell my students, has more to do with asking more difficult questions and less to do with arriving at simpler answers.

Being a good skeptic goes hand in hand with developing critical thinking. To accept what is thrust upon us by fashion or tradition countermands the goal of creative thinking. How was it arrived at? Where is the reason for it? Who or what benefits from it? I'm not satisfied with my students blindly accepting a body of knowledge. We need to work together to hone it, to perfect it, and we do this by developing the habit of doubting that leads to questioning. Critical thinking operates in a controlled way. You make use of your analytical skills; you learn to reflect on things before moving ahead; you apply logic and good judgment; you identify and sort out different arguments that bear on the issues; you learn to apply relevant evidence and exclude what is not germane to a particular situation.

I've found that one of the most effective ways to promote critical thinking is to read about and discuss why old ideas once agreed upon, issues once thought settled, came to be questioned, abandoned, and replaced by new ones. I value teaching rejected knowledge. All of my science courses include a good deal of historical material, which usually takes up a thin section at the beginning of any science survey text. Thus, in "Introductory Astronomy," I spend quite a bit of time on the hypothesis of dynamic encounter, which explained the origin of the earth and planets as the result of the close passage of a nearby star to the sun. Almost universally accepted in the 1920s, dynamic encounter was rejected in the 1950s in favor of the formation of planets as a natural consequence of the formation of stars. I want my students to know *why* that paradigm shift happened.

When we encounter theories of the origin of the universe, I give ample time to the now largely discredited steady state theory. Popular in the 1950s, it postulated an eternal, infinite universe. After discussing steady state, we turn to the reasons why today's accepted alternative, the big bang theory, which explains creation as the result of an instantaneous event that happened nearly 14 billion years ago, replaced the steady state theory. I try to trace with my students why things changed, what questions were posed, and what new celestial observations were acquired that led up to these sea changes. We also deal with the counterarguments that were made and the kind of evidence employed in defense of the established theory. Our goal is to address the big question: How do we understand scientific discovery as part of an expanding, constantly changing set of circumstances that developed out of creative thinking and the habit of raising questions? Students find this deeper inquiry into why scientific explanations change far more interesting than learning only the tenets of contemporary cosmology. They become especially unsettled when they confront the reality that scientific truth undergoes constant change. Many of my students are taken aback when, at the end of my astronomy course, I advise them not to save their notebooks for too long because what's in them will soon be obsolete. My measure of lasting learning is, as usual, correspondence and visitation with alumni ten, twenty, thirty, or more years out of college. This is what they remember best. But they admit that detail helped them focus on the big picture.

Some of my colleagues are critical of my historical approach to science: "How do you have time to cover all the topics you really need to touch upon— infrared astronomy, unmanned extraterrestrial exploration, findings from the Hubble Space Telescope, peculiar galaxies—if you spend so much class time dealing with the history of scientific thought?" Let the historians deal with that, they advise me. Textbooks play to the desire to seek full coverage of a field. I think too many of them lead students to regard science as a static body of knowledge jam-packed with facts and formulas (which they are sure to forget even before the beginning of next term). No wonder students hate science! I'm concerned more about portraying the way science happens.

So, what has all my time in and out of the classroom amounted to when it comes to fulfilling every college teacher's number one goal? To teach students to think critically, you need to teach the argument, the idea, and you need to pursue the process of its development relentlessly, through frequent dialogue and feedback, with those who travel the road of learning with you. Given these lofty goals, I can't claim a high batting average. Considering that only about one-third of all graduates believe the college experience strengthened their capacity to think critically, I'm fully aware that teaching is a low-yield process of refinement fueled by its high-octane successes.

In my half century in the classroom, I can count on one hand the number of times I've been engaged in a serious conversation about how to construct a test that one can feel confident measures what a student has really learned. In big survey classes, especially in the sciences, machine-graded objective tests are the rule.

When I taught such a class on one of my visiting faculty appointments at a large university, I announced on the eve of the first exam that I would put a copy of a test in the library for students to review. I'm a mild advocate of learning by drilling, but by the time I'd spent a few weeks with these well-intentioned, if ill-prepared, college kids, it became clear to me that they would need all the assistance they could get. Given the large number of students enrolled in the class, the test needed to be framed entirely in the true-false question mode. I'd scarcely begun to administer the exam when I heard pained sobs emanating from the back of the hall. Who's crying, I wondered as I made my way toward the source. There I beheld a frail-looking, heavily tanned young woman. (It was well-known that one of the major incentives for enrolling at this particular institution was its proximity to prime surf.) "What's the matter? Are you okay?" I inquired. Tears mixed with black eye liner streaming down her cheeks, she choked out a reply, "You lied to us. You lied to the class." "What do you mean," I replied. "You said you'd put an exam in the library." "Well, I did." "So I went there and studied it and I memorized the answers—true, false, false, true, true, true, false—and then you gave us a different exam!"

Usually, I try to make it a point to minimize testing information recall and maximize how to apply what a student may have learned to a different situation. One of my favorite examples from my astronomy class comes after we learn how the moon rotates on its axis and revolves around the sun and how the moon and the sun as seen from the earth move among the stars. On the test I ask my students to explain how astronauts living on the moon would view the motion of the earth, sun, and stars. (It can be tested by multiple choice in large classes.) This is a more difficult question than the memorizable one that inquires how long the earth takes to circuit the sun or the definition of a day, a month, or a year because it requires students to think. Students need to place themselves in a framework different from the one they learned about in class and from the readings. There is little doubt in my mind that this type of question offers a better assessment of a student's understanding of how an idea works.

To suppress the tendency to cram information into their heads, I permit students, especially in my more quantitatively based tests, to consult a 4×6 index card with anything they choose to write on one side. I'm convinced that the very act of organizing and sorting out what's important, then printing it out or drawing it, aids in the learning process. As you might expect, this generous option often becomes an exercise not unlike the old telephone booth analogy (with words replacing people) of seeing how much information you can cram into a tiny space. For fun, I occasionally run a "most creative info card" contest. Competitors submit their cards (anonymously) for review. One entry consisted of a set of overlapping microscopic texts written in different-colored inks. (It required the use of different-color spectacles to be read—disqualified.) Another contained only a simple prayer from the Koran. Not surprisingly, students with the most elaborate, carefully designed cards ended up making the highest scores on the exams. In proctoring the exams, I also discovered that the students with the most detailed cards were the ones who spent the least amount of time consulting them during the exams.

Assessing writing, critical thinking, and the general acquisition of knowledge through standard testing is part of the pedagogical skill set. I acquired most of my more effective habits (and learned to drop the ones that didn't work) in casual conversation with my colleagues, usually when I shared my feelings—and elicited theirs—about where a class went wrong. But by far the majority of my assessing and reassessing how I can become a better teacher comes from listening to my students.

How To and How Not To Teach

In 1981 the Council for the Advancement and Support of Education (CASE) in Washington, DC, created its first annual selection of National Professor of the Year. Colleges and universities across the country were invited to nominate teachers from their own and other faculties. A select panel read the case files submitted, which included data on classroom accomplishments and letters of recommendation. Hundreds of entries were pared to five finalists, from which a single winner was selected. (Since the early 1990s the competition has been subdivided into awards in various sub-categories.)

I was selected the 1982 National Professor of the Year. I got the call late one summer afternoon when my nineteen-year-old son and I were tarring the garage roof. Like the overjoyed person in the generic TV commercial who's just been informed with a knock on the door "you've just won a million dollars," I was ecstatic. (The monetary prize that accompanied the honor was quite modest.) More important, I was invited to deliver a lecture at the Smithsonian Institution following the awards ceremony, which was held at the Jefferson Memorial (replete with the US Marine Corps band playing as jets flew over the Capitol). It was a big deal for Colgate and especially for my working-class extended family. Many aunts, uncles, and cousins drove down from southern New England to attend the afternoon-long program.

Even the day I learned the good news, I had no doubt in my mind that such an award, like most, was purely symbolic. The World's Strongest Man certainly can't live up to what the title advertises, any more than Miss America connotes the best by any test. I came to view myself as a poster child for the promotion of good teaching. A few years later I gladly contributed to the book *Distinguished Teachers on Effective Teaching,* edited by 1983 awardee Peter Beidler of Lehigh University. Since then, I have never passed up the opportunity to share what I have learned about the classroom experience.[36] I've received several other honors, including selection as one of *Rolling Stone Magazine*'s "Ten Best College Professors" (1991). Most of all, I cherish the 1990 Phi Eta Sigma Professor of the Year Award, given by Colgate's freshman class. It's especially important to me because the students choose the honoree. I have no doubt that awards beget awards, and I have never thought for a moment that I am *the* best teacher.

My teaching accolades over the years, especially the CASE national award, have had a curious effect on how I teach. I've always felt motivated to be in the classroom. I can't wait to get there, and when I'm away from it for long periods, as in the summers I spend writing or during sabbaticals working on research, I genuinely miss my contact with students. But since the CASE award, I've somehow acquired a need to prove that I really am very good at my craft. Many students who enroll in my classes know about the award and expect to experience teaching at its very best. I cannot disappoint. My lectures must be pristine and our discussions engaging to the highest degree. My former Colgate colleague, anthropologist Gary Urton, who received a MacArthur Genius Award in 2002, has shared similar thoughts with me about the effect of such grand accolades. "Of course I'm not a genius," he told me about a year after he was selected, "but everybody seems to think I am." Already a productive scholar, the pace of Gary's quality research publications has increased noticeably since 2002. He tells me that the MacArthur is something he feels he must live up to. He is now a professor of anthropology at Harvard.

Since 1982, the number of people who come to me for advice about teaching has increased. Obviously, the extent of my venerability has lengthened considerably since then. I had been teaching a mere twenty years when I got the CASE award. I think it set me up as a role model, and it's also responsible for the many questions teachers from around the world ask me. For what it may be worth, let me share a few responses.

First, *you teach who you get*. That's a corollary of *know thy audience*. Your job, as Mark Edmundson puts it, is to connect with the students' energy and hopes.[37] Science teachers constantly complain about the poorly trained, mathematically illiterate young people who populate their classes, and humanists decry their students' dislike for reading nonfiction. Social scientists marvel at how out of touch their students are with geography, history, and global politics. Others gripe: "My students can't write." "My students don't talk." "Kids these days have no attention span." "They don't do the readings." These are serious problems (I'll share my thoughts about a host of them in chapter 5). But none of these shortcomings should be sufficient cause for a teacher to shirk from his classroom duty. If my students lack math skills, I do my best to help, especially those who are willing to seek me out to overcome their deficiencies. I try to look for ways to translate the mathematical jargon found in most science textbooks into sentences made up of the English language. To give an example, I use floor tiles to illustrate that the inverse square law (of gravitation or light intensity) amounts to little more than a problem in how you visualize space. The farther away you are from a source, the greater the area over which a signal gets diluted. If you double the distance from the source, the energy that falls on a single tile at a given distance gets spread out over four tiles. After I demonstrate the dilution effect with tiles and a ruler, I sketch it on the board. All of this takes time, but it makes the abstraction to "1 over r-squared" much easier to comprehend.

Second, lay out your goals and expectations, not only at the beginning of every semester but also at the start of every class. Be honest about your likes and dislikes. Personally, I don't like teaching in a classroom with two empty front rows and everyone crowded toward the back of the room. "How'd you feel if you were hosting a party and all your guests huddled around the back door?" I ask my students on opening day (when the front row is usually empty). I want them to know *how* I feel and *why*; consequently, in my large classes I don't allow anyone to sit in the back two rows. I mustn't let my friendliness and approachable nature get in the way of the fact that I'm in charge of the classroom.

Semester's opening may remind some teachers of Clint Eastwood's altercation with a bad guy in the Dirty Harry film *Sudden Impact*. In a tense eyeball-to-eyeball confrontation, the outlaw is about to make a move to draw his gun. Who can forget Eastwood's icy retort: "Go ahead, make my day." Some of the unfamiliar faces I look out at on day one seem to express that classic retort. Does the inherent fear of science motivate the lack of inspiration I read in their glances, or were they victims of some awful previous classroom experience? Maybe it was the subject matter they found boring in the past. I know that many of my students attend college because that's where everyone with decent grades, inspired or not, ends up (more about that, too, in chapter 5). Past scenarios, real or imagined, are irrelevant to my task, which is to turn on and motivate those who now sit before me, whatever their orientation, whatever their educational backgrounds—to get them to read and write and speak and *work*, not for me but for themselves. Their skill level or attitudes do not diminish my respect for them. They motivate me. I relish a bar set high.

Third, though at the outset of every meeting, whether lecture or discussion, I give an outline of where I intend to take each of my classes, I also remind my students—using a short résumé—how our pursuits in today's lesson will follow from where we left off last time. I also make it a point, if I'm lecturing, *not* to follow the text by rote. Yes, I do refer to the reading assignment and I pose questions to the class, but basically I see myself, especially in large classroom situations, as a synthesizer. My role is to try to put things together from the more didactic texts we tend to use in preparation for class. Six decades of teaching in the liberal arts impels me, as does the interdisciplinary nature of my interests, to make broad connections, to raise big questions. So, if you're just beginning to teach, don't be afraid to broaden your range. Try painting with a big brush once in a while. Your students will be the better for it, and so will you.

Despite all efforts to achieve success, failure happens. One of my friends calls our shared profession a "7 percent solution" (the term comes from Sherlock Holmes's percentage dilution of an effective narcotic). The impact of all our efforts in the classroom really doesn't amount to much, he tells me pessimistically. But sometimes there are surprises.

I long grieved over the precious time I had wasted teaching Bob Rodat. An English major in the mid-1970s who managed to find his way into three of my classes, including a J-term experience in Guatemala, Bob was an exceedingly bright guy. He was very articulate and pretty good with the pen, too—maybe too good. He could achieve comfortable Bs (regarded as respectable then) in his courses with little effort. Bob spent a good share of his time partying. All my attempts to shake him into realizing some of the potential I knew he possessed had little effect. "I want to have fun. I want to enjoy college life," he'd tell me. "There's plenty of time to get serious later"—a line I'd heard many times before from my undergrads. When he graduated I told him candidly, out of frustration, "Bob, I have the feeling you're never going to amount to anything."

After leaving Colgate, Rodat got a cushy job in a Washington, DC, government office. He'd call me every few weeks, usually opening the conversation with a line like "two priests walk into a bar . . ." After a few off-color stories, Bob would proudly inform me that he spent most of his time idling behind an empty desk. He usually got most of his work done by noon. As the years flew by, we lost track of each other, the case with most former-student-teacher contact. Twenty years after

Bob graduated, Lorraine and I were settling into our seats at the local movie theater just as the lights started to dim. The title of a movie we were eager to see appeared on the screen, Saving Private Ryan, followed by "Steven Spielberg, etc.," and then the words "screenplay by Robert Rodat." We turned to one another with jaws agape, popcorn spilling all over our laps. "Can it be?" It was! When Bob, now married with children, visited campus that spring to give a seminar on creative writing, he told us what had happened since our last contact.

Somehow, college never taught Bob that one of life's realities lies in the realization of how fleeting and precious one's existence can be. It took the loss of a close relative to cancer to make him aware that there's a time limit attached to setting and pursuing life's goals. Why had he waited so long to get it together? Why, despite all my efforts, had I failed to reach him? Does an incubation period come with implanted skill sets? I'll never know, but I can't stop wondering. I single out Bob's case because it is unusual. But then I wonder whether he might really be no different from any of the other students I've encountered over the years who, despite their grades or social behavior in college, end up later in life creatively applying the latent skills they had acquired early on, whether it be in running their own businesses, teaching, writing, or simply volunteering.

Any seasoned teacher can easily match my stories one for one. You never know who will end up where. That's one of the mysteries of our profession. Sometimes you realize much later that you had an impact on a student you hardly knew you were affecting at the time. I met Dr. Christine Peters (now Cucciarre), a professor of writing in the University of Delaware's English department, at her twentieth Colgate reunion in the spring of 2012. She reminded me that she got a C in my intro astronomy course when she was a junior. As I jokingly braced for a change-of-grade appeal, Christine surprised me by telling me that she was tremendously influenced by what she learned: "I remember Colgate fondly and always knew that I would one day inspire students the way you inspired me." Dare I resort to the Clint Eastwood analogy to tell you how I felt? When I told Christine I had been working on a book about teaching, she offered to read it, share her knowledge of effective teaching, and give me feedback. She did, and this gives me, once again, an opportunity to thank her.

I want to sum up by citing the results of an in-depth study that surveyed the skills and classroom habits of university teachers.[38] There were six major conclusions that exemplify the best teachers: know your stuff, take it seriously, keep your expectations high, create a good environment, be yourself, and never lose sight of your objectives. In closing, let me expand a bit on each of these points:

1. Good teachers know what they are talking about. The best of them are active and accomplished scholars and artists; even if not widely acclaimed for what they write about, they closely follow developments in their fields. They seem to have a capacity for using their knowledge to develop techniques for helping their students think about and act on the ideas and concepts that confront them. They have learned how to clarify, to cut to the heart of things, to simplify without loss of meaning.

2. Good teachers' attitudes toward how they prepare their lectures and discussions are as serious and demanding as what they do when they engage in scholarship. They are less concerned with self-directed issues, such as what material will I include or exclude and what assignments will I give, and more with student-oriented questions, such as what will my students need to understand to answer the important questions raised in this course and how can I help them assess their own work.

3. The best teachers expect more out of their students than most other teachers, but their objectives go beyond the courses and embody the sort of thinking and acting expected in life.

4. These teachers work hard to create a critical learning environment by giving their students opportunities to work together, opportunities to try, fail, get feedback, and try again, and by raising more questions than simply giving answers.

5. When they walk into a classroom, good teachers display a kind of openness that convinces students that their teacher knows they are there because they want to learn. The teachers are self-confident enough to talk about their own curiosity and the obstacles they have faced in the never-ending process of learning.

6. Finally, good teachers monitor their own efforts; they take student feedback seriously, and they make sure they never lose sight of the real objectives of learning.

Now that I've shared my personal thoughts about the whys and hows of the profession of liberal arts college teaching, I want to turn, in the final chapter, to some of the more controversial issues and problems that have arisen on the contemporary academic scene. I pose each of them as a series of questions. My aim will be to offer advice, based on my fifty-plus years of teaching that might be helpful to future teachers, as well as to enrolled and prospective students, about where I believe the learned life is headed.

He's not an intellectual. Intellectuals
start all the trouble in the world.

Peggy Noonan[1]

No system of education known to man
is capable of ruining everyone.

Otto Neugebauer[2]

Are Sound Teaching and Strong Scholarship Compatible?

*June 15, 1965, my dissertation defense—a harrowing three-hour rite de passage in
which each of the four inquisitors who served on my committee saw fit to invite his
or her professional pals to join in devouring my brain. Things didn't calm down
for me until they began feasting on one another. They gestured in agreement and
disagreement on issues ranging from the nature of atomic nuclei to the creation
of the universe, subjects quite remote from my research problem, which had to do*

DOI: 10.5876/9781607323037.c005

with measuring the effects of hot gas clouds surrounding nascent stars and how to calculate the energy that emanated from stellar surfaces.

When, after a lengthy adjournment, the chair told me that I passed and the committee had signed off, I walked out of the examination room clutching my precious two-inch-thick manuscript that had been the focus of the past two years of my life. Caught in the undertow of the intense encounter with a roomful of vultures picking at me, I was still in a daze when I entered the registrar's office across campus to get my final administrative signatures and place the master copy of the dissertation on file. I plopped the tome on the receptionist's desk, then filled out a few forms before moving on to the desk of the registrar's secretary, a stern-looking middle-aged woman with thick glasses and hair wrapped in a bun. "There it is," I said smiling. "I'm done"—sigh. Expressionlessly, she checked over my forms and browsed the opening pages of the fruits of my hard labor to check for the faculty signatures. Then she cast a raised eyebrow over her horn-rims and asked, "Where's your title page with the committee's signatures?" "What?" My blood suddenly rushed to my feet. "That's the top page; it was there when I left the observatory," I said, thumbing in the direction back toward the hundred-yard trek I'd just completed in the hot sun carrying the open-top box full of paper. Could it have been blown off the top of the pile by the draft when I opened the doorway, I wondered. I retraced the steps along my course from the department office to the administration building, looking from side to side, praying silently for the relief that would engulf me at the sight of a sheet of white paper lying along the walkway. No sign of it. Maybe somebody picked it up? My thoughts darted about. How in hell can I get all those signatures again? Aden Meinel had raced to the airport to catch a flight to Chicago, and I'd seen Ray Weymann head for his car immediately after the defense for a trip to California. A major crisis was brewing!

Half an hour later I re-entered the registrar's office on the verge of tears. "It has to be in this room," I theorized aloud. I crawled about the immediate vicinity of the desktop where I had deposited the load. The secretary stood over me, offering little more than a deep exhale at what for her seemed to be typical negligent student behavior. Then a clue—on the floor, sticking out from the edge of the filing cabinet—I glimpsed a small white triangle, the tip of a paper iceberg. I gripped it surgically between thumb and index finger, tugged gently, and out it slid, face-up: page 1. An eccentrically placed ceiling fan had caused the mishap. Evidently, the unnatural wind must have blown the top page off the pile.

Apparently it sailed off and landed on the floor, sliding almost entirely beneath the cabinet. I was saved!

The committee thought my dissertation was worthy of publication, and Aden and Ray encouraged me to draft it up for submission to the *Astrophysical Journal*, or *ApJ* (pronounced "App-Jay" by insiders), the flagship serial publication in the world of astrophysics. The quality of one's professional work can be assessed only by those who have in-depth knowledge of the subject matter—the jury of your peers. Usually, two or three of them are consulted by peer-reviewed journals to arbitrate submitted research papers. "Get it done before you get bogged down with all that fall teaching," Aden advised (I was about to begin my third year at Colgate). Redrafting a highly condensed version of my research would become my major task for the rest of the summer of 1965. I've always found rewriting the most fun part of the research process—that final chipping and polishing of a work, the general shape of which you're already aware. Do sculptors feel the same way? At least it's the easiest part of the process—or so I thought.

I boiled my 320-page magnum opus down to 50 pages by drastically condensing the data reportage, which constituted the bulk of the work, and eliminating the obligatory overview of the literature section that accompanies all dissertations. I sent it off to *ApJ* in late August. Three months and three reader reports later came word from Subramanyan Chandrasekhar, a noted astrophysicist and the editor of the journal. My paper was accepted subject to drastic revision, mainly to make it shorter. Wrote the great "Chandra": "If all our contributors publish papers of this length there will come a day when the front cover of the *ApJ* will travel at the speed of light[!]" Two more drafts and eight months later, my work had been condensed to a barely recognizable version of the original: statement of problem (2 pages), observational data (2 pages), results (2 pages)—6 pages total. Abridgment notwithstanding, I remember the feeling of elation that came from seeing my work in print. I was actually making a valid contribution, however small, to the frontier of human knowledge. What I had accomplished would remain in the written record for posterity, even if much of the data and results would be superseded by higher-quality instrumentation and more progressive ideas years later—always the case in science. Curiously, the issue of the *ApJ* that carried my 6-pager also included a paper titled "On the Relativistic Garden Hose Instability," by S. Chandrasekhar. It was 50 pages long. It's good to be the editor!

As I worked the redrafts of the dissertation in the fall of 1965, I also resumed teaching. It was then that I first began to feel the tension so well-known to all teacher-scholars, a tension I have come to believe is best left unresolved. Two years earlier I had begun to revel in my new-found love affair with undergraduate teaching. I remember thinking how "set for life" I'd be once I got the dissertation out of the way. Then I could hang up my shingle and practice the craft I desired: influencing bright young minds. But I also began to realize that a significant part of my calling came from outside the classroom. So many stones were left unturned in the broader aspects of my research problem. Critiques of my *ApJ* six-pager led me to think more deeply about future lines of inquiry. I got into collaborative studies with one or two close colleagues. I bonded with a group of like-minded researchers, discovering and sharing ideas about the exotic phenomena taking place in the vast, unimaginably remote domain of nature we play in, known as the cosmos. My desire for mutual engagement with my astronomy colleagues and the problems we shared would not abandon me. Two passions: one for teaching, the other for contributing new knowledge to my chosen discipline. Are they compatible? At least for me, active scholarship is a necessary part of cultivating good teaching.

As a way of assuaging my guilt over stealing time from my teaching and devoting it to pure research, I began to think of ways to involve my under-graduates in the process. Joint faculty-student research, a common enter-prise in undergraduate colleges today, was largely unknown in my early days of teaching. I wrote grant proposals so I could set up Colgate's modestly equipped observatory with the latest electronic detection technology. We could collect and analyze data on star formation in-house. I created a course called "Astronomical Techniques" to train students to acquire the requisite research skills in my newly developed astronomy and physics major. I took some of the more qualified members of the class with me to distant obser-vatories to help me gather data. When some of my undergrads coauthored papers with me and even published work under their own names in journals, I shared with them the feeling of seeing one's work in print in a scientific publication. I found that I also needed to check my desire to fashion every student who crossed my path into an astronomer just like me, a habit shared by many of my younger colleagues.

I think the vital connection between teaching and researching emerges out of the dynamic between the ever-changing and, especially in the case of science, progressive nature of the discipline. Professors who are not actively engaged in some way at the vanguard of their discipline are more likely to generate sets of yellowed notes and canned PowerPoint presentations for reuse year after year. True, there are consummate scholars in academia who, though they may not publish in the peer-reviewed journals, nonetheless manage to keep up with their discipline by attending conferences and communicating with their colleagues. Many of them are good teachers. On the other side of the coin, there are excellent researchers who become so consumed in their studies that they leave too little time for achieving balanced success in the classroom. But despite popular claims, there is little evidence from US Department of Education survey data that teachers neglect their students in favor of selfishly pursuing their scholarship. Teachers nationwide spend more than 50 percent of their time on teaching and less than 20 percent on research; half of them publish only one article per year. To dispel another myth: only 25 percent of students do *not* find their profs inaccessible because they are off researching.[3] Research and teaching draw upon different skills, but they come together in the *active mind*. Scholarship is the life's blood that flows in the body of the effective teacher. The excitement of being engaged in the process of acquiring knowledge, coupled with the passion to share and develop the essence of that knowledge—these are the conditions that produce the best teachers.

Gerald Graff has compiled the results of a number of studies on the relationship between scholarly and teaching activities, especially in large universities.[4] In achieving curricular reform, he says, educational institutions need to get away from the notion that professionalism and specialization must somehow remain hostile to one another. His advice? Draw on the university's research culture. Seek ideas related to curricular coherence in debates and disagreements embedded in the ongoing disciplines on campus. Integrate the perennial antagonists, as he puts it, in putting together the common experience. And do this without the necessity of seeking cross-disciplinary agreement on values and beliefs. I remember during the battles I refereed over general education revision—metaphor vs. reality, text vs. context, and which text to use—saying to one of my colleagues: if we could bottle this, it would make an excellent gen ed program all by itself.

This ideal environment, born out of the tension between teaching and research, must always remain in delicate balance. Not all my fellow teachers agree with my opinion on "necessary tension," particularly those vying for tenure at large state universities.[5] I can't blame them. Their world is a far cry from the small, liberal arts college environment I've been privileged to grow up in. Given all the duties of their office, they complain that there is hardly any time left to devote to serious scholarship, except maybe in summer or when they are on leave. Furthermore, many universities offer no leave program. Often bearing the burden of a heavy teaching load, these overworked teachers are also saddled with the necessity to acquire big bucks through grant writing and to put down three or four articles or a book before tenure time—very difficult requirements to meet. Should they publish incomplete arguments or pieces written in haste, the sort of stuff that already takes up too large a portion of what appears in print? "Scholarship is depressing," admitted Peter Beidler, one of my fellow CASE nominees, in apparent despair. "The forces that drive it, its relationship to academic careers, the lack of critical judgment of its worth, and the deceptions and hypocrisies through which it flourishes make the specific manifestations of scholarship even more depressing."[6] Beidler speaks from the point of view of the humanities, which, he argues, have become inhumane because of an excess of unnecessary scholarship. He teaches at an institution like mine, where faculty are judged for promotion and tenure on the quality of their scholarly output as well as their teaching. To all students who answer a question posed them by many of their professors, "Where do you see yourself ten years down the road" with "teaching in a college just like you," let me offer a few words of caution: no job worth seeking is free of tension.

Should My Job Be Guaranteed for Life?

What's tenure? I asked myself that question when, having served for six years on the Colgate faculty, I received, in my seventh (1969), a letter from the dean of faculty starting with congratulations and then "you are hereby awarded continuous tenure." When I couldn't answer my question, I made an appointment with the jocular English professor who had succeeded the great ombudsman (p. 39–40) and put the question to him. "Well, it means that unless you take off your clothes and run around crazed in the classroom, we can't fire you," he replied. Then he got serious and explained to me how this novel concept, often the envy of other professions, came to be.

Academic tenure was designed to protect university professors engaged in research. The idea actually goes back to ancient Greece, when Socrates pled to the Athenian court to permit him to continue his critical inquiries and still be allowed free meals in the Prytaneum, the town's religious and political center where the communal hearth was kept. Free food and freedom go together, especially when you're involved in work that pays little and you need to spend practically all your time in deep thought. The problem of the civil right of free speech developed into the concept of academic freedom when universities were created in the Middle Ages. Then researchers, who also became teachers, or masters—and were still underpaid—were licensed to practice their dual craft. They were given certain "rights and privileges," as stated in their documents. (My old college diploma still certifies that I am "entitled to all the rights, privileges, and honors thereunto appertaining"— whatever they are.) Competence to conduct research thus became linked to competence to teach. Protection against loss of license also resulted in protection against being dismissed from a continuing appointment based on a review of your competence according to standards provided by the particular institution that employed you.

The modern notion of tenure started in 1900 at Stanford University when economist Edward Ross was fired because the widow of railroad magnate Leland Stanford, who served on the board, didn't care for his views on immigrant labor and railroad monopolies. Ross's firing caused a row. Professors protested and some resigned their positions. This set up an ongoing national debate on freedom of expression and control of universities by the private sector. Fifteen years later Johns Hopkins philosopher Arthur Lovejoy and educator John Dewey organized a meeting to form the American Association of University Professors, a union dedicated to the promotion of academic freedom. Basically, it was founded to formulate tenure contracts with universities and to guard against the dangers of being dictated to about how to pursue teaching and research interests.

"Do away with tenure" is among the remedies proposed by most critics who have entered the current debate about what's wrong with our colleges

(I'll deal with that topic in greater detail later in this chapter). The tenure system has been reviled by some as antiquated and unfair, "the last refuge for academic scoundrels and malingerers, guaranteeing them not only life-time appointment but a stranglehold on the appointment and promotion of junior faculty," as one retired Brown University professor bluntly characterizes it.[7] Another unfortunate consequence of tenure is that it risks making you complacent and resistive to change. The longer you can remain ensconced in your way of doing things, whether it involves how you teach or what material you include in your courses, the more you might feel threatened by outside pressure to change or to being judged by those who would tread upon your sacred turf. Having served on a host of tenure committees, I believe that while there have been abusers of the system, tenure does offer a measure of protection to teachers from the will of the administration and the board.

Originally, tenure had nothing to do with teaching. In the early days, university professors to whom tenure contracts applied were those who conducted advanced research. They were distinguished from *college* professors, who were required to transmit knowledge to the "immature." "So," explained the dean in answer to my "what's tenure" question, "tenure is all about academic freedom, your freedom to teach as well as inquire—some compensation for the low rate of pay you get in the university. The university has made a decision to 'marry you' after our six-year courtship," he concluded.

The fact that I didn't know about tenure was a result of everyone at Colgate having achieved it; but then, as you'll recall from the story of my hiring, teachers were pretty hard to come by in the early 1960s, especially in the sciences. I would learn to appreciate what being tenured really meant a few years later when I made my huge leap from the sciences to social science. My academic freedom definitely contributed to my daring to explore and expand my interests. I doubt I would have made my sojourn into a discipline so remote from the one in which I'd trained had I not possessed some measure of job security. The result of that extra-disciplinary trip, I think, has had a positive impact on my students' education. I did it at a time when tenure requirements had been drastically elevated, the result of a glut of fresh PhDs sent out into the marketplace—serendipity.

How Can Teachers Serve the Wider Community?

In addition to teaching and scholarship, service comprises the third branch of the blessed trinity of the professoriate, at least at my institution. This translates to demonstrating an active interest in curricular issues and in the general welfare of the college. Specifically, it includes serving on committees, advising students, and mentoring younger members of the faculty. We used to call it "collegiality." It's good work but in my view no substitute for either excellence in the classroom or making contributions to one's discipline. I worry lately that some of my can't-say-no colleagues tend to get too wrapped up in university politics, much to the detriment of their scholarly pursuits.

A major part of my service consists of efforts to reach a wider community. I spend considerable time writing for, and speaking to, popular audiences. I think these activities enhance my teaching skills because I'm forced to shed scholarly jargon and become more attuned to the level, language, and general understanding of those I seek to address. The outreach program I developed at the observatory brought the world of professional science into the local schools. Over the years a significant number of grade-schoolers who rode the yellow bus to attend my nighttime public lectures and the observatory sessions that followed have written or called to tell me about their lives as engineers, scientists, even artists and journalists. They relate how their trips to real science facilities helped inspire and motivate them. Some of my most memorable experiences have grown out of my relationship with the local community.

Comets are unpredictable. They appear suddenly out of nowhere and slowly streak from night to night against the starry background, most of them never to return. That's why throughout history, often-unscheduled cometary appearances were thought to portend evil omens. Their advent disturbed the otherwise pristine, predictable quintessence. When Halley's Comet appeared in 1301 (it was not then known to be a recurrent sky event), Giotto likened it to the Star of Bethlehem and so painted it in a work he executed on the ceiling of the Scrovegni Chapel in Padua, Italy. The great comet of 1843, visible as a luminous streak across the western sky at sunset for several weeks, was heralded by the Millerite cult, forerunner of the Seventh-Day Adventist Church, as a "sign in heaven" that the biblical Apocalypse was at hand.

How bright a comet will become (and when) is difficult to predict. That depends on its distance from the earth and how close it gets to the sun. Comets shine both by reflected light and fluorescence caused by the sun exciting the molecules that light up a comet's atmosphere, which it sheds in the form of a tail that grows to millions of miles in length. To complicate matters, not all comets possess the same ratio of dust to glowing gas: lots of dust and you get a faint comet; less, and you get a much brighter one.

Of course, I knew all this back in 1966 when I experienced my first naked-eye comet, Ikeya-Seki. It was named after the two Japanese amateur astronomers who first sighted it. Notice of its impending appearance was disseminated through peri-odic leaflets sent to all astronomical observatories by the International Astronomical Union. These bulletins gave daily positions and other aspects of noteworthy astronomical phenomena for telescopic viewers. I recall being particularly attracted to the "brightness" column in a mid-September notice, which indicated that this particular comet would approach minus eight magnitude by mid-October. Minus eight—that's twenty times brighter than the planet Venus! You could witness it in broad daylight—pretty spectacular, I thought. A few days later I received a call from a reporter at the Syracuse Herald Journal, our nearest big-city newspaper. "What's all this about a bright comet coming to town, professor?" the reporter inquired. After a brief conversation, he persuaded me to write a short-op-ed piece about it for Saturday's edition.

Sometimes we say things we're sorry for later. We've all experienced it—that unfortunate, unintended remark spoken in haste and without much thought. When we goof in the media, the result remains indelibly seared in the historical record, waiting to be mined at any time in the future by searching critics. Of course you can apologize or retract your words, but who reads retractions? As I composed the 500-word piece on Comet Ikeya-Seki, my mind was fixed on that minus eight magnitude figure. I did a little checking. There hadn't been a comet that bright since the 1860s. Even Halley's Comet, in its spectacular 1910 appearance, failed to reach minus eight. (Older readers will recall that Halley was a total bust during its last visit to the inner solar system in 1986; that's because it never got really close to us when it crossed the earth's orbit.) So I penned the words I would later come to regret: "Ikeya-Seki promises to be the most colossal celestial spectacle of the twenti-eth century . . . It will have a dazzling tail longer than the Big Dipper."

Late that Saturday night I got a call from a colleague in the education depart-ment. "I just heard on NBC Monitor news that you discovered a new comet with the Colgate telescope." "Me? Must be some mistake." Though I certainly had not discovered Ikeya-Seki, I appear to have been the first astronomer to go public in making predictions about it. The phone rang again and again—and again. As much as I tried to deny that I'd made any discovery, especially at the still dismally equipped Colgate Observatory, I realized why I had achieved instant popularity as soon as I spotted the front page of the Herald Journal. There was an article headlined "Ursa Major Has Rival." Other page-one news from around the country followed: "Colossal Spectacle Expected: Comet, Bright as Big Dipper, Will Be Visible in U.S. Today (Indianapolis Star), "Fiery Comet Speeds into U.S. View" (Tucson Daily Citizen), "Big-Tailed Comet to Zip into View Today" (my hometown New Haven Register), "Look Skyward Tomorrow for Celestial Spectacle" (New York Times).

AP, UPI, Reuters, and every other media outlet in the land quickly spread word that the tiny dome on the side of a hill in rural Madison County, New York, would be mission control for monitoring the comet. I told inquirers that a telescope isn't required and that you don't even need to be near a real observatory to see a naked-eye comet. Regardless, at their collective request I was forced to open the observatory for public viewing of the phenomenon. Ikeya-Seki was scheduled to appear as a morning comet visible in the east just before dawn. A few weeks after brightening considerably, it would disappear behind the sun for a few days, then return to view in the west after sunset for a few weeks. Astronomers had calculated its hyperbolic orbit, which means, like most bright comets, it would put on a one-time-only show, then vanish forever.

The next morning at about 4:00a.m., I drove up the hill to the observatory. There was then no driveway or parking lot at the humble 400-square-foot blockhouse facility. Normally, the handful of visitors would park by the side of the road and walk 30-odd yards across the grass to the building that housed our humble celestial probe. As I turned onto the main campus road and veered uphill toward the dome, I could see several pairs of moving headlights swarming over the dew-covered grass in the pre-dawn dimness. Other cars were parked along the crowded roadside all the way down the hill. A few dozen people milled around the tiny building, awaiting instructions on which way to cast their gaze. I recall one woman breast-feeding a baby. Would her child be blessed by the light of the cosmic portent? A few of my academic colleagues made skeptical inquiries, an attitude well cultivated in their trade. A couple of geeky kids who aspired to be astronauts (there were many of them in the 1960s) were among the onlookers, as was Clem Henshaw, my *ever-supportive department chair. Most of the rest of the spectators consisted of eager Hamilton townies and new-found fans from my public open-house program, now in its fourth year. A significant number of attendees had driven all the way from Binghamton and Syracuse, over an hour south and northwest of Hamilton, respectively.*

Alas, they had ventured out in vain, for there was no comet to be seen that morning. The fact that the sky was blanketed by 70 percent cloud cover didn't help matters. The next morning dawned clear and frosty cold. Even more cars buzzed their wheels over the slippery, dew-soaked grass. The crowd had doubled in size. So did the farthest distance traveled: two or more hours from Rochester, Oswego, Elmira, and Albany. Why didn't they realize they could view the colossal celestial spectacle from their own backyards? I directed everyone's binoculars and our telescope toward the predicted coordinates. We saw little, maybe a faint hazy patch barely discernible through the telescope. Was this one of those very dusty comets, I began to wonder?

The next day, still no comet. Same for the next. A few days of stormy weather followed. Then another viewing window, but Ikeya-Seki failed to materialize. "Haze Thwarts View of Comet," read an update in the Herald Journal. Gradually, eager anticipation turned ritual into ordeal as the cometary no-show pattern repeated itself. After a couple of weeks of faithful skywatching, my once ardent followers began to fall by the wayside. The first dropouts were the skeptical colleagues, followed by the distant sojourners (I thought of the three wise men of biblical lore who were favored with a far better show), then the townies, even one or two of the wanna-be young astronauts. The media led the chorus of doubting Thomases with pieces like "comet, comet, where is it," which didn't help. After three weeks, only a dedicated sixth grader and a retired psychology professor held out, and then there were none, not even me. The comet was a dud. It just hadn't lived up to expectations.

About three weeks after my minus eight prediction, I awoke just before dawn with a start. Patty, our five year-old, had toppled out of bed. After I repositioned her I thought, "Why not take a peek outside?" I stepped out the back door into the chilly autumn, north country air and there it was—an extraordinarily bright fuzzy object just above the faintly glowing, pre-dawn eastern horizon. Ikeya sported a long, curved luminous tail that arced almost all the way up to the overhead point. It was by any account a colossal celestial spectacle!

I felt vindicated, but in whose eyes? Few took notice of the late-arriving Comet Ikeya-Seki. Turned out it was not favorably situated for extensive primetime viewing in northern temperate climes. And it was visible only for a few days around the time I happened to catch it. But I did get letters from people who witnessed the phenomenon. A woman living on the outskirts of Honolulu wrote: "Professor, you were right! This morning my husband and I were treated to the most colossal celestial spectacle we ever saw. Ikeya had a long tail that pointed straight up out of the ocean and it was glittering." Hawaii's tropical location was better situated for observing the comet. Another skywatcher from Ilion, New York, related: "At about 4:15 PM yesterday, a friend and I saw quite a beautiful spectical [sic]! The light was so bright that when we looked at it (with sunglasses) our eyes watered. On the edge of a nearby cloud there were three vertical rays of bright color—orange, yellow, and steel blue. This lasted about ten minutes. We said at the time that we had never seen anything like it and wondered if it had anything to do with the comet." She and her friend had likely witnessed a "sun dog," caused by the refraction of sunlight through ice crystals in the atmosphere—not related to the comet.

Of all my comet-related fan mail, I cherish no piece more than the touching letter I received from Mrs. Linné Konigsberger of Wilkes-Barre, Pennsylvania: "My daughter and I have been following your adventures with the great comet. Gloria is twelve and she constantly talks about being an astronomer. Are there opportunities for women to work as apprentices or secretaries in astronomy? Gloria loves math and she is skilled at typing. Horseback riding and stamp collecting are her hobbies . . . Any advice you have would be welcomed." In my response I tried to update Mrs. Konigsberger's misconceptions about the role of women in astronomy, which would have fit better with the science of the times a generation or two earlier. Her mom's letter led to direct and lengthy correspondence with Gloria, a very bright kid. I counseled her at a distance about what courses to take and how to study. I advised her to concentrate more on calculating and less on typing. Our handwritten missives continued through her college years, into graduate school, and beyond. After she received her PhD, Gloria became a member, and eventually department chair, of the astrophysics faculty at the prestigious National University of Mexico. Her research on the formation of high-temperature stars and binary star orbits is still based there today. Moral? Service to the public community can bestow unanticipated rich rewards.

Postscript: To this day Ikeya-Seki '66 remains the best comet I've ever witnessed— better than Hale-Bopp, better than West, Hyakutake, and Halley all rolled into one. Ever unpredictable, the comet turned out to be more of a sun grazer than the orbital pundits had anticipated. In fact, it had passed so close to the sun that it was captured and thrown into an elliptical orbit. Ikeya-Seki now has a ninety-nine-year period; it's due back in 2065. Whoever the first young astronomer may be to pick up on it, may that person be endowed with the temperament to disallow words chosen to describe it that exceed the rational bounds of reliable scientific prediction.

In Loco Parentis: I'm Not Your Parent—or Am I?

In loco parentis—in place of the parents. That phrase used to be a hot-button issue on campus, especially during my early years at Colgate. "Look, I'm not your father," I recall telling one of my advisees who had been partying harder than average and cutting too many of his morning classes. It showed in his grades. Some parents argue: "We pay a lot of money to send our kid to your elite residential college. Shouldn't you be responsible for seeing to it that my offspring toes the line?" "We're here to educate," is a typical teacher's response. "We're trained to foster the life of the mind. We're teachers, not babysitters. Besides, students should have learned by now that they need to take responsibility for their behavior when they're away and independent from their parents." When I first cut my pedagogical teeth, there was little doubt about my role: a teacher not only instructed—he advised; he was a confidant, an older brother, a father. That's how it was in the private, all-male, Ivy-ish institution where I first flung open my classroom doors.

Take attendance, for example. Well, we *took* it. Over the years I have waxed and waned in the rigor of my enforcement of this now largely antiquated practice. Frankly, I get annoyed when kids don't show up for class. I take a lot of time to prepare my lectures and hone my discussions, and I want my students to know what's going down firsthand. The anti–*in loco parentis* classroom stance on attendance that I seem to adopt periodically goes like this: "You're paying the money (or someone in your family is). It's costing you $600 an hour to listen to me. If you don't want to tune in, that's just fine with me. Oh, by the way, there will be an hourly exam next Monday covering everything we've done so far." At term's end some complain: "This really isn't fair. I came to all the classes. I studied and still I got a C on the exam. My roommate sleeps in, cuts, and he gets a B." "Well, life *isn't* fair," I'm forced to reply. "Maybe we need to discuss *how* you study. Or maybe your roommate logs a lot of book time you aren't aware of. Maybe he just picks up on certain things quicker than you" (I usually try not to say that). Often, when I used to distribute small, disposable aluminum ashtrays to classroom smokers, instead of wasting time calling names off a class list, I'd also pass a sheet of paper around and ask students to sign in. Of course, you never knew who was signing in for whom. One jokester signed his dog into my class on more than one occasion. (In addition to smoking, dogs were permitted in the classroom as well.) But then, I hardly ever bothered to look at the list anyway.

In the days of *de rigeur* attendance taking, all instructors were required to submit attendance records along with their grades at the end of the term. Each course was supplied with a pink sheet on which the instructor was expected to record course grades and a blue sheet to list the number of unexcused (a note from the dean or the doc at the infirmary) absences for each student. Three cuts a term were permitted, with double cuts for Friday and pre-break class day absences. Exceed the number of cuts permitted and you flunked the course regardless of your grades on the exams and assignments. Period!

One of my recollections from the ancient epoch of attendance taking took place in Professor Henshaw's elementary physics class, the one with all the fancy demos7 . Expressly for this purpose, Clem employed the services of Professor Berkey (we met him earlier at dinner [p. 28]), who always seemed a bit servile in the presence of his imperious chairman. Each day Don would show up with the seating plan and a folder full of blue sheets. Berkey was in charge of all the lab sections and needed to sit in on the course anyway, so he'd pop in unannounced to do a systematic seat check as the lecture proceeded.

This particular day, Clem was lecturing on sound waves. In typical fashion he'd trotted out every tuning fork, bell, whistle, and horn—anything that made noise— and placed them on the demo table at the front of the class, along with a tape recording of trains passing through railroad crossings and cars whizzing around speedways. He'd use these devices to demonstrate phenomena like the Doppler effect, or the change of pitch of a signal emitted by an object as it moves toward or away from you (heard any ambulance or police siren noises lately?). I also taught a section of lab that year, so I watched raptly as the professor skillfully demonstrated different sound frequencies—the plucking of a bass guitar and several ranges of pitch all the way up to the top of the piano, hammered out on tuning forks. Then he picked up an ultra-high-frequency dog whistle and announced: "Now, when I blow this whistle, none of you will hear a sound. That's because the frequency of vibration that comes out of it is beyond the range of detection of any human ear. But you can rest assured, lads, that every dog within a half-mile radius will respond to it." With that the professor pursed his lips, put them to the aperture, and blew, whereupon, as if on cue, Professor Berkey entered the room, attendance sheets in hand—accompanied by laughter and applause.

Given such rigid attendance requirements, one might imagine that students who did cut class would need to fashion pretty creative excuses for doing so. I'm not talking about those whose great-grandmother passed away three times last semester. It's the truly novel excuses that stick with you, the ones so exquisitely conceived that they might be pardonable on the grounds of creativity. One of my favorites was that of the hard-partying Wayne Edmunds, a geology major and Colgate football star. He had arrived back in Hamilton a day later than the rest of the team from an away football game. When he finally got around to sallying in late to class following the previous one he'd blown off, I caught him on the way out the door at the end of the hour. I put on a stern face, and asked, "Okay, Wayne, where the hell were you yesterday?" He gave me a lame look, then his eyes widened. "Professor, you're never going to believe this. On the way home I stopped for a beer at a bar in Manlius" (the drinking age in New York State was still eighteen then). "There was this guy down at the end of the bar. He was having a beer, too, a frosty one in a big glass mug." "Get to the point, Edmunds," I responded impatiently. "Well, he put that half-full mug down on the bar. Then he said some funny words I couldn't understand. He put his hands about six inches over the glass and raised them up very slowly, and you know what happened? That glass followed his hands right up off the bar-top and into the air. He levitated that goddam' mug of beer three feet off the bar, and he kept it up in the air for five minutes! I was so amazed I haven't been able to function since then—can't eat, can't drink, can't even think." How could I possibly expect Wayne to make it to class in such a disturbed mental state?

When I shared this story with my colleague Paul Pinet of Colgate's geology department, he topped me. He told me a tale someone told him when he was teaching at Georgia State. One of his students who had missed class showed up at the next one with his arm in a sling, his head bandaged, his face bruised, and both eyes blackened. When asked what happened, he offered an Edmundian retort: you'll never believe this, but "me and my girlfriend went to the Georgia State Fair last Saturday. We see this guy walking around with a muzzled 500-pound bear. He's *got a sign: $2 to go ten minutes wrestling the bear and win $100. I'm a pretty strong guy and I'm always in need of a few bucks, so I figured, lemme try it. Besides, this bear was an old scraggly looking, tired-out critter. What could happen? So I pay the $2 fee. I go up to the bear and I start bear hugging and trying to rassle him. But the bear just stands there gawking at me. Then I try maneuvering around him from the back; still he doesn't move. Then the guy goes, 'You gotta smack him to get him going.' So I punch the bear in the chest. 'Hit him harder. He can't feel it,' says the guy. Then I hit him two-three times in the snout. 'Harder. Hit him a good one.' So, I tighten my fist, rear back, and haul off a haymaker—a powerful shot right to that bear's nose. Next thing I know the bear goes nuts! He roars at me and smacks me in the face with his big paw. He lifts me way up in the air and body-slams me. Then he jumps up and down on top of me until I'm nearly unconscious." Long pause. "What about the $100?" inquired the skeptical prof. "Did you go the ten minutes with him?" "Ten minutes?" replied the student. "I got taken out of there on a stretcher in two minutes flat. I ended up spending three hours in the emergency room down in Valdosta. Sorry I missed class."*

We professors may say we aren't our students' "away parents," but much of what we practice is gleaned from sound parenthood: we prod and cajole our students to do certain things. We assign them tasks with deadlines, and we reward and punish them. Like good parents we offer a structure, one that allows freedom for them to make decisions for themselves when warranted. Today, we've receded from the old days when we were more intimately involved in our students' social lives. For example, when professors were expected to function as mothers, fathers, and brothers of Colgate students, house parties were not allowed to take place without designated faculty chaperones.

In my first fall term at Colgate, the dean of students asked Lorraine and me to chaperone a party at an on-campus fraternity. Three days in advance, his office sent us a manifesto stating all the rules and our assigned duties thereto appertaining; for example, we were expected to make sure no one violated the age-eighteen New York State liquor consumption law. As I scanned the document I noticed that one of the weekend party rules had been amended to read: "All bedroom doors shall remain open only to the extent that a folded towel may be inserted over the top of the jamb" (it didn't state precisely where on the door the towel needed to be secured or how many towel folds were required) and "rooms shall be fully lighted throughout the party." Apparently, this was some sort of administrative concession to an earlier version with a fully open-door policy.

We arrived at the frat house with little intention of checking every room for ongoing hanky-panky. Just before the house president responded to our knock, I remember saying to Lorraine, "I'm not their father, for God's sake," my breath condensing in the cold night air. Once the crew cut–topped, smiling house president greeted us, our cordial response was drowned out by loud hootenanny-skittle music washboarded out by a live musical group. The strong smell of brew wafted up from a thin film of liquid that covered the floor. Our host handed us a bottle each of Canadian Club and ginger ale and said "welcome, Professor and Mrs. Aveni; you can sit over there," pointing to a sofa next to the fireplace. As many women (long hair, sheath, headband, pearl necklace) as men (tie and coat over a white shirt, white bucks) crowded the dance floor. I cannot imagine how so many young women had managed to materialize at our rural, all-male college. Were they shipped in on flatbed trucks? Everyone seemed to be having a raucous good time. We made nice for a while, poured a mixed drink, and talked to some of the boys, but feeling a bit out of our element, we decided to slip away quietly within the hour.

When I told a senior colleague about our brief experience at the frat house and asked whether he had chaperoned last weekend, he replied, "God no! Joanne and I don't do that any more. Once was enough." He told the story of being given an identical assignment back in the late 1950s under the old regime. He and his wife dutifully marched upstairs, intent on systematically enforcing the open-door rule. Room after room they checked: lights on, door open, lights on, door open . . . until they got to the end of the second-floor hallway, where they confronted a closed door. A band of light emerged through the space just above the level of the floor. The professor and his wife stole up to the door, threw it open, and barged in. There they confronted a young couple engaged in one of the more creative postures associated with the carnal act, its visual details enhanced by an unshaded 100-watt bulb that illuminated the scene from above. Before the young couple could react to the surprise intrusion, the professor bolted, his shrieking wife in tow. They flew through the front door and out into the snowy night, never again to set foot in a student living unit.

————————————

The open-door debate actually goes back a long way; for example, in 1898 Harvard president Charles Eliot wrote "Students living in buildings whose doors stand open day and night, or in scattered lodging houses cannot be mechanically protected from temptation."[8] Eliot was emphatic about the need for students to learn to live responsibly by governing themselves; he did not believe it was the university's job to enforce rules of conduct. Eliot's emphasis on self-reliance resonated with his insistence on free electives in the curriculum (discussed in chapter 3). His words of wisdom about student self-responsibility place him well ahead of his time in the diminution of *in loco*.

The "Greek system" (John Rexine, my late colleague in the classics department, so despised the term that he frequently complained in letters to the campus newspaper that frats had nothing to do with Greek civilization) is still alive and well on American college campuses. Can you believe that as late as the late 1960s, Jewish students were blackballed (denied admission by a single vote) by college frats? Frat and sorority rituals, often fueled by excessive alcohol, seem as silly to me now as they did when I attended college—and sometimes they can be downright dangerous. It isn't just about kids having fun. These social practices, often extolled in the media (*Princeton Review*'s annual Top 10 Drinking Schools comes to mind), are simply unacceptable.

The highly praised 1978 cult classic film *Animal House* is an example. It's really a movie about young people who rebel against their establishment elders, but unfortunately the bad guys are those who run the university, while the heroes emerge out of a bunch of miscreants who live in the frat house. A pair of misfit freshman roomies at the mythical Faber College are rejected by the Omegas, the most prestigious (and smug) goody-goodies on Fraternity Row—the guys who live by the rules. They wind up at Delta House, a haven for the mischievous, low-GPA end of the student body. Meanwhile, the evil dean conspires with the Omegas in his quest to revoke the Delta chapter—for too much beer drinking and just having fun—by setting up a fake exam and engineering failing results for the perceived campus low-lifers. With little to risk, the losers respond by putting on the wildest toga party in Faber annals, replete with scenes of drunken projectile-vomiting and exquisite debauchery. In the party's surprise aftermath the wildest of the Deltas, Bluto (short for John Blutarsky, played to a T by John Belushi), delivers an impassioned speech (How did he magically acquire his rhetorical skills?), exposing the ruse and jettisoning the evil administrator. Beneath its silliness and even allowing for the film's well-intentioned message about young people's fears and frustrations, *Animal House*, to judge from Internet responses more than a generation after it first appeared, is heralded as the epitome of having a good time in college through a social club. I don't mean to imply that student-run organizations don't have a positive impact on colleges. Many of them offer opportunities for developing leadership qualities, getting involved in community service, and other collaborative work. Despite attempts at improvements, though, I think the system still tends to promote too much exclusivity.

"Fratitudes" often make themselves apparent in the classroom. My colleague, geographer Jessica Graybill, remarked to me about the "programmed" nature of a small segment of one of her discussion classes. Four women who sat together often responded exclusively and supportively to each other's comments, almost to the point of finishing one another's sentences. Furthermore, they exhibited the same attitude and posture toward every issue raised in the class. It was as if no one else was involved in the discourse—including the teacher. All four were members of the same sorority. Locally, we speak of this tight inclusiveness as the phenomenon of the "Colgate bubble," the socially engineered sphere of inquiry out of which many students are reluctant to venture. We need to find ways to encourage them to burst the bubble.

Though my institution still harbors fraternities and sororities, the intervening years have seen the abolition of a large number of long-standing rules, such as those I was expected to enforce in my chaperoning incident at the frat house. Within a decade of my arrival, Colgate adopted coeducation; that was followed a decade later by coed dorms (alternating floors by gender and alternating rooms a decade after that). As noted earlier, mandatory chapel attendance was abolished long ago. Our college even did away with the annoying classroom bells that preceded and ended every class. The bells were equipped with electronic vibrators that produced a low buzzing sound intended to warn instructors that there were two minutes remaining in the hour, and then the bells would toll. The episode began when a group of revolutionaries muffled the old dingers by stuffing them with rags. It ended a year later when the administration honored a petition presented by the student senate, though the vibrators survived the assault on the bells and remained operational for some years afterward. Every once in a while a curious student would inquire on the way out the door, "Professor, how come the clocks make those weird noises just before the end of class?" "That, James, is a very interesting story. Got a few minutes?" I'd reply.

Since the early 1980s there has been considerable retrenchment in liberties allowed our students; for example, today there are fewer pass-fail options and independent study courses. Personally, I think that's unfortunate because some of my best work with students came out of guiding them to pursue their own interests. In addition, a greater percentage of students is required to live in dorms rather than in apartments in town. Today, many students tell me they feel oppressed, reined in by an administration that intervenes in their freedoms. Responding to the more litigious attitude in American culture today, universities feel they must be more cautious about the conduct of the lives placed in their care, even if they aren't parenting. We teachers play a role in the overall lives of our students, especially at a residential college. How we relate to them is crucial to fostering learning. We need to know when to intrude and when to hold back, both inside and outside the classroom—a delicate balancing act.

Can We Really Measure Good Teaching?

Twenty years ago a senior member of our economics faculty showed up for a curriculum committee meeting. As he burst through the door, an angry, hurt expression on his face, he complained bitterly, "Goddammit, I'm *not* 90 percent worthless." He had just read his Student Evaluation of Teaching (SET) forms. During the first ten minutes of his final class, students had filled in bubbles with number two pencils in response to statements such as: I studied for this class "not at all" (1) up to "more than for any other class" (10) and relative to my other classes I got "nothing" (1) to "much more" (10) out of the experience. Other questions probed instructor preparation, enthusiasm, and accessibility, all expressed on a decadal scale. Finally: briefly stated, rate percentagewise the contribution of your instructor to your overall learning experience, from (1) "worthless" up to (10) "extraordinary." What had set the professor off were the responses to the last statement, in which the value of the way he practiced his livelihood, in the eyes of the students, was relegated to a single number on the baddest side of the continuum.

The slightly more expansive version of the Colgate SET form that was en vogue from the 1980s up to a few years ago consisted of four "short response" questions confined to a single page:

(1) Why did you take this course?

(2) Describe the effort that you put into this course.

(3) What did you get out of this course? How has this course contributed to your intellectual growth or education? (This question at least requires students to reflect on their own understanding of their intellectual maturation.)

(4) Please describe in precise terms your opinion of the quality of teaching in this course, giving special attention to what you consider important strengths and/or weaknesses.

In classes smaller than twenty-five students, the results are usually typed out by a staff member, a deterrent to teachers with a detective mentality who might hire a handwriting expert to determine which responders dared hurl a barrage of invective at them.

One of the most common responses to Question 4 is: she really knows her stuff, but she doesn't know how to teach. This translates to an instructor's inability or unwillingness to understand the mental capacity of his students and how to work with them effectively. In part, I think, this is a result of the deficiency of teacher training in most new hires. Like me, novice teachers usually come straight out of graduate school where they have focused solely on research. It's a bit like training to practice oral surgery without learning anything about how to deal with your patients as people. Let me reiterate that more graduate schools need to think about including mentorships in teaching as part of their curricula.

Colgate's new SET form, typical of what you'll find at most liberal arts colleges, includes twenty-two quantitative items to be answered by one of six ratings ranging from "strongly agree" to "strongly disagree." About two-thirds of the items are instructor-centered. Example: The instructor explained the material clearly and understandably, was approachable, made grading standards clear, graded fairly, presented material in an interesting way, showed respect and concern for students, was well organized and pre- pared, was open to contributions from all class members, handled questions well, and had high standards. Other questions focus on the course and the student: my interest was motivated and inspired by the material, my appreciation of the topic has increased, it challenged me, I have grown in conceptual understanding/critical thinking, I put a great deal of effort into it.

A qualitative section, consisting of responses to five brief questions on learning reads: describe the effort you put into this course; how did it contribute to your appreciation and understanding of the course subject; in what ways did it contribute to your intellectual growth; how did the instructor's teaching contribute to your learning; and, do you have any specific suggestions that might improve the quality of the teaching? The survey sheet ends by asking the student to state her anticipated grade.

Another form, now up for adoption, deals in far greater depth with the effectiveness of conveyance of course material, teacher-student interaction, grading, and student self-related learning than the document it may replace. These sorts of exhaustive survey tools are symptomatic of the contemporary campus trend—I would say preoccupation—with assessing how well we do our jobs. In the past decade or so, colleges have paid more attention to learning assessment than ever before. How can any teacher regard "how am I doing" as a bad question to ask? But it can be carried to extremes. For example, this past semester, as part of our expanded program of teaching evaluation by peer review, I was required to sit in on two or more classes of each of four junior faculty members and to keep a set of notes for consultation. Each senior faculty member must submit letters of evaluation to the third-year and tenure review files following meetings at which the student evaluations and results of personal classroom visits are assessed. The cases are discussed in full by the department, summarized by the chair, then passed on to the dean of faculty and his review committee of elected faculty. At the same time, the college has been reviewing and reformulating its mission statement as well as redesigning its website. I wonder: Have we become so neurotic about whether we're really doing right by our students that we feel compelled to devote almost as much time to assessing our teaching as to doing it?[9]

But expanded SETs are only part of self-assessment. Many state-supported colleges are being pressured by policy makers to justify, by metric means, whether and how taxpayers' dollars spent on education can be judged effective. The New Leadership Alliance for Student Learning and Accountability, a recently formed coalition of higher-education groups, has asked American colleges to gather evidence related to student learning; for example, giving standardized tests to entering students and repeating the same tests prior to graduation is one suggested way to measure improvement. Critics argue that standardized tests are too narrow. They don't measure what students gain in the areas of problem solving or working collaboratively.[10]

Another way to measure the efficacy of higher education was proposed by a voluntary group representing 300 allied state colleges. Known as the Voluntary System of Accountability (VSA), it would require that in the sample of students tested, learning be measured on a "value-added" basis that takes students' academic baselines into account.[11] The results would be made public so colleges could be compared in the open. The VSA constructs a College Portrait that includes requirements for admission, graduation percentages, academic programs, what the community is like, even a College Affordability Estimator for each participating institution. These data are used to meet requirements for accountability to governing boards, as well as student learning outcomes and institutional improvement applied to the college accreditation process.

This is all very helpful, but the corporate language employed in the proposal annoys me. It seems to imply that we can assess learning the same way we measure success along the ladder of achievement in a big-business enterprise. (Recall our discussion of online learning, where we find the same sort of techno-jargon used in the sales pitch.) We are already aware of the inadequacy of the standardized tests that emerged out of the No Child Left Behind law in elementary, middle, and high schools. Unfortunately, the desire of legislatures to get to a quick, quantitative bottom line, combined with the current cloak of suspicion and distrust cast over American educational institutions (I'll talk about that later), led in part by the corporate sector, places us too close for comfort to the government imposition of standards in my view.

In all aspects of assessment, I think we suffer today from a "metric malaise." We're too obsessed with acquiring quantitative results related to the efficacy of our teaching. Learning is a process that takes place in the mind. For some, it is slow and difficult; so much depends on student attitudes, backgrounds, openness to new things, and an innate willingness to experiment. It's hard to measure. Hyping the value of my lectures or discussions to get better SETs is no substitute for my spending more time trying to figure out who my students really are.

Education just isn't a commodity, and I don't think students in the midst of a classroom experience can fully judge its value. They haven't had the time to determine whether what they learned will make any difference in their lives. I agree with the educator-humanist Stanley Fish, who thinks "deferred judgment" is the best way to evaluate teaching.[12] Unlike the immediate response you might give a waiter to the question "was everything okay," when a student completes a class, it may be years before she knows whether she got her money's worth. I think Fish's restaurant example holds true. I recall one of my fellow teachers, described repeatedly by his students as "just plain boring." Yet when alums ten, twenty years out visit me, they frequently bring up his name and praise him in hindsight for how much they learned in his classroom. Too many college professors teach to the evaluation forms the way public-school teachers teach to the test, says Fish; but, despite his cynical view of SETs, he concedes there is value to evaluation, especially if you include questions like: Does the professor grade assignments in a timely fashion? Does he hold office hours? Does he show up for class on time?

Questions on websites such as the popular Rate My Professors focus more directly on the teacher. You get to voluntarily grade your teachers on a zero-to-five scale in four categories: helpfulness, clarity, easiness, and overall interest. Finally, there's a yes-no category of "hotness" symbolized by a chili pepper (it's colored red if you're "hot"). Wonder what that means . . . ? There's space to add a brief explanatory statement to accompany the numbers.

In studying these data, I discovered an interesting correlation between grades awarded to professors in the "easiness" and "overall" categories. Those who scored highest overall (4.0–5.0) also tended to rank highest in easiness. For teachers perceived as difficult or demanding, that is, scoring 2.5 or less, I found few examples of a high overall rating. Anyone who doubts that grades have anything to do with good classroom ratings needs to look past the numbers; for example, I read the comments that went with the scores of the overall top ten professors, those who racked up scores in the high fours in all categories. I was surprised to find statements like "by far the easiest teacher in the school"; "everyone gets an A"; "it's ridiculous; he tells you the answers to the questions that will appear on the exam"; and "hate to call her a disgrace to the college because she's so nice." The recipients of such comments, need I repeat, are judged to be the *best* teachers.

I don't mean to imply that teachers won't benefit from reading student comments. I read my SETs all the time, even though I cringe when I see phrases such as "he gives too much busy work" or "I came to all the classes, did all the reading, and got only a B—not fair." Surveys and SETs can help the instructor. Many of the lengthier comments students write about my courses point out weaknesses; for example, some assignments that need further crafting by the instructor, ideas and concepts that require clearer explanation, some tangential readings that ought to be dropped. Clarity, organization, and a good sense of humor constitute much of the SET subject matter of inquiry. Overall, I manage to score pretty well although, perhaps because of my bent-over senescence, I haven't managed to qualify for a chili pepper on Rate Your Professors.

In a sense, times haven't changed. The earliest teaching evaluations were conceived back in the 1920s by professors interested in studying how effective they were in the classroom. When I arrived, Colgate had its own underground rating sheet, known as the *Grapevine*, which offered the lowdown on who and what to take. Widespread adoption of SETS didn't occur until the late 1960s and early 1970s at most universities, when they gradually began to be given serious attention in deciding tenure and promotion. Except at the large research-oriented universities, damnation or salvation in the academy today hinges more than in the past on what students write on SETS, especially in smaller colleges that pride themselves on quality teaching. Some professors respond by doing all they can to rack up the highest possible scores. Grading leniently or bringing sweet treats to class on SET-form day are common strategies. One study by educational psychologists found that students offered chocolate prior to filling out SET forms gave more positive evaluations.[13]

Responding to style is another problem with SETs. In a well-known experiment, an actor was hired to give a lecture on "Mathematical Game Theory as Applied to Physician Education." It was an articulate presentation delivered in a highly stimulating manner, accompanied by much charismatic hand waving. The presenter punctuated his delivery with clever witticisms. But the talk also contained a lot of meaningless, irrelevant content. Following the lecture, the distinguished-looking professor answered questions in double talk, frequently contradicting what he had said during his presentation. Evaluations of the pseudo-prof by various audiences, including one composed of professional psychiatrists and graduate students in education, were highly positive.

Despite the skepticism and controversy about SETs and their being likened to popularity contests, psychologist Wilbert McKeachie, who has traced their evolution, concludes that students who learn the most tend to give the most credit to those who taught them.[14] If a teacher's job is to knock students off their preconceived mental rails, one of the problems with student evaluation of teachers is that some students may not be interested in buying what's being sold. A common criticism on sociology and political science SETs is that the teacher disagrees too much with, or has no respect for, students' views. Studies show that students say they learn less from such professors.[15] Basically, we don't like to listen to people who disagree with us or challenge our views. Of course, SETs don't address questions based on any sort of deferred judgment. Rather, they only ask you to assess the product the way you might judge how good your lunch tasted—it's all about immediate customer satisfaction.[16]

Better Grades for Better Students?

My grandson brought over his fourth-grade report card to show me. "I made honors," he said. When, after congratulating him, I asked how many other kids in the class got honors, I received frowning glances from his mother and grandmother. Grade inflation is rampant in American education today. In the early 1960s at Colgate the overall GPA, or grade point average (on a scale of 0 for F to 4.0 for A), was 2.3, a C+. You had to work hard for a "gentleman's C," as those enrolled in my then-all-male institution called it. Between 1963 and 1969 the average GPA shot up to a B, or 3.0. Since then it has slowly ascended to 3.2 (a B+ is 3.3). Grades are generally highest in the humanities, lowest in the sciences. Economics and chemistry, among the most competitive disciplines, bolster the downside.

Colgate is not alone; other small liberal arts colleges display similar trends. For example, at Reed College, 33 percent of the students in fall 2007–8 classes received As (up 3% in the last decade), while 51 percent got Bs. DePauw registered 45 percent As (up 10% for the same period) and 41 percent got Bs. Hope College instructors were more generous (57% As, 30% Bs); compare that with its 1960s numbers (19% and 44%, respectively). At Brown, 95 percent of students registered either an A or a B; at Macalester 91 percent; Grinnell 90 percent; James Madison 90 percent. Following a pledge in 2004 to battle grade inflation by capping A grades at 35 percent, Princeton still registered 41 percent As (down only 6%) and 49 percent Bs (up 6%). Graders at large universities were only marginally more difficult; for example, compare University of North Carolina at Chapel Hill (45% A, 37% B), Georgia Tech (42% A, 34% B), and Penn State University (44% A, 33% B). PSU's 1951 numbers offer a stark contrast in grade distribution trends in the American university (21% A, 37% B, 29% C).[17] To make itself more competitive, one not-so-prominent law school recently elevated all student GPAs by 0.3.

Competitive high schools routinely name multiple valedictorians; for example, a suburban Houston institution recently graduated thirty of them, 6.5 percent of the class. Eight schools in a Colorado district had a total of ninety-four, and another in Southern California awarded valedictory status to all students who achieved a GPA of 4.0 or better; there were twenty-three in that category.[18] Why these trends?

"We're getting better students now." That's the refrain we hear from many who dole out more As than Bs. But leniency in grading may have as much to do with the general rule-bending tendency in universities. I think it goes along with the lassitude exhibited by many teachers who routinely allow students to turn in late or incomplete assignments without penalty. Overburdened with administrative duties and writing assignments of their own, some faculty members become poor role models; many arrive in their classrooms late and insufficiently prepared. Like busy parents who feel they neglect their children, they make amends for their guilt by rewarding their students more generously.

I think the perception that education is a commodity is also related to grade inflation. Recently, one of my freshmen who failed to excel on her midterm charged into my office in tears and complained indignantly: "How could you give me a B? I've never received a grade below an A in my life." I invited Valerie to look through the test with me. In the midst of our postmortem she burst into an even higher-voltage throb: "What do you expect? I came to every class. I did the reading. I took notes. Why did you give me such a low grade?" Valerie was only expressing the widely held idea in most students' minds that "A is for effort." I'd heard it before: if I do everything you ask, from completing the assignment to attending class, and my maximum effort nets me a B or a C, then what's the point; how else can you evaluate me other than by the effort I put in? Now, most of my students are well aware that if intercollegiate athletics were based on such principles, all sports teams would end up league cellar dwellers. Why, I wonder, do students find it so difficult to translate the importance of performance, achievement, and concrete results from the athletic to the academic field?

"*Engagement* is what I expect," I explained to Valerie after pointing out several answers on her exam that proved she didn't really *get it*. "A grade isn't *what I give*; it's *what you earn,* and that's determined by how successfully you engage the subject matter. In my class it isn't work alone that determines the value of what you achieved," I tried to convince her. "It has more to do with how you *perform*—it's mostly about the *quality* of the work you do in my class." Like many students, Valerie felt entitled. Her family had paid a lot of money for her education. As her service representative, why was I defaulting on the deal? She expected an A. After talking with her, I realized that one of Valerie's problems was that she hadn't learned the importance of listening (recall the discussion on p. 110). The anticipation of high grades blocks any real desire to listen. If buying an education were no different from buying a car, she'd have a legitimate complaint. Unfortunately, in today's world education has become a commodity. One study on why students exhibit this sense of entitlement concluded that increased parental pressure and competition among both peers and family members contribute to a greater sense of anxiety about the need to achieve.[19]

Marketing and vocationalism play a huge role in the issues of grade pressure and perceived student entitlement. Today, going to college is viewed as an inalienable right. It's what you do after you graduate from high school, not to mention it's the key to a good job. Lately, however, a new generation of students thinking about college is beginning to sway from this doctrine. This may account for why, in 2010, the United States fell to twelfth place worldwide in the percentage of people awarded college degrees. Colleges respond to this competitiveness by "developing their brand" with elaborate websites, extended campus tours, ad videos, and campus visit days for prospective students. These were never part of the college scene when I was a student. Today, students and parents are attracted to places where they know they stand a better chance to acquire a degree that looks good—provided they can afford it. The equation "education equals opportunity" still remains fixed in American life. There's a happy ending to my story about Valerie, by the way. After extended tutoring during office hours, she became motivated to work on her weaknesses. She redoubled her effort and finally *earned* an A.

One of the largest, most thorough surveys of data on how college has actually affected students since the 1980s paints an optimistic picture. Educational analysts Ernest Pascarella and Patrick Terenzini report that, in fact, students made "statistically significant freshman-to-senior-year gains on a variety of discussions of learning and cognition," especially in verbal and speaking skills.[20] When these authors reviewed the comparative literature going back to the 1960s, they discovered that "consistent cognitive, attitudinal, value, and psychosocial changes have occurred over the past fifty years."[21] Large or small, urban or rural, our colleges *do* teach students to think in more critical and reflective ways, to acquire more tolerant values and attitudes, and to attempt to cultivate an interest in cultural and artistic activities. College *does* help them acquire a better sense of identity and expand their "interpersonal horizons,"[22] as well as their intellect. On the practical side, the one that continues to matter most to investors in the collegiate enterprise, those who attend college achieve long-term positive gains, such as higher occupational status, earnings, and quality of life—and so do their children. Regarding deferred judgment, according to a survey involving 24,000 participants, college alumni report that their undergraduate experience was either positive or highly positive (75%).[23]

Are students brighter now than when I first started teaching? Grades aside, yes, even if the quantitative and reading skills they bring to my classroom are somewhat diminished. As a result, I have been forced to dummy down my classes a bit. And even though I admit to such academic heresy, I still receive a dismal 2.6 easiness grade on "Rate Your Professors."

Why Are Professors under Siege?

The early 1980s, one of my J-term projects. My students and I were traveling in vans across the Yucatan Peninsula surveying Maya pyramids. When we got to the ruins of Uxmal, we decided to splurge by spending one night at the new Club Med hotel across the road from the site. Before dinner a few of us gathered around the pool to relax. I was fairly exhausted from three long days of trekking through the brush and climbing up and down unexca-vated mounds trucking loads of measuring equipment. As I lay stretched out on a chaise, half-asleep in the late afternoon sun, I overhead the kids chat-ting. Matthew, one of my seniors, casually remarked, "Well, four months left after we get back. Looks like I gotta get serious about facing the real world." I mulled over his words: Had I contributed to making Matthew's col-lege engagement seem *unreal*? Isn't college supposed to consist of a gradual immersion into learning how to live a responsible and productive life? Maybe Matthew thought of college as some sort of holding tank, a protective buffer against what life's really like on the other side. (Do supermarket lobsters think the same thing as they peek out the glass window of their tank?) Had Matthew not thought seriously about the college experience during the past three-and-a-half years? But most important to me was the question, what are we doing (or not doing) to give him that impression?

Why, despite the increased perception that we all must go to college to succeed, has the experience of *being* in college become so devalued? That's a subject about which much has been written and discussed, especially since the beginning of the 1980s, when the balance of power in US politics took a conservative tilt. The fact that the 1980s produced the loudest anti-curricular complaints makes sense. The turmoil that had centered around question-ing American ideals and institutions began early in my career. The late 1960s and early 1970s were tension-filled years on American college campuses. The spring term of 1968 witnessed the assassination of Martin Luther King Jr. (on April 4). A few months earlier, one of our Jewish students had been blackballed by a fraternity. Just days after the assassination, a racial incident took place: the firing of blanks from a gun as one of our thirty-five enrolled black students walked by a fraternity house. Led by the recently formed on-campus Association of Black Collegians, a rally was held and a protest march on the Administration Building ensued. I was one of a minority of faculty who joined the sit-in that followed. The group that occupied the Ad Building demanded that the Colgate Board of Trustees revoke the charter of the offending frat. Unlike similar encounters with perceived establishment forces at other universities over pressing social issues—Columbia, Wisconsin, and UC Berkeley come to mind—our affair was settled peacefully. The board suspended the charter. But other campus demonstrations followed in suc-cessive years, as the college campus became the focal point for elevating the national conscience regarding social justice and our country's questionable involvement in world affairs: protests against the bombing of Cambodia, the march on Washington, and the Kent State massacre.

Challenges to our educational mission came in the 1970s with the feminist movement and an increase in the diversity of cultures attending American universities. The altered mix within student bodies began to seek curricular change by pushing to make room for issues, texts, ideas, and authors that mattered to them (see my discussion of Core in p. 56). In the ensuing backlash, conservative educators argued that, ruled by an attitude of political correctness, such curricular inclusions—many of which were already beginning to be implemented—are far less important than those that define our long-held Western ideals. New curricula only promote causes that come and go with the fashion of the times.

The title of Allan Bloom's timely best-seller cuts to the soul of the attack on the "New Left" curriculum from the conservative quarter.[24] Published in 1987 and with over a half-million sales in hard copy, Bloom's book was the talk of the campus. It had followed a blistering essay he wrote for the *National Review* in which he charged universities with abdicating the needs of their students. He linked the rise of cultural relativism to the abandonment of reason and the cancerous growth of a new pseudo-philosophy, an ideology based on commercial pursuits. Bloom even lashed out at pop music, calling it erotically sterile and designed to convince students that their rebelliousness constituted genuine politics. One liberal reviewer called Bloom an academic Ollie North (of Iran-Contra fame during the Reagan administration)—hostile, reactionary, and anti-democratic.

The culture wars I talked about in chapter 3 were in full swing then. Within academia, *The Closing of the American Mind* accused those who devised the new college curricula of having no focus, no integration, and no idea of what an educated person should know. Bloom believed colleges were ruled by specialists who cared mainly about research and too little about the quality of their teaching, merely casting bones to anyone outside their field in the form of a smattering of disconnected electives.[25] But above all, what Bloom and fellow detractors[26] feared most was the academy's disregard for the old standards—the "great books" that had long represented academic ideals, like the Old and New Testaments and books by Homer, Aristotle, Milton, Shakespeare, and so on.

Love, as well as the pursuit of honor and glory—the qualities Bloom cherished—can be pursued only in the study of Western literature, he argued. I disagree. Having immersed myself in interdisciplinary learning, I believe they are real and present in varied forms in literature from all over the rest of the world. One only need seek them out and engage them. Let me offer an example. I spend quite a bit of time in my seminar "Comparative Cosmologies" discussing the qualities of the hero in the Popol Vuh, the Maya story of creation. My students are fascinated to read that the Maya hero possessed a different set of attributes than his Greek counterpart. They are fascinated, too, when they discover that Maya mathematics is in many ways quite unlike the mathematics of the West—but it is still mathematics. Bloom's intense focus on teaching Western truths is accompanied by his failure to take seriously, indeed to acquaint himself with, other valid ways of knowing. Immersion in the qualities of character extolled in the literature of *non*-Western cultures, alongside the study of the great literary works of the Western canon, can serve as a mirror through which to view our own culture. Bloom might have learned something had he sought to focus his deep interest in Nietzsche through a comparative cultural lens.

Traditionalists cling to the idea that there are specific works acknowledged over the ages that deal with the deepest issues of human meaning and that we all should read them. Precisely which ones make the top ten list depends on whom you ask. Which texts do we choose to define legitimacy in the university curriculum on literature? Which are indispensable in the canon to which all educated liberal arts students ought to be exposed? Which periods are the most important? Does excluding a particular work make it unworthy?

Or, ask progressives, is the very idea of a canon of excellence prejudicial, elitist, and hierarchical? The idea that traditionalists should represent the entire species by reference to the contributions of the West seems to me both unwarranted and insular, especially when it's professed by many whose backgrounds demonstrate a profound lack of inquiry into cultural ideals other than their own. How can you pass judgment without acquiring knowledge? We should also ask what we mean by Western, especially in a time of vastly changing diversity in both the nation's and the university's populations. Isn't the traditional notion of what we mean by that term always changing? As the interpretation of the US Constitution is bound to change with historical circumstances, shouldn't an educator's view of what's most important, what's indispensable, change too?

Just as the US Constitution has strict constructionists, so does the literary canon. Conservatives say the loss of objectivity is embedded in the philosophy of the literary left, which inspires a loss of rigor and constraint. On the other side of the coin, if that steadfast canon appeals to the idea of excellence and addresses the most deep-seated issues of meaning to the upper-class white males who created it, can it really deal with the thoughts, ideas, and passions of women and people of color? Though their worldviews can be palpably impacted by the canon, their inclusion in the curriculum can enrich the process of acquiring knowledge with another kind of aesthetic. And so, the revisionists, or anti-traditionalists, envision an ever-changing canon.

Professors in the humanities have emerged as the most embattled sector of the campus culture wars. Facing declining enrollments (Harvard and University of Virginia English majors down 20 percent over the last decade, and departmental closures in German, philosophy, and world languages and culture at Penn),[27] the humanities are looking for new ways to reshape their programs. A generation after Bloom, Harvard English professor Louis Menand highlighted the continued lack of agreement on a paradigm for the humanities.[28] He did a contrast of 2010 English department requirements at two first-rank liberal arts colleges. The traditional approach, taken by Wellesley's English department, required ten courses for the major (part of the more-is-better philosophy), eight of which must be in literature and at least two of which must deal with pre-1900 texts and one with pre-1800 texts. In addition, all students are required to take a course each on literary criticism and Shakespeare. Interdisciplinary courses, with a single exception, are not counted. At the other extreme, Amherst's anti-traditional English department loses both the Core and period requirements. Their students take only one lower- and one upper-level course out of a total of ten. Courses may come from outside the department, but students need to argue to the department the interrelatedness of the three courses in the package they choose.

Menand is careful to note that the contemporary uncertainty about what the canon ought to be that has percolated down to the undergraduate curriculum is part of the intellectual revolution that has taken place in research and writing in humanistic disciplines as a whole. He refers specifically to the period between 1970 and 1990, when the humanities "helped make the rest of the academic world alive to issues surrounding objectivity and interpretation and to the significance of racial and gender difference."[29] This happened as a result of "boundary suspicion" between the disciplines replacing "boundary respect," and it coincided with a loss of respect for professionalism in general. Anti-disciplinarity gave way to inter-disciplinarity.

The scientific canon also came under attack during the culture wars era, especially following the 1980s and early 1990s in works such as *The Flight from Science and Reason* and *Higher Superstition*.[30] Einstein, Copernicus, and Galileo are all old, white European males, noted detractors from the left. Retorted the deconstructionists: defining objective truth is an impossible task.

Is science an objective way of knowing, an enterprise that seeks to reveal the *real* workings of the natural world, or is it a projection of social or cultural forces—that is, a mere social construct? (Recall my story about the course I co-taught on "Evolution" [p. 68].) Nobel laureate physicist Sheldon Glashow takes the ideology of the universality of science to the extreme end of the continuum. He thinks the underlying truths about nature are "objective, extrahistorical, socially neutral," that they are knowable, and that they constitute "verifiable, genderless, inviolate, invariable" natural laws that are verifiable not only by us but by any hypothetical, intelligent alien who might hail from any part of the universe. Anyone, says Glashow, would discover the same logical system as our own to explain the structure of protons and the nature of supernovas. He concludes his credo with the words "this is my faith."[31] Many of my students are surprised to learn that a scientist's belief system can embrace *faith*, a word usually confined to religious thought.

If you sensed a defensive posture in Glashow's words, it's probably because he wrote them at the frontline of the assault on science by an anti-reductionist brigade of humanistic scholars, among them Sandra Harding[32] and Bruno Latour.[33] Harding, a philosopher, charged that science is hierarchical, authoritarian, and dominated by men. That claim has been answered in the two-plus decades that have passed, in which the number of women in science has increased dramatically.[34] For example, between the mid-1980s and the mid-20 aughts, the number of BAs in all science fields achieved by women has risen from 45 percent to 55 percent. But do these complaints speak to the way science is done? Harding claims there are non-Western and feminine ways to do science that are different from the traditional ways.

As a person who has dedicated himself to the study of the pursuit and means of acquisition of precise knowledge in other cultures,[35] I can sympathize with Harding to a degree. Assuming that science incorporates hypothesizing how nature will behave by testing one's ideas through the gathering of relevant data, logically subjecting it to quantitative analysis, and using the results to certify or modify the original hypothesis, I have shown that the ancient Maya behaved no differently. They constructed the Venus Table in the Dresden Codex, an algorithm capable of predicting the time of the first appearance of Venus in its cycle to an accuracy of one day in 500 years. In my view, Harding's quarrel has more to do with the ends to which acquired scientific knowledge would apply. She shares a stage with environmentalists who attack the techno-aspects and invasive practices of the scientific enterprise.

Latour, a French sociologist, is a social constructivist. He assails the very roots of scientific epistemology acquired during the historical Enlightenment: the separation of subjective and objective thinking, or what amounts to the social and the natural, which he regards as a wrong turn. Latour postulates nothing less than a new "politics of nature."[36] For him, the natural world isn't just "out there" to be engaged "such at it is"; and making a distinction between *facts* and *values* gets us nowhere because what we mean by nature is itself socially constructed.

As comparative literature professor Oscar Kenshur points out, Latour's critique is really aimed at the historical development of his own sociological discipline.[37] He doesn't deal with the core issue of whether the basic reality out there, defined by Glashow, is addressed by science. What we really need to decide, argues Kenshur, is whether, on a case-by-case basis, there is any ideological dimension to a particular scientific theory or there is or is not a belief that serves ideological interests that are scientifically plausible, apart from how useful that belief is.

Where does the debate about canonic science fit into the curriculum? Today, both Core and elective science courses in the colleges reviewed in chapter 3 reflect the interdisciplinary approach to the acquisition and transmission of knowledge that grew out of the culture wars. Though it deals primarily with non-Western cultures, my own work in archaeoastronomy is now called "cultural astronomy." What I once thought of as the merging of archaeological and astronomical skills that might lead to objective knowledge of the practice of astronomy in ancient cultures has expanded to address contemporary indigenous societies as well—call it *ethnoastronomy*. In effect, cultural astronomy, as practiced in contemporary academia, reflects the role social, political, and religious issues play in our attempts to understand nature.

In the closing decades of the twentieth century, turmoil in the American professoriate passed well beyond the issue of curricular content. America's corporate-dominated culture forces higher education to focus on how to help students get jobs, which detracts from what a college's mission ought to be—namely, to teach students how to reflect thoughtfully and independently on problems and issues. Advocates for progressive change point out that the trouble with most of their detractors is that they offer no alternative beyond advocating returning things to the way they were. To when—ten, twenty, thirty years in the past? Fear of change permeates most objections—fear of loss (of standards), fear of deterioration (of sound curricula), and fear of neglect (of students). Despite the data I quoted earlier on student improvement since the 1980s, a worried attitude pervades us—that America may pay the price for the flimsy diploma that will result from this cheapened, diluted form of education and that will impoverish our future leaders.

How Do We Teach in a Dummied-Down Culture?

As a student of ancient Maya civilization, I became particularly fascinated with the extraordinary attention post-Y2K American pop culture devoted to predictions about the apocalyptic end of the world. Said to have been foretold in the ancient Maya inscriptions, the latest version of apocalypse was due to take place on December 21, 2012, according to a number of self-styled prophets who increasingly flooded the Internet with doomsday predictions—close to a billion hits if you Googled "Maya 2012" just prior to that date: giant flares will erupt on the sun and cause the earth's magnetic field to overturn; a planetary lineup will produce massive earthquakes; we'll collide with a giant comet. In response to many e-mails from people genuinely frightened by what they had been reading, I decided to write a book on the 2012 phenomenon.[38]

I tried to explain why archaeologists and epigraphers have roundly dismissed these claims, which are based on distorted, misunderstood evidence from the Maya record, along with wild conjecture about the occurrence of catastrophic natural phenomena. The scientific side of me found it especially interesting that those who claim access to secret knowledge have developed the skill of pirating scientific lingo to impress the uninitiated reader. One such statement I'm fond of quoting has to do with a universal bliss-out slated to occur on 2012's winter solstice: "This would be the most opportune time for us to reconnect with the heliotropic octaves in the solar activated electromagnetic field," which will "cause the senses to attain new revelations."[39] I expected smiles when I read this meaningless statement to one of my classes until one student raised a hand and asked, "What's wrong with that?" His response gave me a real sense of not only how low the level of science education in American schools has sunk but also how easy it is to impress people with sophisticated language—all style, no substance.

In his book *The Dumbest Generation*, Mark Bauerlein quotes a number of howlers from Jay Leno's "Man on the Street" interviews with twenty-somethings:[40]

Q: Do you remember the last book you read?
A: Maybe a comic book.

Q: Where does the pope live?
A: England

Q: Where in England?
A: Paris

Q: Do you ever read any of the classics?—pause—Anything by Charles Dickens—pause—*A Christmas Carol*?
A: I saw the movie. I liked the one with Scrooge McDuck better.

Author Susan Jacoby cites these relevant statistics: 27 percent of *college graduates* think all living beings have always existed in their present form.[41] Nearly half are not aware that the original thirteen colonies are located on the East Coast. When it comes to scientific literacy, the stats are just as appalling. A 1988 National Science Foundation survey of 2,000 adults over age eighteen revealed that one of four respondents didn't know whether the earth goes around the sun or the sun goes around the earth. Only half said it takes a year for the earth to orbit the sun (17% said one day, 2% said one month, and one in ten didn't know). Just under half believed (correctly) that electrons are smaller than atoms, and ⅔ thought lasers work by focusing sound (not light) waves.[42]

Okay, more amusing anecdotes and stats, but if we reflect on them, they portray a culture that knows shockingly little about history, civic affairs, science, literature, and current events. Bauerlein blames the fact that people read less during the extraordinary amount of time they spend in front of computer screens. Like Sherry Turkle (p. 110), he makes a strong case that the techno-digital revolution has decreased the size of the social universe of the younger generation, who carry on a narrow, self-absorbed dialogue that excludes almost everything that matters in the real world. To put it simply, "The more they attend to themselves, the less they remember the past and envision a future."[43] Survey data back Bauerlein up: in 1966, 60 percent of college students believed it was very important to keep up with political affairs; by 2005 that figure had dropped to 36 percent. Performing arts attendance has declined noticeably; so has that in museums and libraries. Statistics on time spent studying are relevant here. In the University of California system, for example, students said they spent, per week, an average of twelve hours socializing, eleven hours playing computer games, six hours in front of the TV, six hours exercising, five hours on hobbies, and thirteen hours studying.[44]

Cyberphiles argue that there's a lot more to e-literacy than downloading tunes and consulting your iPhone or tablet. It isn't all fun and fantasy. Screen time offers new skills and presents novel aptitudes, they argue; for example, video games speed up and enhance spatial intelligence, and reality games help develop a young person's capacity to work with others. The new brain that multi-tasks is just different from the old one that fixates on one thing at a time. But tests show that whatever lessons stem from the avalanche of information acquired through screen time don't last long—the learning doesn't stick. According to Bauerlein, students enrolled in schools that use computers in the classroom performed no better on reading, writing, and quantitative skill tests than those who did not.[45]

What types of info make up the information revolution? Jacoby thinks there are two kinds of "junk science"; first there's pseudo-science, or unsubstantiated allegations based on erroneous "facts"; then there is the politically derived form of that term, which, she claims, has been applied by extreme politically conservative groups to studies that run against their agenda (Jacoby includes global warming and DNA testing in her long list).[46] "Junk Science II" is part of an anti-intellectual demeanor that runs through much of American culture. She places it under the broader heading of junk thought in general, defined as anti-rational, contemptuous of countervailing facts and expert opinion, and "thriving on accusing the other of being the sole source of irrationality."[47] According to Jacoby, the media promote junk thought by feasting on the opportunity to air bizarre theories, along with the public appetite for controversy. Cloaking it all in meaningless scientific jargon makes it look more impressive. The proliferation of the Internet, a domain where anyone—expert or non-expert—is accorded equal access and treatment, makes it very difficult for the common citizen, especially one deficient in quantitative reasoning, to discern truth from fiction (recall my inquiring student in the 2012 example). Peggy Noonan's classification of the mental state of America's forty-third president in this chapter's epigraph is echoed in Harold Bloom's characterization of the "aggressive ignorance" of those who aspire to public office as one of the dismal consequences of America's waning higher-education programs.[48]

Dissing the expert is another trait associated with junk thought. Anyone who presents scientifically established evidence in a peer-reviewed journal is open to being accused of bias based on political motivation, usually by someone with an opposing viewpoint. So much expert bashing goes on in the media that the public becomes conditioned to the likelihood that *nobody* is really telling the truth—whether it's a TV meteorologist arguing against the existence of global warming, a climatologist arguing for it, or someone alleging that NASA conjured up the moon landings as a hoax. Hollywood adds to the confusion by annually dealing out disaster and conspiracy films by the dozens.

How does all this shake out in my workaday world? When I enter the classroom today, I get the sense that I am less regarded as a learned individual to be sought after for knowledge and truth—the way I thought of my professors when I attended college. Today's popular version of the so-called egghead is more in tune with President Eisenhower's well-known characterization of the intellectual as one who uses more words than he needs to in order to say more than he actually knows.[49] In today's anti-intellectual environment, the academic is generally reviled as too liberal, socialist (which used to mean Communist), not at all acquainted with the lives of real people, and godless for sure. Would you place your innocent child under the influence of such a monster?

Rutgers philosophy professor Bruce Wilshire attributes student disconnectedness and aversion to inquiry to a combination of their sense of a rampant betrayal of trust affecting American society and a general cynicism about intelligence acquired through schooling.[50] Many young people believe that beneath the carefully worded speeches of our leaders lie selfishness, greed, and ambition. This cynical attitude conditions apathy and leads most students to think of education as a mere commodity. Money buys everything, so your best bet is to pay your dough, shut your mouth, serve your time, and get your ticket to success—a college degree. "The possibility that knowledge could only be earned through diligent and at times drudging effort to come up to the standards native to the enterprise of knowing oneself had apparently never entered most of their [students'] minds," writes Wilshire.[51]

Teaching is a more challenging profession today than it was when I began my career over fifty years ago. The writing and reading skills and especially the ability to carry on face-to-face conversation are impoverished in most of my students compared with those of, say, thirty years ago. So, too, is the fund of general knowledge they come equipped with, especially history, world affairs, and geography. On one of our J-term visits, we were driving east from Belmopan, the Belizean capital, toward Belize City. As we entered the urban area and sighted the coast, one of my students pointed to the vast body of water before us and inquired, "Professor, what's the name of that ocean?" When I told next semester's class our forthcoming field project in archaeo-astronomy would include a visit to the Maya ruins of Copan, Honduras, another asked, "Is that in Peru?" Why didn't my students acquire such basic skills in high school?

In his book *The Knowledge Deficit*, educator Eric Hirsch makes a case for the common knowledge base he believes ought to be taught in our schools.[52] He claims that it should consist at least of what any good newspaper writer would assume her readers already possess. On the other hand, experiences have taught me that while there will always be a lot of stuff my students don't know, I often find they know things I never guessed.

The Life of Mind and Body: Do They Really Go Together?

What are the odds of the same person getting struck by lightning twice? (One in 9 million.) What are the odds of getting hit by a meteorite? (One in a quadrillion.) That did happen to Mrs. Hulitt Hodges of Sylacauga, Alabama, in 1955. She was sitting in her living room watching afternoon soaps on her small-screen black-and-white TV when, all of a sudden, a 9-pound falling star crashed through the roof, bounced off the top of a dresser, and smote her a blow on the left thigh. Thanks to the intervening furniture she received only a nasty purple bruise about 2 feet across on her hip and buttocks. What about the probability of having a metal staple driven into your scalp on successive New Year's Eves? That happened too—to me.

There aren't many venues for New Year's Eve parties in tiny Hamilton, New York—population 3,600. One common gathering for faculty at the college, especially back in the old days, was the Faculty Club BYOB potluck. On the last night of the year we'd gather there, dance to 45 rpms on a little portable record player, and make merry until the wee hours. At the stroke of midnight we'd go around with our silly hats and noisemakers greeting one another. Needless to say, some of us libated beyond the norm, but that's a common occurrence at the end of a major cycle of time—in this case the semester—in all cultures, civilized or not. Think of it as a way of letting off steam before the purification ritual of making New Year's resolutions that accompanies the start of a new life cycle the morning after.

"Crazy Ed" Ashnault was a fixture at practically all of these parties. That's what members of his ever-struggling basketball squad affectionately called him because of his emotional courtside passion. Ed could out-protest and out-yell any coach, and he could throw a chair twice as far as the legendary furniture mover Bobby Knight. Off court he was a good friend, a great golf partner, and pretty well-read. Ed would lovingly weave his way through the party scene on New Year's Eve, hugging the ladies with a "Happy New Year" and back-slapping all the guys. On one such occasion he flailed his way over to my side of the room. "Aveni," he shouted from a distance (for some strange reason, athletes and scientists at American colleges have a habit of calling one another by their last names), "Happy New Year, old partner!" As he approached me, his hammy hand loomed ominously over my right shoulder. I turned and dropped down a bit to avoid the anticipated blow, and the paw landed on the tip of my cone-shaped chapeau. The force flattened the cone, and the single staple that held it together penetrated the epidermis of my skull. There was too little hair on my head to cushion the strike, which made the contact all the more painful. I reached a finger up toward the offending pain center and could feel the tiny U-shaped piece of metal embedded at its two end points in my scalp. It took some effort to pry the offending object loose with my thumbnail, and for several days thereafter I nursed what resembled the sting of some tiny asp descended from the sky.

Fast forward 365 days. New Year's Eve at the Faculty Club. There we were, having broken all our resolutions long ago, letting off steam once again. Same setup. Tiny phonograph sounding out a few new tunes. Same excellent potluck fare and, as usual, more than enough to drink. Usual crowd. Some we hadn't seen last year had returned from sabbatical, and there were a few young initiates. Lots of old-timers and, once again, my ever-affectionate friend Ed. At the stroke of midnight I skillfully positioned myself at the antipode, thinking I might escape his uncontrollable embrace. But he spotted me. "Aveni, Happy New Year," his hug-seeking limbs flailing. As he approached I tried a new maneuver, positioning myself behind Jerry Balmuth, my colleague in the philosophy department. "Hey Jerry, Happy New Year," Ed croaked, momentarily redirecting his salutation. Then, as if casting a dragnet, he swept his arm out over both our heads. Twixt armpit and elbow he made contact with the philosopher, who deftly deflected the lower portion of the arm between ulna and wrist toward me. The palm slammed onto the top of my head, once again flattening my silly cone-shaped hat and driving the staple home—a mere two inches from last year's strike! This time, however, only one end of the staple penetrated my skin (the other half was flattened). I still consider it a direct hit, though. I figure, as with lightning, there's no way you're half-struck.

I have not attended a Faculty Club New Year's party since. They were discontinued a few years later; that was three years after dear Ed was let go when our team fell below 500. Besides, I couldn't imagine getting my noggin stapled three years in a row. What are the odds?

One of the social pluses of teaching in a small college is that I get to know colleagues well outside my discipline. It gives me a chance to appreciate ways they all contribute to the same educational mission that engages me, even if some of them reside in the Division of Athletics. To judge from any college catalog, one might get the impression that sports have little to do with the business of learning. But visit a campus or read a college newspaper (ours devotes more than 25% of its content to athletic contests) and you will learn otherwise.

When, how, and why did this strange marriage between mind and body take place in the academy? It stems from the basic moral goal that a sound mind deserves to be encased in a sound body. Back in the early nineteenth century, in addition to doing gymnastics, college students were encouraged to spend time outside class digging ditches and helping plant and harvest local products. But many chose to expend their physical energy roughhousing. After 1850, athletics in American colleges acquired a history of violence and corruption. Intramural class "rushes" paired teams from different dorms in rugby-like football, which eventually became ritualized hazing in which young men would seek fellows of like sort to exercise with. One dictionary definition of haze, "to intimidate by physical punishment," seems to me quite consistent with another, "to season or mellow."

Historian Brian Ingrassia traces the first intercollegiate athletic contests to the 1870s, when students and local supporters, not university administrators, began to see competition on the field—first football, then baseball and basketball—as a source of school and town pride.[53] It wasn't long before physical fitness became part of the college curriculum. All the schools with which I have been associated have had two- to four-year phys ed requirements.[54] Recently, Colgate removed it from the curriculum, along with the graduation requirement that all students must swim a complete lap in the Olympic-size natatorium.

Ingrassia argues that progressive reformers and professors saw competitive athletics as a way of making colleges seem less elite. Yale, Harvard, Princeton, and later the University of Chicago led the way in fostering athletic competition among schools as university policy. This happened in the 1880s and 1890s. Regional goodwill was accompanied by revenue intake, which led to the construction of bigger and better stadiums and gyms, along with the appointment of athletic directors who had developed a knack for recruiting superior athletes. Many of them, like Amos Alonzo Stagg at Chicago and Walter Camp at Yale, became the forerunners of Paul "Bear" Bryant of Alabama, Joe Paterno of Penn State, and John Wooden of UCLA—men who operated successful sports empires with little supervision from the rest of the institutions willing to pay exorbitant salaries to retain them. Unsavory characters in town businesses and the Vegas interest, along with pride-filled, wealthy alumni boosters and other commercial enterprises, helped ratchet up the level of competition. As intercollegiate athletics spread south and west, along with the increased violence bound to accompany intense physical competition, winning at all cost became the only thing that mattered. Rampaging on the field to attain that goal actually led to a presidential intervention to tone down violence in sports. In 1901 Theodore Roosevelt convened university presidents at the White House and issued an ultimatum to that effect. His action led to the formation of the National Collegiate Athletic Association (NCAA).

Conferences, bowl games, March Madness, and vast TV revenues—today they're all part of what most Americans think of when they hear of Notre Dame, Louisiana State University, Duke, or Syracuse. Despite the diminution of Division I athletics in the Ivies, THE (Yale-Harvard) game is still the most notable biannual collegiate event in New Haven and Cambridge. Even tiny I-AA Colgate achieves occasional national recognition, especially in hockey. Rabid fans from gown and town fill our 2,000+ capacity Starr Rink, their communal way of coping with north country winters. Title IX, introduced in 1972, has resulted in a stream of incoming women athletes. Recently, we restored athletic scholarships to our program; so athletic competition is alive and well, at least at this small liberal arts college.

What's it like teaching academics to athletes in a competitive program? Problematic. On the plus side, student athletes are among the most highly disciplined people in my classroom, a fact I owe to their coaches. But many of them are worn smooth by the exorbitant demands placed on them, including daily practice beginning at 4 p.m., away games mid-week, and extended tournament play, especially toward the end of their competitive seasons. Student athletes are among the most exhausted-looking attendees in my Monday classes. My disdain for those who sleep during classes doesn't help foster my relationship with them. As one might expect, these students always give preference to their duties on the field over those in the classroom. "If I don't show up for practice, coach won't let me play," or "I can't attend the study session because it's the night before the game," they tell me. My athletes are shocked when I offer to write a note asking coach to excuse them from practice to attend an academic extracurricular; yet they present stacks of similar documents penned by their coaches asking me to allow them to miss class.

"Yes, Whitney. I understand that your coach needs you in the game because you bat cleanup. He *needs* to win. He doesn't have tenure and I do; but believe me, even though my job isn't at stake, I need your brain more than he needs your body," I told one of my brightest kids who attended Colgate on a four-year women's softball scholarship. I know Whitney would have made an excellent prospect for further study at one of the better schools with a good cultural anthropology department, but unfortunately her thirty-seven–game schedule left her with barely enough time and energy to muster a B in my class. Like the many athletes I teach, she is one of the 99.9 percent whose dream of a career in professional sports is not likely to materialize. Update: she's now five years out, bored with her menial job, and seriously thinking of further study. Will I write her a recommendation?

There are those who succeed in integrating their athleticism into their life's work. My former student Christine Cucciarre, once a runner at Colgate, has developed a course titled "Running and Writing." She and her students, all runners, talk about writing as they run, even compose and meditate on writing and thinking as they do so. She cites brain research that shows collaboration between the two activities: students learn better when moving. Maybe there's something to all my pacing and gesticulating when I lecture. There *is* a synergy between the life of the mind and body.

But let me not complain. At Arizona, South Florida, and Colorado, where I've spent semesters, the situation is far more worrisome. Many athletes in the mega-versities are barely literate; their graduation rates are abysmal— part of their sacrifice for entertaining the American public and enriching the coffers of our academic institutions. Rutgers is one recent example of a quality institution that has sold out to the ballyhoo and glory that come with collegiate sports. That institution now spends $26.9 million a year subsidizing its athletic programs. It has also capped faculty salaries, removed phones from many offices, and postponed repairs and renovations—all in the quest to elevate its national sports status. (There was a time when the Colgate-Rutgers rivalry was a big deal in the east.) Buffalo, Connecticut, and South Florida, to name just a few, have taken a similar track.

"Academics first." This is the mantra my athletes relay from their coaches; but I have found precious few student athletes who really believe the life of the mind trumps the extreme demands placed on the student body. I think the worlds of sports and academia would both be better off if the National Basketball Association and the National Football League, like Major League Baseball, set up farm clubs instead of using educational institutions to recruit their players.

As an academic, I find it difficult to compete against the Division of Athletics. Coach Bear Bryant once said that it's kind of hard to rally 'round a math class. Over the century-and-a-half since they were installed in the American academy, team sports have succeeded in teaching the progressive value of subordinating the individual to the community. Sports is a ritual based on belonging, an activity far removed from the largely solitary act of deep thinking the learning process requires.

How Can We Improve Our Colleges and Universities?

Outside the campus there isn't much interest in educational issues, and there's not a lot of discussion about how to improve the overall quality of undergraduate education—a sad state of affairs. Today, the public eye is more focused on steps to limit the increased cost of education in a financially troubled world. Who can blame a prospective college parent: a year's tuition at the highest-ranked, small liberal arts colleges has escalated well beyond $50,000. I think America's loss of commitment to public education is partly to blame for the escalated costs of state-supported schools; for example, currently only 8 percent of the operating budget at the University of Virginia comes from the state. The only choice left for flagship institutions—UC Berkeley is another example—to sustain quality is to raise tuition, and even under these conditions salaries remain frozen and budget cuts enormous.

Some argue that a three-year degree could save that much per annum. What's so magical about the number four? Why not pack four years of curricular content into three years? Would such a program deprive students of time for intellectual exploration? As we saw in chapter 4, online learning is another option; but, as I argued, screen time doesn't really substitute for the face-to-face experience that comes from interactive classroom instruction.

Derek Bok believes that, though well intentioned, many of the university's goals are too often pursued unrealistically, and this contributes to the underperformance of our colleges.[55] Among these, he lists foreign language courses that fall short of proficiency, writing classes taught by unqualified instructors, the lack of basic courses in science designed for the non-major, and concentration requirements that have expanded at the expense of free electives. Teachers, he further notes, are not willing enough to experiment with new ways of learning that have been proven effective; for example, engaging students more actively in the learning process. He cites too little instruction in quantitative methods and moral reasoning as other problems.

One of the criticisms leveled against Bok's analysis is that there is little agreement on how to teach value-laden courses, even on whether they should be taught; for example, Harvard humanist Louis Menand believes all undergrads should be required to take a Core course in "Reason and Faith" in which they confront big issues in religion, such as intelligent design and radical Islam.[56] Menand's detractors include Harvard psychologist Steven Pinker, who argues that the pursuit of truth through rational inquiry appropriately leaves no place in the college curriculum for the study of religion.[57] Though religious studies thrive at a number of elite institutions, I find it curious that there is no religion department at Harvard.

Bok does offer some possible solutions to deficiencies in the American college; for example, conducting comprehensive evaluations of gen ed programs and including more helpful questions on survey forms, such as, how much has this course helped you improve your ability to think critically and analyze problems. (We're already doing that at Colgate.) Granted, measuring progress in such areas is difficult, but at least this sort of inquiry gives a hint of whether students are responding to one of the primary goals of all gen ed programs. Moreover, comments that accompany such a question can give those who design the curriculum an idea of how students perceive critical thinking. I think one of Bok's most sensible suggestions for the improvement of teaching, is to encourage more institutions to introduce preparation for teaching and aspects of student learning into their PhD programs. After all, these are the institutions that produce our college teachers.

Self-study involves hard work, but despite my awareness of the general inertia on American campuses that trends against critical introspection when it comes to initiating change, I agree with Bok that both government and private agencies can help by funding efforts to measure existing program outcomes and looking into ways to improve them. Finally, just as inspirational teaching can move students to great intellectual heights and outstanding productivity, inspirational leadership from the college administration can serve as a call to action by the faculty. Presidents and deans need to challenge their professors; they need to offer them incentives to think more about the business of teaching. A major study of the efficacy of teaching concludes that those institutions that exhibit a desire to increase their instructional effectiveness can do so, but the will must be there and all sectors of the university, from administration to faculty, must be conducive to this goal.[58]

If professors need good ratings to secure their jobs, universities need them too if they want to remain competitive in the marketplace. This is why administrators and boards pay close attention to the *US News and World Report* college rankings. These rankings are based in part on the SAT scores of entering students and on the scholarly reputation of the faculty as judged by competing institutions. In the liberal arts category, to which Colgate belongs, two ways to move up in the standings are by offering a sizable number of classes with small enrollments (capping at nineteen students per section is advertised as the most effective way) and by squeezing as much of the budget as possible into merit scholarships. Some question the relevance of such tactics for the overall quality of their programs.

Among the offbeat solutions about how to improve America's colleges and universities is a plan proposed by conservative Texas regents. They want their professoriate in the University of Texas at Austin evaluated on the basis of how many students they teach and how many research dollars they attract. They are asking college administrators to figure out a way to offer a four-year degree for under $10,000 tuition. It's no secret that expanding online classes is part of the mandate. Meanwhile, North Carolina's governor is pushing legislation to fund state colleges based not so much on "butts in seats" as on "how many of those butts can get jobs."[59]

To supplement standard evaluative tools, such as the SET forms discussed earlier in this chapter, Bok advocates participation in the National Survey of Student Engagement, which asks students to respond to questions about interactive forms of learning they have experienced.[60] Examples include: How often do you speak in class; talk to a professor outside of class, write a paper, give a talk, or participate in group projects and community service? How much does your coursework emphasize memorizing, analyzing, synthesizing, applying and making judgments? The obligatory question about how your course or institution has contributed to your personal development is broken down into sixteen parts, including working with others, writing, speaking, and thinking critically, as well as contributing to the welfare of the community and developing a sense of spirituality. Students are also asked how long it takes their teachers to return feedback. Schools can use these results to target areas of improvement in their programs. I believe writing should be a big part of this effort. My students are more engaged and acquire deeper learning when they write in my class. Unfortunately, only one-quarter of America's accredited colleges, most of them in the small liberal arts category where significant efforts in program evaluation are already being made, have participated.

When I think of the almost impossible demands we teachers place on ourselves, it's a wonder we don't set ourselves up for more criticism than we already receive. We must teach values while at the same time question the values we teach; we must deal with the practical, everyday concepts and ideas our students need to acquire to become functioning citizens, but we are also expected to move beyond the practical to the transcendent.[61] I believe the will to improve on the work we do is there. I see it in energetic discussions with my younger colleagues every day at Colgate and at the other colleges and universities I visit.

Why College Anyway?

In *The Sheepskin Psychosis*, freelance writer John Keats suggested that the necessity of going to college was basically a con-job perpetrated on the public and that it has little to do with what a functioning citizen learned or needed to learn.[62] That was back in 1963. Keats was not the first skeptic of academic book learning. In the mid-nineteenth century Henry David Thoreau thought he'd get more out of living in the woods, where he would learn the fundamental facts of life—*real* experiential learning. A century before him, French philosopher John Jacques Rousseau thought the best way to get an education was to read *The Adventures of Robinson Crusoe*.

I find it ironic that America, which by all accounts offers the most sought-after college experience, also harbors a never-ending skepticism toward it. That may be what makes the experience such a meaningful one. Today, we live in the midst of the most anti-college atmosphere I've breathed in my half-century in the classroom. A steady stream of popular books complains about the all-time-high dropout rates, the decline in the quality of instruction, the lack of proof of the efficacy of the product, and the staggering increase in the cost of attending college.[63] Rutgers, Ohio State, Florida State, Wisconsin, and Iowa, for example, all have four-year graduation rates just under 50 percent and six-year rates around 75 percent. Only the elite private colleges top 90 percent in the latter category. The cost of attending college has reached budget-crippling levels for the average middle-class family, especially since the 1980s. Even at public institutions like Michigan and Penn State, tuition and fees for an in-state freshman top $25,000. You'll need to more than double that if you want to attend a select private college. Americans now owe

$1 trillion in student loans, more than their credit card debt.[64] Despite the punishing cost, college attendance remains at an all-time high, with more than 40 percent of Americans age eighteen to twenty-four attending the 5,000 two- and four-year American academic institutions.

Meanwhile, university investments in building better-appointed dorms and fancy gyms, not to mention hiring a cadre of counselors to tend to the personal and social needs of enrollees, are on the increase. Amid the contemporary consumer-oriented mentality, educators already relegated to lower priority and status in the academy come to be thought of as mere suppliers of knowledge. And so, the theory goes, the college's clients tend to seek out the path of least resistance to attain the credentials they, or their parents, have paid for. Always right, customers hold the upper hand when it comes to evaluating those who serve them. They are not afraid to punish teachers severely should they become too rigorous or demanding. In discussing the entrepreneurial mode, Jeff Selingo, editor-at-large of the prestigious *Chronicle of Higher Education*, writes: "American colleges and universities seem to be in every business but education. They are in the entertainment business, the housing business, the restaurant business, the recreation business, and on some campuses, they operate what are essentially professional sports franchises."[65] Is the diploma really worth it at any cost? Selingo foresees a financial collapse of the system just around the corner.

Columbia humanities professor Andrew Delbanco likens the rising cost of college to a progressive disease.[66] The prosperity of a good college is linked to the quality of the faculty it hires. The more prosperous it gets, the higher the cost of maintaining the best faculty members, placing them in small seminar classes, and having them supervise senior theses. I recently had the rare privilege of teaching, with my colleague Robert Garland from Colgate's classics department, Colgate's High Distinction Senior Core seminar. We enrolled twelve students, chosen through interviews. All were high honors candidates engaged in writing their senior theses. We selected readings structured around the theme of the "so what" question, which the more daring members of my classes have occasionally put to me. Example: Why should I care about whether the universe was created all in a flash 14 billion years ago (give or take a billion) or has existed for all eternity in the same condition it's in right now? I just want to be a CPA, so what does it matter to me? It's my job to deal with that question. Reframing the senior theses in their concentration, students in our seminar were asked to address the "so what" question in a liberal arts context by rewriting their theses and discussing them with the class in a language we could all understand. That's an expensive proposition—two full professors and only a dozen students; but Delbanco thinks that sort of activity is worth it, and if our best colleges stop supporting small classes and seminars, our educational system will be the worse for it.

At the community and state college levels, quality control is far more challenging because politics is involved. Budgets have risen even as government administers funding cuts. Political decisions to treat higher education as a public good can turn things around, but they are anything but forthcoming in the current atmosphere of distrust in the system. I think this has helped fuel the notion that technology's cheap delivery—"disruptive innovation devices," as ed blogger Karine Joly terms MOOCs—can remedy the situation.[67]

Sociologists Richard Arum and Josipa Roksa complain that college students are taught by fewer and fewer full-time, tenured faculty and more and more by adjunct teachers who are generally less qualified and much cheaper to hire.[68] They back up their sweeping critique of the current status of the undergraduate experience with a study based on the College Learning Assessment (CLA) test they created to assess learning growth. The part of the test on which Arum and Roksa base their conclusions has to do with performance tasks, such as writing memos to an employer they are advising about purchasing a type of airplane that has recently crashed. Students acquire their advice from various documents, including news articles. Their written work is graded on the basis of analytical ability, critical thinking, writing, and problem solving. When the test was administered to the same group of 2,000 students at the beginning of their freshman and the end of their sophomore years, Arum and Roksa found that nearly half of the students' test scores had not improved significantly. They concluded that for a majority of students, little learning actually takes place in American colleges. A more reasonable conclusion might be that no learning took place as measured by their particular test, which may not have assessed student skills adequately. Louis Menand noted this point as well.[69] He looked at the CLA test and concluded that while it correctly monitored some skills, it dealt with none of the other factors that might have been implicated, such as social attitudes and acquired knowledge. Moreover, the study took no account of the sophomore leap in development, witnessed by many of us who interact closely with students over an extended period (recall my discussion in chapter 2).

Arum and Roksa's conclusions have also been questioned by UCLA Emeritus Professor of educational studies Alexander Astin. He finds that they do not square with his own long-term studies.[70] Astin is also critical of Arum and Roksa's statistical methods; for example, they don't report scores or state how many students showed any degree of improvement, only that 45 percent of the two-time test takers failed to significantly improve their reading and writing skills in their first year of college. Astin also questions the arbitrariness of their statistical definition of significance. Arum and Roksa's conclusions also fare poorly when measured against the three-decade study by Ernest Pascarella and Patrick Terenzini.[71] On the basis of an extensive body of work that included several kinds of tests, they concluded in 1991 that compared with freshmen, college seniors have better oral and written communication skills, are better at abstract reasoning and critical thinking, and are more skilled at applying reason and evidence to address poorly structured problems that don't have correct answers subject to verification. Moreover, those studies exhibited an increase in intellectual flexibility in being able to understand more than one side of a complex issue.

Like Arum and Roksa, sociologist Andrew Hacker and journalist Claudia Dreifus have joined the pile-on.[72] They think our once rigorous colleges have been transformed into resorts for corporate-directed adolescents. Salaries commanded by college presidents and competitive athletic coaches are exorbitant, and too many student amenities, such as climbing walls and duplex-apartment dorms, are way out of line—a far cry from the more Spartan cell-like sleeping quarters of old, with hard beds and shared bathrooms down the hall.

In The Basement of the Ivory Tower attacks the American college from the inside.[73] Written by the anonymous "Professor X," a member of the faculty of a fictitious four-year private community college who does his professing part-time as an adjunct appointee (he teaches creative writing), this book is damningly critical of both students (most are unqualified to attend college and, when it comes to writing and literature, unreachable) and their teachers (they are too low on rigor and too high on consciousness-raising). Professor X says the entire system is geared to pushing through job seekers deluded by the worn-out post–World War II myth that everyone ought to have an education. The anonymous professor's advice: save yourself time and money. If you're not ready for an advanced educational experience in the liberal arts, go straight into vocational training. It's still done today in central Europe, and, as Louis Menand has pointed out, it was done in the United States up to the twentieth century. Menand regards the undergraduate college as a requirement for law or medical school as "the most important reform ever made in American higher education."[74] Not only did it raise the status of these professions, it also elevated the liberal arts to a position that made American-style higher education the envy of all forms of learning practiced in the world. Incidentally, regarding Professor X's claims about teaching quality, a recent Northwestern University study revealed that non–tenure-track teachers received higher SET ratings than full-salaried employees. The fact that they are evaluated solely on teaching ability may be a contributing factor.[75]

Other recent players on the crowded anti-college, don't-waste-your-time battlefield include venture capitalist crusaders like Peter Thiel and James Altucher. Thiel, a billionaire college dropout, created a fellowship in his name that awards twenty students under age twenty $100,000 each to stay out of college and instead be mentored by Silicon Valley entrepreneurs like himself.[76] Thiel views college as a kind of insurance policy that keeps people from falling out of the middle class. Having to cope with college debt years later is very stressful. It also sets you on a career track that prevents you from diversifying your options. College is too impractical and too expensive, he says, and besides, the liberal arts education it offers doesn't apply in today's real world. Thiel unabashedly make clear that his core theory of purpose-directed education rests on the credo that getting rich lies at the base of success in life. He seems unconcerned about where intellectual development fits into the picture.

As far as Altucher is concerned, college is a scam perpetrated by college graduates to produce more college graduates.[77] Playing on the myth that, like owning a home, getting a college degree is a *sine qua non* mark of success, he sees the escalation in costs as part of a college conspiracy. Altucher recalls his college days and what he learned: how to drink and socialize with members of the opposite sex. As far as critical thinking and skillful writing are concerned, he claims to have figured out all of that on his own when he studied the ways and works of the great financiers, like Warren Buffett. Altucher's message to high-school graduates, like Thiel's, is: don't go to college. At the receiving end of the migration away from the humanities lie the "STEM disciplines" (science, technology, engineering, and math), for which business is pleading. These are the fields that supply us with "broadly shared economic prosperity, international competitiveness, a clean energy future, and longer healthier lives for all Americans,"[78] as a recent White House press release put it.

Former US secretary of education William Bennett also thinks there are too many people on campus.[79] And of those who do go to college, too many are studying irrelevant material—read, non-vocationally oriented courses. Bennett adheres to the business-commodity model of education. He wants all students, before taking the plunge, to study *all* the data—in other words, evaluate loan debt, the return on investment, lifetime monetary earnings, how well people performed, what skills they acquired, and so on. I can't think of a better way to kill the curiosity of a motivated young person.

Want my advice? Visit as many institutions as you can. When you talk to students and professors you can, without much difficulty, get a sense of the character and quality of the place, what motivates them to study or teach in their chosen area, why they want to contribute to society or develop their artistic or scientific skills. Look, listen, and ask about what's really important. Don't be dazzled by the glitzy campus tour. You shouldn't judge how an institution and its people might shape your life by the size of the climbing wall, the number of clubs, or the variety of social activities. Beware of words like "leadership," "partnering," "excellence," and "incentivizing," warns Mark Edmundson. Used by many people in pitching a university, excellence, he says, usually implies world distinction. It means "we're smart, we're accomplished, we're successful."[80] It says nothing about ethics. Finally, take a critical look at what you read about going to college, including many of the books I've mentioned in this chapter. Judge for yourself.

Like me, Edmundson is well aware of the dominance of the economic market in shaping many critiques of American higher education. He likens the way we think of college to the idea of putting money into the stock market or a mutual fund.[81] If you didn't need that degree to end up with the job you have, then it must have been a bad investment. That may be true for some people, says Edmundson, but not with those who have "hungry hearts" (drawing on Bruce Springsteen's song). They are the ones I know so well, the ones with the "burn to learn," who seem to have been born with a desire to want to know and do everything. They may not be the most gifted, they may even be slow learners, but they never stop pestering their instructors with questions. They're adventurous, not because they are secure or uncertain or because their parents saddled them with great expectations. Quite the opposite: these inquiring young people somehow seem to have acquired enough self-confidence to be willing to risk their values and beliefs. They are already possessed of the love of learning and the willingness to experience things strange and new, the very essence of what I strive for in my classroom. Cabbie, caterer, chemist, or classicist; it really doesn't matter where you end up. The real value of an education is measured not by your salaried outcome but by your desire to engage it.

Louis Menand, an ardent defender of the rewards of going to college that rise above the cost-benefit–based attack launched by the anti-college crowd, cites three theories—all of which may apply at the same time—concerning what going to college means. First, it's about developing and demonstrating your intellectual ability across a range of subjects, which at the same time sorts students by aptitude for various areas. Under this theory, grades are all that really matter, provided the courses you take are rigorous, regardless of subject matter. Second, college introduces the citizens who will determine the course of the world in the near future to matters that will not only empower but also enlighten them. As Menand puts it, you're there to learn things that "if you don't learn them in college you are unlikely to learn them anywhere else."[82] Of course, Menand would need to exclude the likes of extraordinarily motivated individuals like Thiel and Altucher, who claim they are quite capable of acquiring all the knowledge they need for their particular aptitudes on their own. What matters more than grades is what you actually learn.

Menand believes American education since the end of World War II has been committed to both the "merit-based" theory no. 1 and the more "democratic" theory no. 2. Those who attack theory no. 1, like Arum and Roksa, for example, think most students are unfit for the proposed rigorous procedure and that their test results prove it. So, the value of the degree is cheapened even as the dollar cost of getting it skyrockets. Theory no. 2 is open to attack by people like Altucher and Thiel, who think most of the professed knowledge worth knowing that's dispensed on campus isn't worth much. Throw in the sticker price and it's worth even less.

Menand's theory no. 3 on why go to college is currently the most popular. It goes like this: our complex, high-tech economy demands specialized skills and knowledge. College is the place to get both, so you can become competent in your vocation. He offers the amusing example of a beverage management major at a large state college that requires courses in philosophy and a pair of humanities electives in addition to other liberal arts courses. Now, how much effort do you think a student in the culinary arts is going to put into a lit course if his life goal is to become bar-master at Vegas's Bellagio resort? This addresses Professor X's griping. All most students who go after the college degree care about as a gateway to getting a good job is a good grade. Yale comparative literature professor Peter Brooks, winner of the Andrew Mellon Distinguished Achievement Award and one of the prime initiators of the dialogue on the teaching of the humanities and professional education, writes: "Universities when true to themselves have always been places that harbor recondite subjects of little immediate utility—places where you can study hieroglyphics and Coptic as well as string theory and the habits of lemmings."[83] No country needs that kind of stuff *more* than the United States, where pragmatism has always dominated our thinking. Given the rampant anti-intellectualism in America, I come away surprised that we have the quality universities we do.

Brooks views the new crisis rhetoric (the old one being the 1980s culture wars) as an angry response to the increasing gap in American society between haves and have-nots, a system "rigged to benefit a tarnished elite that no longer justifies its existence."[84] While Harvard, Yale, and Princeton offer high salaries to faculty and numerous amenities to students, state colleges languish in a limbo of frozen salaries and increased class size. In hard times, more students who would otherwise have gone for the high-price spread are forced to opt instead for community college.

On students and professors, Brooks agrees with Menand that most of the critical accusers, like Arum and Roksa, use vocationally oriented testing to determine learning capacity, all the while advocating the study of the liberal arts. Further, he doesn't think Hacker and Dreifus's opinion of the "professoriate" as a bunch of lazy, self-serving hacks interested only in sabbaticals, selfish pursuits, and often irrelevant research—and with little interest in teaching and students—matches the professoriate he has known. I agree with Brooks that the university is in far better control of itself than most other American institutions. It has replaced the old elite with new blood. (Of those hired at Colgate before 1985, I am the only individual remaining in either of the departments I serve.)

Others argue that finding common ground with the professions cheapens the meaning of a liberal education. For example, English professor Lisa Colletta thinks deferring the value of an education in terms of market price cuts the experience back to a service role and further supports the widely held American notion that only the market can determine what's useful.[85] A liberal mind is supposed to be *disinterested* (that oft-misinterpreted word you'll recall from chapter 2). It means independent. The liberal mind is thoughtful in the sense that it weighs ideas in the context of the history of thought; it understands complexity and ambiguity and is naturally inquisitive. The liberal arts constitute a record of the human desire to understand the world and an account of the ideas and events that brought us to our present historical moment.[86] This is *real* knowledge and it has little to do with professional training, which is not necessarily informed by this sort of thoughtfulness.

The liberal arts is *not* utilitarian precisely because it is designed to give you a sense that there have been other ways of understanding the world in different times and under different circumstances; it is designed to show that value itself is ever-changing. For the humanities specifically, Colletta thinks this translates to cultivating an understanding in students of the many layers of history, a sense of the aesthetic, and an awareness of the power of human creativity. Students know they have succeeded, not by how much they contribute to the development of a moral code but rather when, perhaps later in life, something in their immediate experience—for example, looking at a work of art or a historical marker, or reading a poem—"stops them cold on the street and demands that they look beyond themselves."[87]

Lisa Colletta, Mark Brooks, Louis Menand, and I all agree with those who believe that college marketing, driven by the credo of making education relevant and useful, lies at the core of academia's current pragmatic trend. Today's college catalogs stress the three Is: innovation, integration, and interdisciplinary education. Shall we college teachers focus more and more of our courses on things practical out of fear that students and their parents, who are paying the bill, might accuse us of offering impractical knowledge? The same was true in Athens 2,500 years ago. In Book 2 of *The Republic* Plato puts this question to the class: "So what shall we engage next?" Glaucon, a bright kid in the circle, raises his hand. "Why don't we talk about navigation? It's useful, practical, helps us develop skills we can make use of in life." "You make me laugh, Glaucon," Plato replies. "Are you afraid of being accused by your peers of acquiring useless knowledge?"

So, is it all worth it? A recent survey conducted in China listed thirty-five American universities in the top fifty worldwide (eight in the top ten). More than 600,000 of the world's brightest foreign students elected to attend American universities in 2007. After having spent a year in residence at the US Library of Congress, one Chinese leader was asked what memory he would take back to his home country. He replied: "The American University. The greatness and autonomy of the American University. There is nothing in the world quite like it."[88]

In my half-century in the classroom, I've never experienced a time when the value of an undergraduate education in the American university has been questioned more, even as the percentage of the population enrolled in institutions of higher education has begun to fall behind that in other nations. But let me restate what I said earlier. Colleges aren't just domains where knowledge is transmitted. They are also places that *create* knowledge. The process of becoming educated, of learning to become both critical of received knowledge and innovative at its very horizon, can be painful. From a teacher's perspective, learning is a process that requires listening thoughtfully and carefully, then responding to many different voices—voices that, in the best learning environments, can diverge considerably from one another. I have seen generations of teachers enter and leave Colgate, and I've had the opportunity to visit hundreds of academic institutions around the country and meet their faculty. They are extraordinarily dedicated, passionate, hardworking people who care deeply about and respect their students. To the students, let me put my own spin on education as a commodity: attending college ought to be like visiting a vast open-air market, one where goods are replaced by ideas fervently hawked by avid pitchmen. The more you experience the feeling of being knocked off the path you walked in on, of truly being disoriented while shopping, the better chance you stand of leaving this treasure trove of wondrous gifts of sustenance fully supplied to subsist on your own.

6 | Epilogue: Class (Not) Dismissed

"So, when are you gonna retire?" If you've been around the college awhile, greying around the temples, maybe forgetting to come to a meeting once in a while, you've probably been asked that question. I have for the past decade or so.

My answer is this: not as long as I have Bridget and Miri and Alex and Kayla and Sam and David and Peter and Amy and Steve and Ron and Mitch . . . I remember my exceptional students as well as I recall my favorite teachers. I just parsed out some of the most memorable in five-year blocks going back to 1963, the year I came to Colgate. The names get more masculine-sounding as I write them in retrograde. (Remember, Colgate didn't enroll women during my first ten years.) Wish I had space to tell stories about all of them.

I cut my pedagogic teeth on Mitch. I'd just begun to write the National Science Foundation proposal to acquire Colgate's new telescope when a member of the admissions staff called and told me they had a kid with an interest in coming to Colgate to study astronomy. Would I talk to him? Of course! Ten minutes later there's a knock on my open door, and the front end

DOI: 10.5876/9781607323037.c006

of an eight-inch-wide, twelve-foot-long metal tube with a starry-eyed kid from Bedford-Stuyvesant at the other end of it enters the room. "I made it myself," Mitch said. Then he showed me other optical instruments he'd cobbled together with his own hands to hook onto his scope. When the interview was over, I phoned the Ad Building and told them, "I don't care what this kid's record is—admit him." Mitch's inspiration almost wore me down. He thrived at Colgate, even if he paid little attention to his non-astronomical courses. He graduated with a respectable 3.2 GPA and went on to earn an MA and a PhD in optical sciences. Later, Mitch designed the dome lenses for the Gemini Spacecraft and he *invented* Revo sunglasses, still the best defense against ultraviolet and infrared light. He ran an optical design firm in Tucson, where he did major work on NASA's satellite and telescope technology. Despite his nerdiness, he became pretty conversant in the liberal arts, even learned to play piano. We stayed in close contact for over forty years. As I was about to submit this manuscript to the University Press of Colorado, Mitch called. I knew he had been battling leukemia for the past two years because he would send weekly reports of his "numbers," as he called them. This time the news was bad. He sounded frail, his voice cracked, his energy dissipating. "This is totally backward, Mitch," I told him. "*You* should be consoling *me* on my imminent departure." "Yeah, it's like *Tuesdays with Morrie,* except I'm Morrie," he responded. Humor had always been a tie that bound us. A week later, Mitch died.

Amy is Amy Silva, my first Latina student and one of the first women to come to Colgate. She just finished a long career directing the education program for kids at the Metropolitan Museum of Art in New York City and is beginning a second career as a special education teacher at the Theater Arts Production Company School. Amy is still with her husband—the guy she met at Colgate just before our Mexico field study group, in which they had both enrolled. Amy struggled at Colgate. Hamilton isn't the Upper Bronx, and Amy was not a high-school valedictorian. She had trouble writing. But Amy had a hungry heart and she never stopped badgering me to help it grow. When she got something wrong on a test, she persisted until she got it right. When I was recently featured in an article in the *Colgate Scene* (yes, it had to do with my longevity at the college), Amy wrote to tell me that her fourteen-year-old had asked why she faithfully read Colgate's alumni magazine. "I read for news of Aveni," she replied. Then, she said, she opened it and "there you were, staring back at me. See, here's my mentor. How wonderful to be able to share my passion for learning with her, a passion which you fueled. Know that I hope to inspire and teach my students, like my children, to believe in themselves the way you believed in me. Thank you for giving me a voice. Con mucho cariño, Amy."

Today, there's Bridget. She's a senior English major who suffers from the malady of extreme modesty. It took me quite awhile to approach her because of her shyness. Never does Bridget ask the usual questions: What's gonna be on the exam? Am I responsible for this material? Instead, it's, do you have any books on magical thinking or I want to discuss some questions that really interest me about the crossover between faith and science. Bridget loves to write and she's pretty good at it, getting better. Over the summer following my course "Astronomy in Culture," she sent me a voluntary 2,500-word essay titled "Trying to Find the Light down a Blind Alley." It ended with the words, spun off van Gogh, "I know nothing with certainty, but the sight of the stars makes me dream." Bridget added, "If the universe is a place for dreams, I think I'll survive." I got out my green pen, struck the last word, and replaced it with "thrive."

Chapter 2

1. Claudius Ptolemy, *Syntaxis Mathematica* [AD 150], ed. John Ludwig Heiberg (Leipzig: Teubner, 1898), preface.

2. Quoted in Jay Parini, *The Art of Teaching* (Oxford: Oxford University Press, 2005), 86.

3. William James, *The Varieties of Religious Experience* (Oxford: Oxford University Press, 2012), 294. Actually, the statement comes from William Inge, "Charles Kingsley's Life," in William Inge, ed., *Christian Mysticism* (London, 1899), 341.

4. Mark Edmondson, "Geek Lessons," *New York Times Magazine*, September 21, 2008, 7.

5. Ibid.

6. Plato, *The Symposium* [ca. 350 BC], tr. and ed. Christopher Gill (New York: Penguin, 1999), 47–48.

7. "Speech of Pausanias," in ibid., 184c.

8. Peter Beidler, "Loving Teaching," *Journal on Excellence in College Teaching* 1 (1990): 1–8.

DOI: 10.5876/9781607323037.c007

9. Ibid.

10. Derek Bok, *Our Underachieving Colleges: A Candid Look at How Much Students Learn and Why They Should Be Learning More* (Princeton, NJ: Princeton University Press, 2006), 114.

11. William Perry, *Forms of Ethical and Intellectual Development* (San Francisco: Jossey-Bass, 1999). Perry further subdivides the four stages into nine levels.

12. Lev Vygotsky, *Mind in Society* (Cambridge, MA: Harvard University Press, 1978).

13. Plata quoted in "Why I Teach," *The Colgate Scene* 36, no. 5 (2008): 2.

14. Carl Weiman, "The Curse of Knowledge, or Why Intuition about Teaching Often Fails," *APS News* 16, no. 10 (2007): back page.

15. Charles Anderson, *Prescribing the Life of the Mind: An Essay on the Purpose of the University, the Aims of Liberal Education, the Competence of Citizens, and the Cultivation of Practical Reason* (Madison: University of Wisconsin Press, 1993), 81.

Chapter 3

1. John Stuart Mill, "Civilization," *London and Westminster Review* (April 1836).

2. Catherine Rampell, "It Takes a B.A. to Find an Job as a File Clerk," *New York Times,* February 20, 2013, 3.

3. Bok, *Our Underachieving Colleges*, 70.

4. Ernest Pascarella and Patrick Terenzini, *How College Affects Students: A Third Decade of Research* (San Francisco: Jossey-Bass, 2005), 502–3.

5. Ibid., 505.

6. Rebecca Mead, "Learning by Degrees," *New Yorker*, June 7, 2010, 21.

7. Beidler, "Loving Teaching," 25.

8. Quoted in Bok, *Our Underachieving Colleges*, 15.

9. At http://www.gawker.com/297435/what-are-the-gut-classes-at-Yale (accessed July 20, 2014).

10. Quoted in http://www.flapperjane.com/September04/running_wild (accessed July 24, 2014).

11. Alexander Astin, cited in Bok, *Our Underachieving Colleges*, 26.

12. James Storing, "A Modern Design for General and Liberal Education on a College Campus," *Journal of General Education* 18, no. 3 (1966): 156.

13. George O'Brien, *All the Essential Half-Truths about Education* (Chicago: University of Chicago Press, 1998), 74.

14. Colgate University catalog (1948).

15. W. B. Carnochan, *The Battleground of the Curriculum* (Stanford, CA: Stanford University Press, 1993), 76.

16. Veblen quoted in ibid., 114.

17. Letters, *New York Times Sunday Review*, May 6, 2012, 2.

18. Ibid.

19. Allan Bloom, *The Closing of the American Mind* (New York: Simon and Schuster, 1987).

20. Charles Sykes, *ProfScam: Professors and the Demise of Education* (Washington, DC: Regnery Gateway, 1988). See also R. Kimball, *Tenured Radicals: How Politics Has Corrupted Our Higher Education* (Chicago: Ivan R. Dee, 2008).

21. Cf. Alan Wolfe, *Moral Freedom: The Impossible Idea That Defines the Way We Live Now* (New York: W. W. Norton, 2001).

22. Mark Bauerlein, *The Dumbest Generation: How the Digital Age Stupefies Young Americans and Jeopardizes Our Future* (New York: Tarcher Penguin, 2008).

23. At http://www.gawker.com/297435/what-are-the-gut-classes-at-Yale (accessed July 20, 2014).

24. Ibid.

25. Henry Rosovsky, *The University: An Owner's Manual* (New York: Norton, 1990).

26. Charles Percy Snow, *The Two Cultures* (Cambridge: Cambridge University Press, 1959).

27. Ibid., 4.

28. Gerald Graff, *Beyond the Culture Wars: How Teaching the Conflicts Can Revitalize American Education* (New York: W. W. Norton, 1992).

29. Colgate University catalog (1988), my italics.

30. Ibid. (2012).

31. Bok, *Our Underachieving Colleges*, 224.

Chapter 4

1. David Edmonds and John Eidenow, *Wittgenstein's Poker* (New York: Ecco, 2001), 291.

2. Ernest Bloch, "History Lessons," *Saturday Evening Post* (September-October 2013): 43.

3. N. Scott Momaday, *Archaeoastronomy JAC* 12–13 (1996): 32–37.

4. Robert Hazen and James Trefil, *Science Matters: Achieving Scientific Literacy* (New York: Doubleday, 1991).

5. *Newsweek*, February 25, 1991, 7.

6. Personal correspondence, Lesley Marcus Carlson, June 1, 2013.

7. Joseph Katz and Mildred Henry, *Turning Professors into Teachers: A New Approach to Faculty Development and Student Learning* (New York: American Council on Education and MacMillan, 1988), 161.

8. William Lammers and John Murphy, "A Profile of Teaching Techniques Used in the University Classroom," *Active Learning in Higher Education* 3, no. 1 (2002): 54–67.

9. Horowitz cited in "The Science and Art of Listening," *New York Times,* November 11, 2012, 1.

10. Sherry Turkle, *Alone Together: Why We Expect More from Technology and Less from Each Other* (New York: Basic, 2012).

11. Victoria Rideout and Ulla Foehr, *Generation M²: Media in the Lives of 8 to 18 Year-Olds* (Menlo Park, CA: Kaiser Family Foundation, 2010).

12. Hannaway cited in Elizabeth Green, "Building a Better Teacher," *New York Times Magazine,* March 2, 2010, 1.

13. Bauerlein, *Dumbest Generation,* 186.

14. Ibid., 188.

15. Doug Lemov, *Teach Like a Champion: The 49 Techniques That Put Students on the Path to College* (San Francisco: Jossey-Bass, 2010).

16. http://www.edu/openbook, How People Learn: Brain, Mind, Experience, and School, Commission on Behavioral and Social Sciences and Education (accessed July 11, 2013).

17. Parini, *Art of Teaching,* 131.

18. Terry Doyle, "Learner Centered Teaching: Real World Model of Classroom Discussion," *Active Learning,* at http://www.learnercenteredteaching.wordpress (accessed August 12, 2013). At the same site Doyle also offers "Eight Steps to Active Lecturing."

19. Nathan Heller, "Laptop U," *New Yorker,* May 20, 2013, 82.

20. Tamar Lewin, "Universities Reshaping Education on the Web," *New York Times,* June 17, 2012, A12, A14.

21. Arnold Jacobs, "Two Cheers for Web U," *New York Times Sunday Review,* April 21, 2013, 1, 6.

22. Tamar Lewin, "Duke University Withdraws from Online Course Group," *New York Times,* May 1, 2013, A14; Tamar Lewin "After Setbacks, Online Courses Are Rethought," *New York Times,* December 11, 2013, A.

23. Ibid., A7.

24. Editorial, *New York Times,* February 19, 2013, A22.

25. Mark Edmundson, *Why Teach? In Defense of Real Education* (New York: Bloomsbury, 2013), 207.

26. Ibid.

27. Amanda Ripley, "Reinventing College: A Special Report on Higher Education," *Time* (October 29, 2012), 41.

28. Ibid.

29. Jacobs, "Two Cheers for Web U," A1, A16. This was the first of a series of pieces on free online college-level classes and how they are transforming higher education.

30. Sebastian Thrun, at http://www.blog.udacity.com (accessed September 27, 2012).

31. Alexander Astin, *What Matters in College: Four Critical Years Revisited* (San Francisco: Jossey-Bass, 1993); Pascarella and Terenzini, *How College Affects Students*, 2: 573.

32. Jacob Bronowski, *Science and Human Values* (New York: Harper, 1956), 27–31.

33. Ibid.

34. Ken Bain, *What the Best College Teachers Do* (Cambridge, MA: Harvard University Press, 2004), 22–23.

35. Anderson, *Prescribing the Life of the Mind*, 81.

36. Peter Beidler, ed., *Distinguished Teachers on Effective Teaching*, New Directions for Teaching and Learning 28 (San Francisco: Jossey-Bass Inc., 1986).

37. Edmundson, *Why Teach?*, 6.

38. Bain, *What the Best College Teachers Do*, 15–21.

Chapter 5

1. Peggy Noonan on George W. Bush, quoted in Rebecca Mead, "Learning by Degree," *New Yorker*, June 7, 2010, 22.

2. Historian of science Otto Neugebauer, as told to Princeton history professor Anthony Grafton, "Can Colleges Be Saved?" *New York Review*, May 24, 2012, 22.

3. Bok, *Our Underachieving Colleges*, 31–32.

4. Gerald Graff, *Beyond the Culture Wars: How Teaching Conflicts Can Revitalize American Education* (New York: W. W. Norton, 1992), chapter 9.

5. Cf. John Hattie and Herbert Marsh, "The Relationship between Research and Teaching," *Review of Educational Research* 66 (2009): 507–24; "Student Learning and Faculty Research: Connecting Teaching and Scholarship." *American Council of Learned Societies* (May 2007).

6. Beidler, "Distinguished Teachers on Effective Teaching," 38.

7. Letters, *New York Times*, September 20, 2009, 5.

8. Carnochan, *Battleground of the Curriculum*, 11.

9. See the intriguing survey report on how we actually spend our time: John Eiher, "Focusing the Research Lens on the Professor's Own Schedule," at http://www.thebluereview.org (accessed May 10, 2014). We work an average of 61 hours per week, and 30 percent of our time is spent on administrative details (p. 7).

10. "Trying to Find a Measure for How Well Colleges Do," *New York Times*, April 8, 2012, A14.

11. Ibid.

12. Stanley Fish, "Deep in the Heart of Texas," http://nytimes.com/2010/06/21 (accessed July 20, 2014).

13. Todd Oppenheimer, *The Flickering Mind: The False Promise of Technology in the Classroom and How Learning Can Be Saved* (New York: Random House, 2003), 321.

14. Wilbert McKeachie, *Learning, Cognition, and College Teaching* (San Francisco: Jossey-Bass, 1980). See also *Improving Undergraduate Education through Faculty Development* (San Francisco: Jossey-Bass, 1985).

15. Oppenheimer, *Flickering Mind*, 34.

16. Online Opinionator, *New York Times*, June 21, 2010, 2.

17. Christopher Healey, *Teachers College Record* (New York: Columbia University, 2009); Educational Supplement, *New York Times*, April 18, 2010, 8, at http://www.tcrecord.org (accessed June 16, 2012).

18. "30 Valedictorians: Too Much of a Good Thing?" Letters, *New York Times*, June 27, 2010, 1.

19. Max Roosevelt, "Student Expectations Seen as Causing Grade Disputes," *New York Times*, February 18, 2009, A15.

20. Pascarella and Terenzini, *How College Affects Students*, 2: 572.

21. Ibid.

22. Ibid., 577.

23. Astin, *What Matters in College*, 276.

24. Bloom, *Closing of the American Mind*.

25. Cf. Charles Sykes, *Profscam*.

26. E.g., William Bennett, "Foreword," in *Education and the Public Trust: The Imperative for Common Purpose*, by Edwin Delattre (Washington, DC: Ethics and Public Policy Center, 1988), 1.

27. Tamar Lewin, "As Interest Fades in the Humanities, Colleges Worry," *New York Times*, October 31, 2013, A1, A18.

28. Louis Menand, *The Marketplace of Ideas: Reform and Resistance in the American University* (New York: Norton, 2010).

29. Ibid., 91.

30. Paul Gross, Norman Levitt, and Martin Lewis, *The Flight from Science and Reason* (New York: New York Academy of Science, 1996); Paul Gross and Norman Levitt, *Higher Superstition: The Academic Left and Its Quarrels with Science* (Baltimore: Johns Hopkins University Press, 1994).

31. Sheldon Glashow, "Does Ideology Stop at the Laboratory Door?" *New York Times*, October 22, 1989, 247.

32. Sandra Harding, *The Science Question in Feminism* (Ithaca, NY: Cornell University Press, 1986).

33. Bruno Latour, *We Have Never Been Modern* (Cambridge, MA: Harvard University Press, 1993).

34. Committee on Women in Science, Engineering, and Medicine, at http://www.nationalacademies.org (accessed July 27, 2013).

35. Cf. Anthony Aveni, *People and the Sky: Our Ancestors and the Cosmos* (London: Thames and Hudson, 2008).

36. Bruno Latour, *Politics of Nature: How to Bring the Sciences into Democracy* (Cambridge, MA: Harvard University Press, 2004).

37. Kenshur, in Gross, Levitt, and Lewis, *Flight from Science and Reason*, 288–97.

38. Anthony Aveni, *The End of Time: The Maya Mystery of 2012* (Boulder: University Press of Colorado, 2009).

39. Jose Argüelles, *The Mayan Factor: Path beyond Technology* (Santa Fe, NM: Bear, 1987), 184.

40. Mark Bauerlein, *The Dumbest Generation* (New York: Tarcher Penguin, 2009), 11–12.

41. Susan Jacoby, *The Age of American Unreason* (New York: Vintage, 2009), 23.

42. "A Twenty-Year Survey of Science Literacy among College Students," at http://www.astronomy101.jpl.nasa.gov (accessed July 29, 2013).

43. Bauerlein, *Dumbest Generation*, 10.

44. Ibid., 21.

45. Ibid., 93–95.

46. Jacoby, *Age of American Unreason*, chapter 9.

47. Ibid., 211.

48. Harold Bloom, "Get Lost in Books," *New York Times,* September 5, 2009, WK10.

49. Jacoby, *Age of American Unreason*, xii.

50. Bruce Wilshire, *The Moral Collapse of the University: Professionalism, Purity, and Alienation* (Lanham, MD: Lexington, 2006).

51. Ibid., 14.

52. Eric Hirsch, *The Knowledge Deficit: Closing the Shocking Education Gap for American Children* (Boston: Houghton Mifflin, 2006).

53. Brian Ingrassia, *Higher Education's Uneasy Alliance with Big-Time Football* (Lawrence: University of Kansas Press, 2012).

54. "History of Athletics in US Colleges and Universities," at http://www.state university.com (accessed July 29, 2013).

55. Bok, *Our Underachieving Colleges*, chapter 12.

56. Menand quoted in Lisa Miller, "Why Harvard Students Should Study More Religion," *Newsweek,* February 10, 2010 (updated March 13, 2010), at http://www.newsweek.com (accessed May 14, 2014).

57. Pinker quoted in ibid.

58. Pascarella and Terenzini, *How College Affects Students*, 652.

59. Frank Bruni, "Questioning the Mission of College," Week in Review, *New York Times*, April 21, 2013, 3.

60. Bok, *Our Underachieving Colleges*, 328.

61. Catherine Gilpin-Faust, Book Review, *New York Times*, September 6, 2009, 6.

62. John Keats, *The Sheepskin Psychosis* (New York: Dell, 1963).

63. Here are just a few of them: William Bowen, Matthew Chingos, and Michael McPherson, *Crossing the Finish Line: Completing College at America's Public Universities* (Princeton, NJ: Princeton University Press, 2009); Nancy Folbre, *Saving State U: Why We Must Fix Public Higher Education* (New York: New Press, 2009); Benjamin Ginsberg, *The Fall of the Faculty: The Rise of the All-Administrative University and Why It Matters* (Oxford: Oxford University Press, 2011); Anthony Kronman, *Education's End: Why Our Colleges and Universities Have Given Up on the Meaning of Life* (New Haven, CT: Yale University Press, 2008); Christopher Newfield, *Unmaking the Public University: The Forty-Year Assault on the Middle Class* (Cambridge, MA: Harvard University Press, 2008); Nancy Riley, *The Faculty Lounges: And Other Reasons Why You Won't Get the College Education You Paid For* (Lanham, MD: Ivan R. Dee, 2011).

64. Anthony Grafton, "Our Universities: Why Are They Failing?" *New York Review*, November 24, 2011, 38–42.

65. Jeff Selingo, *College Unbound: The Future of Higher Education and What It Means for Students* (New York: New Harvest, 2013), 5.

66. Andrew Delbanco, *College: What It Was, Is, and Should Be* (Princeton, NJ: Princeton University Press, 2012).

67. Karine Joly, at http:www.collegewebeditor.com (accessed July 30, 2013).

68. Richard Arum and Josipa Roksa, *Academically Adrift: Limited Learning on College Campuses* (Chicago: University of Chicago Press, 2011).

69. Louis Menand, "Why We Have College," *New Yorker*, June 6, 2011, 74–79.

70. Alexander Astin, "In 'Academically Adrift,' Data Don't Back up Sweeping Claims," at http://www.chronicle.com (accessed May 14, 2014).

71. Pascarella and Terenzini, *How College Affects Students*.

72. Andrew Hacker and Claudia Dreifus, *Higher Education? How Colleges Are Wasting Our Money and Failing Our Kids—and What We Can Do about It* (New York: Times, 2010).

73. Professor X, *In the Basement of the Ivory Tower: Confessions of an Accidental Academic* (New York: Viking, 2011).

74. Menand, "Why We Have College," 79.

75. "Are Tenure Track Professors Better Teachers?" at http://www.nber.org/papers/w19406 (accessed July 3, 2013). See also, John Gross and Edie Goldberg,

Off-Track Profs: Nontenured Teachers in Higher Education (Cambridge, MA: MIT Press, 2001); and the discussion in *New York Times Sunday Review,* November 17, 2013, 2.

76. Peter Thiel at http://www.thielfellowship.org (accessed May 14, 2014).

77. Joseph Altucher, "8 Alternatives to College," at http://www.jamesaltucher .com (accessed June 5, 2011).

78. Thomas Frank, "Easy Chair: Course Corrections," *Harpers* (October 2013): 10–13.

79. William Bennett and David Wilezol, *Is College Worth It? A Former United States Secretary of Education and a Liberal Arts Graduate Expose the Broken Promise of Higher Education* (New York: Thomas Nelson, 2013).

80. Edmundson, *Why Teach?*, 109.

81. Mark Edmundson, "Education's Hungry Hearts," *New York Times Sunday Review,* May 31, 2012, at http://www.nyt.com (accessed May 14, 2014).

82. Menand, "Why We Have College," 74.

83. Peter Brooks, "Our Universities: How Bad? How Good?" *New York Review of Books* (March 2011). 12–13, at http://www.nybooks.com/articles/2011/march24 (accessed May 14, 2014).

84. Ibid., 3.

85. Lisa Colletta, "The Ultimate Utility of Nonutility," *Academe* (September-October 2010): 29–31.

86. Ibid., 30.

87. Ibid., 31.

88. Lamar Alexander, "Why College Should Only Take 3 Years," *Newsweek,* October 26, 2009, 27.